German Pioneers
of Montgomery County, Ohio:
Early Pioneer Life in Dayton, Miamisburg, Germantown

By H.A. Rattermann

Translated and Edited
By Elfe Vallaster Dona

Foreword
Don Heinrich Tolzmann

CLEARFIELD

Copyright © 2014
Elfe Vallaster Dona
All Rights Reserved.

Published for Clearfield Company by
Genealogical Publishing Company
Baltimore, Maryland
2014

ISBN 978-0-8063-5706-5

Contents

	Foreword by Dr. Don Heinrich Tolzmann	i
	Introduction	ii
	Acknowledgements	viii
CHAPTER 1	History of the Original Settlement of Montgomery County, Ohio	1
CHAPTER 2	Small Town Life of Early German Settlers	11
CHAPTER 3	Small Business Endeavors in Germantown and Miamisburg	21
CHAPTER 4	German Pioneers bring Musical Entertainment to Ohio	27
CHAPTER 5	German Social Clubs, Singing Societies and Early Newspapers	35
CHAPTER 6	Jakob Köhne's Pioneer Memoirs of Germantown, Ohio	43
APPENDIX A	Index of German Newspapers & Papers in Dayton, Ohio	54
APPENDIX B	Index of German Newspapers & Papers in Germantown, Ohio	57
APPENDIX C	Index of German Newspapers & Papers in Miamisburg, Ohio	59
	Images	60
	Notes	71
	Sources	119
	Bibliography	122
	Index	137
	About the Author	152

Foreword

In 1879, H.A. Rattermann traveled several times from his home in Cincinnati to nearby Dayton to deliver a series of lectures on the German pioneers of Montgomery County. He was invited to speak there by the German Pioneer Society of Dayton, an affiliate of the German Pioneer Society of Cincinnati, which had been founded in 1869 for the purpose of recording the history of German immigration, settlement and influences in America, especially in the Ohio Valley. Its historical journal, *Der Deutsche Pionier*, which was edited by Rattermann, is a veritable gold mine of information on these topics.

In his Dayton lectures Rattermann describes the social, cultural, and religious life of the German pioneer settlers of Montgomery County, often providing detailed biographical information on them. His treatment of German churches, societies, and newspapers reflects the meticulous research that he was known for. Especially interesting is his coverage of the German-language press; altogether more than thirty German-language newspapers were published in Montgomery County, mainly in Dayton. Shortly after they were presented, Rattermann's lectures appeared as a series of articles in the *Pionier*, but have not appeared in translation until this time. Taken together, they project a vivid portrait of the county's German element.

Fortunately, Elfe Vallaster Dona took on the task of translating and editing Rattermann's articles. Her translation succeeds in capturing the spirit and flavor of Rattermann's colorful nineteenth century German text, while her extensive notes explain and define the many persons, places, terms, etc., which he mentions. Her translated edition of Rattermann's history definitely contributes to a greater understanding of the richness of the German heritage of the state of Ohio, opens up new venues for further research and study, and demonstrates the importance of German-language source material for regional and local history.

Don Heinrich Tolzmann
Cincinnati, Ohio
Author and Editor of German-American History and Culture
http://donheinrichtolzmann.net/about.html

Introduction

The purpose of this book is to add to the understanding of the local history of Montgomery County, Ohio, by making information accessible to a larger reader base as the text was only available in German up to now. This book contains some details of the history of Montgomery County, Ohio, from before its founding in 1803 through 1879, which are generally not found in history books. Many historical books dealing with Montgomery County, Ohio, refer to the German immigrants and their contributions only marginally or in passing and references to their German heritage, traditions, and contributions are obscure. German-Americans were involved in every aspect of city and community building. One historian, Heinrich Armin Rattermann (1832-1923), was concerned about the missing German element in Anglo-American historical scholarly works, and wanted to preserve that heritage and contribute to the self-esteem of the Germans. Rattermann was a German-American author, poet and amateur historian of the 19th century who wrote about the early German pioneer life of Montgomery County. His amateur status might make some professional historians cringe, but when looking into Rattermann's historical writings one finds them to be well-documented, drawing on multiple resources, and providing the reader with a wealth of small bits of information that evoke a more complete image of our local history. Rattermann included stories about life, events and people of the past. This oral story-telling element adds color to the local history, because witnesses' accounts are usually not present in history books. The author tried to verify those anecdotes and find cross-referenced sources when possible. When checking Rattermann's sources, it became obvious that he carefully recorded and annotated his research findings. He also used a variety of records, such as land records, church records, immigration dates, maps, and testimonies of the German settlers. There are few witnesses who can speak for the early German-speaking settlers, the dangers and difficulties they faced when settling this area, the joy of the first child born in their small platted town, even the shame they faced when they had to try their first fellow-countryman as a criminal in Newcom's house. He still knew some of the earliest German settlers whose anecdotes he faithfully recorded. He actually witnessed some of the events he writes about. Rattermann had the foresight to preserve that knowledge and with it the values, traditions and memories of the German settlers. By doing so he provides us today with a more connected and immediate access to our local history.

Intriguing Finds/Facts

Did you know that the first court case in Dayton involved a German pioneer who was ordered to pay a fine of six dollars and court costs? Did you know that the Newcom tavern was a jail and courthouse in 1803 and prisoners were "housed" in an empty well? Did you know that there were plans to call present-day Dayton *Venice* and the Mad River should have been named the *Tiber*? Did you know that the first *lager beer* in America might have been brewed in Germantown, Ohio, in 1830 by a German pioneer? And did you know that Dayton's first hospital, St. Elizabeth, was started by German Catholics? Did you know that Colonel Robert Patterson brought his slaves from Kentucky to Ohio and caused quite a controversy? Did you ever imagine Dayton as being a wild, thorn-studded place covered with thick bushes, but few trees? No wonder it took the early German pioneers one week to get from Cincinnati to Dayton. Once here they started to clear the land and built log cabins, schools, churches; infirmaries; created German newspapers, and established many social clubs where they preserved their cultural heritage.

Rationale for the Book

Why should we care about these early settlers? What do we have in common with some of the first German-speaking settlers in Montgomery County, Ohio? What do the documents of the past have to do with me and my city? What do the memories and traditions of an ethnic group have to do with a democratic culture? The answer is that the past and present are related. Have you ever found yourself driving in the greater Dayton area and wondered about names such as Gunckel, Emerick, Wellmeier, Kastle, Schiller, Heinke? You passed a park on your way to work called Waldruhe. Have you ever wondered why a German-sounding name was given to a park in Miamisburg? We are surrounded by history. We can learn from the early pioneers, the masters of improvisation who could create a makeshift log cabin that would serve as a home, a tavern, a grocery store, a jail, and even a courthouse. We can be astounded by their sense of friendship, their loyalty to each other, their understanding of the meaning of civic duties, as well as their ways of coping with the dangers they encountered while settling a wild country.

German Heritage

Rattermann managed to make local history come alive. He shared anecdotes he heard, biographical incidents, historical dates and names he researched, and cultural traditions of German and other ethnic immigrants. According to Don Tolzmann, it was important for German immigrants to be valued as contributing to American civil and political life and that meant for German-American historians in the 19th century to begin "the task of recording and writing German-American history."[1] Since the writing of American history books was dominated until the 1920s by Anglo-American historians, Tolzmann points out, the German pioneer historian, mostly self-taught, meticulously collected primary source materials and recorded historical dates, names and events in order to document the contributions of German-Americans to history alongside the Anglo-Americans. Few references are made in the local history books of Montgomery County, Ohio, to the German element, although a significant number of the early Ohio settlers were German. According to Faust, "the German settlements were thickest in the present county of Montgomery, centering in two places, Dayton and Germantown, which as late as 1825 were rival cities, each hoping to surpass the other."[2] However, Miami County, specifically the city of Piqua; Auglaize County with towns like Wapakoneta, New Bremen, and Minster had a large German population. Faust also mentions the German settlements in the city of Glandorf, Putnam County; the city of Delphos, in Allen/Van Wert counties; he points to Toledo, Columbus, and Cincinnati as having a large concentration of German settlers; Highland, Brown, and Hamilton counties had a large population of German-speaking immigrants as well.[3]

According to the 2010 *American Community Survey* of the U.S. Census, German-Americans make up 15% of the population of the United States.[4] German-Americans in Ohio represent 26% of the population which makes them the largest ethnic group.[5] Making some of the German-

American historical documents available that illustrate the beginnings of the formation of Dayton, Miamisburg, and Germantown will add to our understanding of Ohio's German immigration and the cities we live in. Rattermann was the historian who recorded this information.

Heinrich Armin Rattermann

The first in-depth investigation into the biography and works of Heinrich Armin Rattermann (1832-1923) was a dissertation completed by Sister Mary Edmund Spanheimer in 1937.[6] When Don Heinrich Tolzmann correctly identified the value of the Rattermann's historical information about German immigrants and their value for America, he re-published Spannheimer's work, when it was no longer in print, in the *New German-American Studies* series.[7] Henry Willen wrote a dissertation in 1939 emphasizing Rattermann's life and lyrical work.[8] Marc Surminski wrote his master thesis on Heinrich Armin Rattermann and *Der Deutsche Pionier.*[9] Praised as one of "Cincinnati's, and perhaps German-America's, most productive author," Rattermann was not only an author, poet, and historian, but also the editor of two sizable German-American journals in Cincinnati (*Der Deutsche Pioneer* and the *Deutsch-Amerikanisches Magazin*) which are still accessed by historians and genealogists today.[10] In these magazines he urges German-Americans to document what their forefathers have done for America in the areas of culture, literature, art, science, and medicine. In the seventy-eight years that Rattermann lived in the United States, he himself was interested in preserving the German heritage as can be seen in his lectures, presented to the German Pioneer Society of Dayton.

German Pioneer Societies

The German Pioneer Society of Dayton was established in 1878 and was modeled after the first German Pioneer Society of Cincinnati. The German Cincinnati Society was formed in 1868 and dissolved in 1961.[11] The Cincinnati membership was initially limited to men who were German immigrants, lived in Cincinnati or vicinity for at least 25 years, were over forty, and paid a membership fee of one dollar. The first issue of the *German Pioneer* magazine, which appeared in March 1869, states that it is the purpose of the organization to renew the bonds of old friendship and to preserve the history and experiences of the German pioneers for future generations by collecting documents and testimonies. Cincinnati, which had a large German-American population in the early nineteenth century, was the ideal place for the publication of such a German magazine. One of the editors from 1874 to 1885 was Heinrich Rattermann, born in Ankum, Germany, who came with his family to Cincinnati, Ohio, in 1845. Although he never wrote a complete history book, he became known as a German-American historian who meticulously documented all aspects of German life. Some of Rattermann's writings have not yet received the attention they deserve. This is the case of the Dayton lectures. The Rattermann Dayton lectures will be of interest to people trying to find out who Dayton's first settlers were, how Dayton looked and how the first churches, schools, clubs, charitable organizations, and hospitals were established. The essays also contain hundreds of names of German and German-American pioneers. Genealogists will find a wealth of information in these lectures as well as in the eighteen volumes of the *German Pioneer* magazine,[12]

Goal of this Book

This book concentrates on six lectures Rattermann presented in German to the *Deutsche Pionier Verein* (*German Pioneer Society*) in Dayton, Ohio, in 1879.[13] The lectures were more like historical essays. They appeared in written form in installments in *Der Deutsche Pionier*, a monthly magazine, established in Cincinnati in 1869 and published by the *German Pioneer Society of Cincinnati* until 1887. The magazine was published monthly from 1869 to 1885 and quarterly until the end of its publication in 1887. From 1887 to 1938, the society published annual proceedings.[14] The editors of the magazine changed throughout the eighteen years of the publication of the journal. Rainer Sell summarizes the contents of the journals by stating that "each issue usually included poems on pioneers, pioneer experiences, and memories of the fatherland; biographies of famous German-Americans; historical essays and sketches of German life, language, and settlements in the United States; the proceedings of the DPVC and its Zweigvereine in Covington, Newport, Dayton, and Toledo; usually excerpted or complete speeches given during the Stiftungsfest and the celebration of Washington's Birthday; statistics on German immigration to the United States; short biographies of deceased members of the DPVC under "In Memoriam" and famous German-Americans elsewhere under "German-American Necrology"; and book reviews of literature pertaining to German-America."[15]

The subject matter of the journals was geared towards the immigration population. The information in the Dayton lectures will be made available in English for the first time through this translation. The focus of this study will be to show how German immigrants made their mark on Dayton, Miamisburg, and Germantown. What makes these lectures significant from a historical perspective is that they were written at a time when German cultural, civic, and political life was still present in those cities. The lectures provide us with a first-hand look into various areas of German-American culture in the United States. According to Tolzmann, "Rattermann's work is of value since it focuses exclusively on the early settlements of Ohio and Cincinnati, and places this account within the context of other early reports of the area."[16] What make Rattermann's Dayton lectures so intriguing are the narratives about early German settlers and their daily life, the description of German pioneer settlements in Montgomery County, court disputes, religious tolerance issues, anti-slavery discussions, and philosophical discussions about the German cultural heritage. The importance of preserving the German language and the German traditions are a major theme.

Principles of Translation and Editing Process

The basis of this book are Heinrich Armin Rattermann's Dayton lectures, which were written in German, and published in the United States in 1879 in *Der Deutsche Pionier: Erinnerungen aus dem Pionierleben der Deutschen in America*, a German monthly magazine. They were never available in English or received any commentary or attention. This book is a translation from German into English using a copy of *Der Deutsche Pionier* preserved in the German-American Collection of the Blegen Library at the University of Cincinnati, Ohio. All eighteen volumes of the German-American magazine are available there both in microfilm and printed form. The former curator of the German-Americana Collection and well-known German-American researcher, Dr. Don Heinrich Tolzmann, brought these treasured lectures to my attention and after reading them I noticed how valuable they are for a better appreciation of the local history of

Montgomery County and especially the seat of the county, Dayton, Ohio. Useful information is also provided about Germantown and Miamisburg. While Cincinnati is generally known as a settlement with a large German population in the 18th and 19th centuries, Dayton and the surrounding areas also had a high concentration of German-speaking immigrants. The Ohio Germans are the descendants of German-speaking emigrants who arrived in Ohio in the eighteenth and early nineteenth centuries.

Every effort was made to ensure that the information and the historical sources are complete and accurate. Rattermann's collected materials and all his footnotes, that formed the content of his Dayton lectures, were researched, substantiated or completed. The inclusion of the numerous annotated, explanatory endnotes was designed to increase the value of Rattermann's Dayton lectures and shed more light on the German-Americans named in Rattermann's essays. By adding information to the original lectures and making them accessible to English-speaking researchers of German-American studies, American historians, genealogists, students or anybody interested in the early American history or the German element in western Ohio, will find some interesting information. In order to increase the reading ease of the book and to distinguish who added the footnotes, the author marked the annotations with "HAR" for (Heinrich Armin Rattermann) or "EVD" (Elfe Vallaster Dona) at the end of each endnote. Similarly, it was a decision to add all the footnotes of the original lectures to the end of the book to make reading easier.

It was the intention of the author to preserve the writing style of the 19th century German historian and any unusual formulations might result from that effort to remain true to the source. German names, as provided by Rattermann, were not Anglicized, which happens often in established local history books. This practice often obscures the German heritage of early settlers. My intention behind retaining the German-sounding names was an effort to preserve evidence that points to their German heritage. Some German terms remained within the main body of text, with either a translation added in parentheses or explanations in the endnotes. Those words can be identified because they are written in italics. Poems and songs were translated, but a list of German publication titles of one of the German settlers, provided in the main text by Rattermann, remained untranslated for easier tracking of those German resources by scholars.

Book Organization

This book is comprised of six major sections, an extensive endnote section, an appendix highlighting some German newspapers and an index. Each section was a lecture provided by Rattermann to the *German Pioneer Society of Dayton*, Ohio. The first, "History of the Original Settlement of Montgomery County, Ohio," includes an overview over the beginning of the Dayton settlement and township histories. The second section, "Small Town Life of Early German Settlers," provides an insight into how the German pioneers survived and how the strong German pioneer women contributed, how they celebrated their traditions, and established a community with priests and churches. The third chapter, "Small Business Endeavors in Germantown and Miamisburg," concentrates on Germantown's newspaper productions, Miamisburg's early settlers, and the establishments of breweries. The fourth section, "German Pioneers bring Musical Entertainment to Ohio," provides an insight into the cultural life, especially the musical life, of the early German settlers. The first music teacher in Dayton was

German and taught many musical instruments. Chapter 5, "German Social Clubs, Singing Societies and Early Newspapers," concentrates on the club activities of the Germans. Finally, the last section, chapter six, "Jakob Köhne's Pioneer Memoirs of Germantown, Ohio," consists of various German immigrant stories. An appendix was added at the end of the book. It contains some supplementary materials that would interrupt the flow of the book, yet could add value to the publication. A search of early German newspapers and papers of Dayton, Germantown and Miamisburg was conducted and the findings are presented in tabular format.

Three sources were consulted: an online newspaper database from the Library of Congress, *Chronicling America*; Karl J.R. Arndt and May E. Olson. *Deutsch-Amerikanische Zeitungen und Zeitschriften, 1732-1955* (Heidelberg: Quelle und Meyer, 1961); and Augustus Waldo Drury, *History of the City of Dayton and Montgomery County, Ohio* (Chicago-Dayton: S.J. Clarke Publishing Co., 1909). The name index should assist researchers with their search of specific people.

Future Direction

There are numerous studies about Heinrich Armin Rattermann's importance to understanding the role German-speakers and German-Americans played in this country. In this book readers can discover a bit more about their own local history, about people who lived here before them, about actions of people who influenced history and local history. Finally, it is essential that Rattermann's documents about Montgomery County, Ohio, are made public to complete, correct or even scrutinize the image provided in established local history books. Understanding the regional history can lead to a closer sense of community, civic participation, local engagement and mutual appreciation of contributions made by any of our ethnic communities.

There is still a substantial need for further research regarding the German element in Montgomery County, Ohio. According to Tolzmann, further investigations could start with two German Dayton newspapers, the *Gross-Daytoner Zeitung* (1866-1947) and the *German-American Bulletin* (1933-1941). The *Gross-Daytoner Zeitung*, "one of the major newspapers in the history of the German-American press," contains a "wealth of information on the history of the Dayton Germans."[17] The role of the pioneer woman in the opening of the West and in settlements of the Montgomery County, Ohio, needs to be explored. Rattermann mentions women, German, Irish and Anglo-American women, only in passing or in anecdotal stories. Their names, dates of origins, or biographies are rarely recorded and little is known about their extraordinary stories, their hardship while traveling the prairie or their perspective on emigration. During the editing process the author has added many secondary sources that might be useful for any German-American researcher or genealogist.

Elfe Vallaster Dona
Wright State University

Acknowledgements

First and foremost, I would like to thank Dr. Don Heinrich Tolzmann, former Curator of the German-Americana Collection and Director of German-American Studies at the University of Cincinnati, for his expert advice, collaboration and encouragement throughout the project. He assisted me in research and provided me with the source material for this book. Dr. Jerry Glenn, Professors Emeritus of Germanic Languages and Literatures at the University of Cincinnati, inspired my interest in this topic and played a crucial role in my academic development.

Throughout the process of writing this book, numerous individuals from the community have taken time out to assist me. I am grateful to the following institutions and staff members: *Dayton Liederkranz-Turner Society*, *Ohio History Connection*, *Warren County Genealogy Society*, Glenn Bowman of *Germantown Historical Society*, Gwen Haney of *Dayton History*, Gillian Izor of *Germantown Public Library*, Mr. & Mrs. Petticrew and Ed Hiehle of *Miamisburg Historical Society* for their support in data collection and verification for this book. The staff of the *Special Collections and Archives at* Wright State University granted me access to their records and allowed me to use their holdings. It is a pleasure to acknowledge the assistance of several individuals from the *Dayton Liederkranz-Turner Society*, Dayton's oldest German organization: Ulrich Gaertner, current President; Louise Gaertner, Chairperson of the *German Genealogy Group*; Lois Lynch, Secretary and *German Folk Dance Instructor*; Judith Schneider, *Jugendchor* Director; as well as Carla and Bob Hall, my Germantown, Ohio, friends and connections. The *Eintracht Singing Society* and the *German Club Edelweiss* are two of the other thriving German organizations in Dayton. Special thanks to Suzanne Maggard, Reference Librarian of the *Archives and Rare Books Library Collection* at the University of Cincinnati. Katharina Hargot, who volunteers to transcribe obituaries in old German newspapers at the *Dayton Metro Library*, deserves my appreciation, since she found many images of the early German settlers for me. I highly appreciate Nancy Horlacher, local history specialist at the *Dayton Metro Library*, for making rare books and archival collections accessible to me, and contributing her expertise.

I want to express gratitude for the generous help afforded me by Wright State University in giving me the faculty development leave. Without this time, the project could not have been completed. My former student, Jacob Hellickson, deserves a thank you for his inspiration.
A special thanks goes to my good friend and colleague at Wright State University, Dr. Nancy Broughton, who shared my excitement at the onset of the project and kept me going when it became difficult to complete it. This book project would have been impossible to finish without the support of Dr. Margaret Thomas Evans who quickly edited the early drafts of the manuscript.

Finally, I would especially like to thank my family, our two daughters, Nicole and Krista, who both listened patiently to all those German-related immigrant stories and historical facts I uncovered, and my husband, Steven, for his encouragement and outstanding support, to whom I dedicate this book.

The book is also dedicated to all those who have a fundamental interest in their local history and are curious enough to become aware of the many diverse groups of people who represent our community.

Chapter 1
History of Original Settlement of Montgomery County, Ohio

After General Anthony Wayne signed the Treaty of Greeneville on August 3, 1795 with the United Western Indian tribes[1], thereby finally determining the status of the Miami countries, the persisting settlers, who did not dare to venture far into the land, staying close to the protective Ford Washington by Cincinnati, during the Indian unrests, immediately began to take possession of the fertile land by the two Miami rivers.[2] Seventeen days after the conclusion of the above-mentioned treaty, General Arthur St. Clair, at the time governor of the Northwest Territory; General Jakob Wilkinson; Jonathan Dayton and the surveyor Israel Ludlow signed an agreement with John Cleves Symmes according to which the seventh and eighth ranges of the Miami countries, between the Little Miami River and the Mad River, were assigned to them. In the contract, however, it was determined that the buyers should immediately start three settlements on the land in question, namely one at the Little Miami River in the seventh range, the other in the seventh row at the mouth of the Mad River, and the third at the river mentioned last in the eighth row.[3] Already on September 21, 1795 Daniel C. Cooper and John Dunlap began to define the boundaries of the contracted land. They finished their work on October 4. Cooper and Ludlow then laid out the city of Dayton, which they finished on November 4. After that they offered one hundred building lots to genuine settlers free of charge in Cincinnati, from where the settlement was launched. The building plots were assigned by lottery. After great effort 46 settlers were recruited; however, most of those were deterred in the course of the following very severe winter during which a great food shortage befell the western settlements.[4] Therefore in the spring of 1796 only the following 19 people went to the new settlement: Wm. Gahagan, Samuel Thomson, Benjamin Van Cleve, Wm. Van Cleve, Salomon Goß, Thomas Davis, John Davis, James McClure, John McClure, Daniel Ferrell, Wilhelm, Salomon and Thomas Hammer, Abraham Glaßmeier, John Dorough, Wm. Chenoweth, James Morris, Wilhelm Neukomm (Newcom) and Georg Neukomm (Newcom).

Jonathan Dayton (1760-1824)
Namesake of Dayton, Ohio

Daniel C. Cooper (1773-1818)
Founder of Dayton, Ohio

Benjamin Van Cleve (1773-1821)
Pioneer Settler of Dayton, Ohio

Georg Neukomm was the son of Christian Neukomm from Zweibrücken who came with his parents to America in the year of 1754 or 1755. They initially settled in the vicinity of Philadelphia; later they settled near Wilmington, Delaware, where they received the name

Newcomer, which was later changed to Newcom. The second wife of Neukomm, an Irish woman, Margaret McCarthy, might have contributed to that. After the death of his father, Georg Neukomm settled in Washington County, Pennsylvania, where he married Mary Henderson, also an Irish woman. It may stem from this that the brothers were listed as Irish.[5] Wilhelm Neukomm, the younger brother of Georg, was born in Delaware. He was approximately twenty years old when he came to Dayton.[6] Wilhelm Hammer came with his family, wife and two sons, Salomon and Thomas Hammer, from Fredericksburg, Maryland, to Cincinnati and later to Dayton. At the time he was approximately 45 years old. His place of birth is unknown.[7] Fredericksburg, however, was settled by Germans almost exclusively. One does not have to doubt his German nationality even if the name was later changed to Hamer which certainly stemmed from the fact that he wrote his name with a dash over his m, which clearly appears in the court records of Hamilton County (Volume A, p. 267). Hammer later settled on a farm at the Springfield "Turnpike," approximately three miles north of Dayton. He was a close friend of Heinrich Böhm, the patriarch of German Methodism, and he later became a preacher too (1810), the first preacher of the Wesleyan doctrine in Dayton and vicinity. The church service was held in Hammer's house for a long time where Böhm himself preached on Sunday, October 15, 1809, which was without a doubt the first sermon in the German language which was ever held in Dayton.[8] Salomon Goß soon moved away from Dayton again. It is unknown where he relocated.[9] Abraham Glaßmeier was a German weaver. He moved to Honey-Creek in the year 1802.[10]

Colonel George Newcom
(Neukomm) (1771-1853)

Heinrich Böhm (1775-1875)
Bilingual German Methodist Preacher

As soon as the first pioneers settled in Dayton, cleared out the forest and built block houses on their building lots, they were challenged by a legal matter concerning their properties. John Cleves Symmes had originally received from Congress a right of purchase for two million acres of land, located between the two Miami Rivers, which was soon changed to one million acres.[11] According to this, his purchase should encompass the land which is east of the Great Miami River with a width of twenty miles and reaching as far north until one million acres were covered. However, because the contractor could not raise the money for the entire area, he received a patent for only 248.540 acres in 1792.[12] Although the borders of this land complex were now exactly defined, this did not deter Symmes, the "smart Jersey man," to also sell land that was east and west of his borders. He relied on his original contract with Congress. However, Congress amended the first "irregularities"- concerning the width of over twenty miles – through an act in 1792, but Congress resolutely refused in 1796 to recognize the land sales made by Symmes to the north of his territory border because these were conducted without any authority.

Because now both of the aforementioned townships were affected by this refusal, this naturally caused a huge agitation among the settlers of Montgomery County, who were all threatened with losing their land and all their invested labor.[13] They appealed to Congress with a petition that granted them in 1799 a preemption right for payment of two dollars per acre. The first landowners of Dayton had therefore to pay one additional dollar to Congress because their building lots encompassed each one half of an acre.[14] A number of citizens complied with the decision but the largest number of them left the land entirely outraged because they were forced to pay twice.[15] Therefore, in 1799 Dayton only had nine residential houses, among them the Georg Neukomm tavern on the south-west corner of Water and Main Street; Georg Westfahl's block house on the east side of Main, between Water and Front Street; and Thomas Arnetz' house on the south-east corner of Wilkinson and Water Street.

John Cleves Symmes (1742-1814)
Pioneer in the Northwest Territory

Map of Symmes Purchase in what are now Hamilton, Butler and Warren Counties

Newcom's First Log Cabin, Built in 1796
Still standing in Carillon Historical Park, Dayton

Arnetz was the first shoemaker in Dayton. Westfahl belonged to a party of four brothers who came to Cincinnati in 1797: Andreas, Georg, Jobst and Cornelius. Andreas remained in Cincinnati, where he lived with his wife, however, not at ease because she ran away from him around the middle of April in 1800.[16] Cornelius Westfahl was the first schoolmaster in Dayton.[17] In the fall of 1804 he established a private school based upon subscription. The school hours were from 9 to 12 o'clock in the morning and from 2 to 6 o'clock in the afternoon. He charged two dollars per three months per student: "a third of the school tuition in approved trade, the rest in cash." The history of this school is preserved in the court files of the county because it soon turned out that not all of Westfahl's subscribers made their payment on time. But because a schoolmaster, as well as any other human being, cannot live on mere promises alone, and because a certain George F. Tennery (who was at that time the only attorney in the county) owed him the school tuition for his three children for two quarters (from September 8, 1804 to March 8, 1805) and because he finally refused to pay this, Westfahl appealed to the court of law and was awarded on August 8, 1805 by a jury (of which the German Peter Felix and Johannes Gewert were members) a verdict of $12.00 and the court costs, together $18.74 against Tennery.[18] Jobst Westfahl was a surveyor who carried out measurements in the upper Miami countries. His older brother, Georg Westfahl, was the first carpenter in Dayton. Georg Neukomm established the first tavern in Dayton.

When the first settlers came to Dayton, the land was densely covered with acorn brushwood, hawthorn and other lower shrubbery; there were only very few large trees.[19] The place looked a little bit like the lower shrubberies which one can find in the middle of the great western prairies. All the settlers lived along the river, with the exception of John Welsh who built his block house at the southeast corner of Fifth and Main Streets. Main Street was the only fairly passable street because it was cleared from shrubberies by Cooper in 1795. Therefore, it happened occasionally that strangers coming from the south to Dayton and walking past Welsh's house unnoted, had walked through the entire municipal area of the town when they arrived at houses of Westfahl or Neukomm asking how far it still may be until the city of Dayton? They were then informed that they have just now crossed the city from one end to the other and they had arrived at the outer limit of this city. That seemed strange to them and they remarked that the city might have been laid out too large and it should only consist of a smaller part. The citizens of Dayton back then oftentimes shared this opinion with them.

The Landing of the First Settlers in Dayton, Ohio, April 1, 1796. The wood of the pirogue was later used to build the first log cabin. The passage from Cincinnati to Dayton lasted ten days. Two small camps with friendly Indians were already there.

First House in Dayton, Built from Lumber of the Pirogue

However, in the year 1803, on May first, Montgomery was separated from Hamilton County and was elevated to a separate county.[20] At that time it included the area of the present-day counties: Montgomery, Preble, Miami, Darke, Shelby, Mercer, Van Wert, Paulding, Defiance and Williams, and the largest part of Auglaize, Allen, Putnam, Henry and Fulton counties. The first hearing in the new district was held on July 27, 1803 in the home of Georg Neukomm.[21] The people of the justice were Francis Dunlavy, president; Benjamin Archer of Centreville; Isaac Spinning, who lived on his farm four miles east of Dayton; and John Ewing of Washington Township, associate judges. Benjamin Van Cleve served as clerk, pro tempore; Georg Neukomm as sheriff; Jacob Müller as coroner and Daniel Symmes as court prosecutor. The entire population of Dayton and vicinity was present during this first court session in order to enjoy the fun. No transactions existed, however, and therefore the high court of justice adjourned until November of the same year.

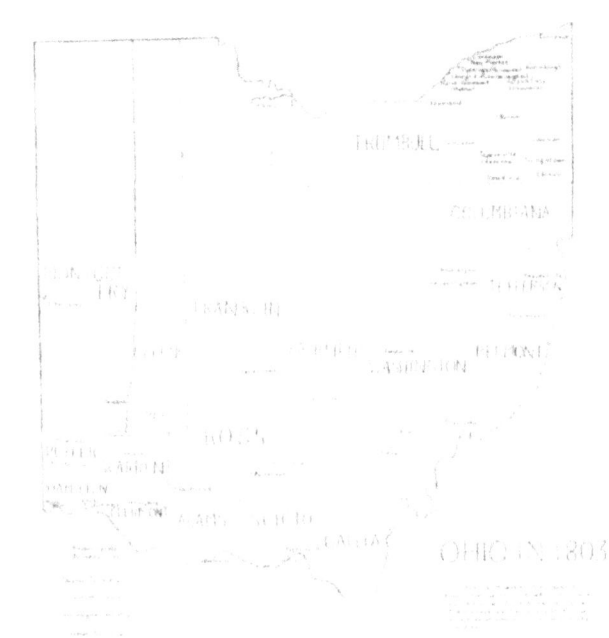

This map was drawn by Mildred K. Fillers, Dayton Public Library staff, based on R.C. Downe's *Evolution of Ohio County Boundaries*, 1803

On November 22, 1803 the court re-convened. However, this time complaints were already presented. The first case that was tried was a complaint against Peter Sunderland, who had beaten a certain Benjamin Scott. Sunderland pleaded guilty of giving the meddlesome neighbor, who had insulted him as "Dutchman" and challenged him to a boxing match, a strong German slap in the face in the process of which, unfortunately, the nasal bone of the Yankee boy was somewhat moved to the side. The defendant pleaded guilty and was fined to pay six dollars and the court costs. However, Sunderland turned the tables and sued Scott for irritation that lead to a breach of the peace, a claim, which was heard in June of the next year. The jury, however, which also consisted of the following Germans: Georg Kuntz, Bernard Baumann, Georg Jaunt and Hans Bansell, exonerated Scott from the accusation.

Georg Kuntz (born 1863 in Dayton, Ohio)
Owner of meat market and President of
the Dayton Grocers' Baking Company

At the same time that Dayton was settled, a German settlement on the left bank of the Great Miami River, about ten miles south of Dayton was established. It was founded by Jakob Hole already in 1792 and was called Hole's Station after him. In 1796 several German families from Berks County, Pennsylvania, settled here calling the settlement Miamisburg. Only a few names of the settlers, who came here before 1800, are preserved. Among them are Philipp and Daniel Gebhart[22], Heinrich Huet, Jacob Kirchner[23] and Anton Chevalier[24]. It is peculiar that in the almost entirely purely German Miami Township[25], as all the sources report, only very few names of the first German settlers are preserved. On the other hand, the names of the few Anglo-Americans who were among them--Dodds, Lamb, Adams, Vernosdell--are well recorded.[26]

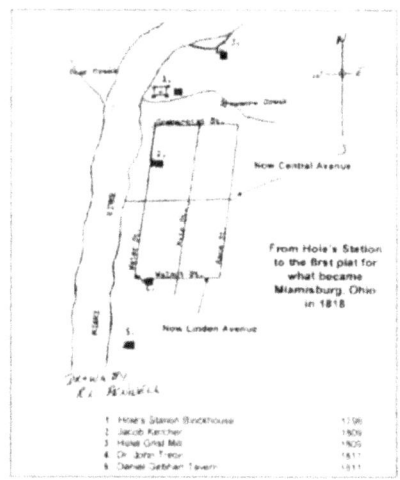

Starting from Miamisburg or rather Hole's Station, Washington Township was also settled. In this township Germans too were the first settlers: among them Friedrich Nutz, Dr. J. Hole[27], Manger, Kelse, Hutfeld, Harries, Malby, Stammel, Peter Sunderland[28] and so on. The first marriage in this township was between Peter and Anna Sunderland; the first child born here was Franz Nutz (Nut); Maria Stammel was the first death of the township. Most of the German settlers here belonged to the Reformed Church whereas the Americans and English considered themselves to be Baptist.

Return from Indian Captivity

Dr. Isaias Hole, son of captain Jakob Hole, the pioneer of Miamisburg, was born in Berks County, Pennsylvania where his father and his father's parents had settled in 1765. Jakob Hole had fought in the War of Independence and came together with Major Ziegler to the West in 1790. Dr. Hole was an educated doctor who studied in Philadelphia under Dr. Rush.[29] In his youth Dr. Hole had to survive a fight with an Indian which he describes as follows: "I went hunting one day with Stephan Williams near Blue Licks in Kentucky. About dusk, feeling tired, we lay down to rest. I had just fallen asleep when the sound of a rifle woke me up again. I jumped up, saw my friend lying dead at my feet and I quickly ran behind the nearest tree from where I spotted two Indians hidden halfway in the shrubbery. After a minute of breathless suspense I recuperated from my initial shock and managed to regain my courage. Then I took aim at the nearest savage (after they had fired several shots at me in vain) and shot him through the heart whereupon the other took to flight. I pursued him for a while without being able to catch up with him or fire at him. I returned to the place where my dead companion was, buried him, scalped the slain Indian and quickly returned to Cincinnati where I lived at the time."[30]

Besides Mad River Township, in which the original part of Dayton is located, there were settlements established before 1803 in the townships of Harrison, Butler, Madison and German. Dilley and Wagener settled in Mad River. Besides Mr. Westphal, a certain Beck was the schoolteacher here in 1805 who gave lessons in both German as well as English.[31] The German pioneers of Butler Township were Heinrich Jaunt, Georg Zink, Thomas Neumann and Johannes Quillian.[32] They came from York, Pennsylvania, and settled at the left bank of the Stillwater River. They called their settlement Little York. Daniel Huber (Hoover) owned the first store in the township; Andreas Wehmeier built the first flourmill at Stillwater, which was at that time called, the northwest branch of the Miami. Joseph Küfer constructed the first sawmill.[33] Next to the Germans settled several Quaker families; Abijah Jones was the first preacher of the township.[34] Madison Township was settled by the German Dunkards from Pennsylvania.[35] The first German-style barn was built by Sultz. Michael Post established the first store. Daniel Miller built the first mill at Wolf Creek, two miles west of Randolph Township.[36] Joseph Flickersdorf was the first person who died in the township. The Dunkards or *Tunkers*, as they were called, always held their church service meetings originally in private homes, later they built a small church at Wolf Creek; Christian Baumann was their first preacher in Harrison Township, which was originally a part of Dayton Township and was settled soon thereafter. Colonel Robert Patterson, one of the co-founders of Lexington and Cincinnati, was the first landowner in the township.[37] He designed Miami City which is now a part of the city of Dayton (the eleventh ward).

Col. Robert Patterson (1753-1827)
Early Settler of Dayton, Ohio

Living Room of Patterson's Log Cabin in Lexington, KY, 1776

Also the neighboring Jefferson Township was settled early. A certain Fulcus was the surveyor. In 1804, Jakob Gripe built the first log cabin which was followed in the same year by the second log house of Peter Weber.[38] Weber constructed likewise the first grist and saw mill. The settlers were almost all German Lutherans and they had already built a small log cabin church approximately three miles from Miamisburg. Naturally, a small settlement gathered around this church, the little village Göttersburg or Gettersburg. Decheron was the first preacher and Oehlinger the first schoolmaster who offered lessons in both English and German.[39]

The southwest township of the county is called German township and it was organized in 1804.[40] It derived its name from the numerous German settlers who located there. The first of those were Philipp and Mathias Schwartzel, Heinrich Mayer, Michael Pfautz, Johann Hähnle, Balthasar Schmidt and others. In 1804, Philipp Gunkel and Wilhelm Emerich[41] settled here and in 1805 Martin Schewe, Leonhard Stumpe, Daniel Fischer, Mathias Ringel, Johann Holland, Martin Meyer, Daniel Pressel and Jakob Kuntz also settled here. The flourishing little town of Germantown was later built in this township.

Philip Gunckel (1776-1848)
Founder of Germantown, Ohio

Randolph Township was settled almost at the same time as German Township. Jacob Kienzle, Senior, settled here in 1805 together with Michael Keck. The first white child born in the township was Jacob Keck. Among the first settlers was Hans Benz (not Bench as they are calling themselves now) who opened the first grocery store in Salem Springs. Hans Benz was an enterprising person; already in 1806 he had built a flourmill and sawmill at the Salem River and he also had a saloon, and waited on customers with groceries and textiles, shoes, hats, hardware and agricultural machines. As a farmer he planted his farm and preached the gospel on Sundays. The first settlers were all Dunkards, who moved here from Lancaster County, Pennsylvania. In the year 1810, the first church was built and Emanuel Flory was then the regular preacher.[42] Until the year 1839, the sermon was only delivered in the German language in this township. The German Dunkards lived peacefully with the Indians whereas the English dwellers quarreled constantly with the savages. Kienzle was the first carpenter of the area. In 1812 Johannes Ledermann designed the little city of Salem.[43] He was the son of Heinrich Ledermann who had already settled in 1800 at Little York.

Shortly after the settlement of Randolph, the Dunkards and Lutherans, who came from Pennsylvania, took possession of the township at the western border, which they called, according to the predominant clay soil, Clay Township. Among the first settlers were Joseph Mickesell and Jakob Gripe who relocated here from Jefferson Township.[44] The first wedding in the township was between Reinhart Gripe and Elisabeth Heidrich, but the young woman died shortly thereafter; the first death of the township. In the southern township of Perry, which was first settled in 1819, a group of the United Brethren Church made their home.[45] They also came from Pennsylvania. The minister was a Mr. Boonbrick (Beinbrecht ?). Among the first settlers were the families Clemer, Müller (the first school teacher), Tobe (after whom the church, Toby's Church, was named because he contributed the majority of the money), Hauser and König. Joseph König was the first white child born in the township. The Königs now call themselves King.[46]

A little bit earlier Jackson Township, located between Perry and German, was established. Jacob Kunz, who bought the 7th section on October 1, 1804, was probably the first landowner of the township. His patent issued by President Jefferson is registered in Volume B, page 9, of the land property books of Montgomery County. Kunz lived, however, in German Township and legend has it that even years later, the township remained a dense forest. The first settlers did not arrive until 1813. In 1816 Stephan Müller built the first "frame" house and Adam Schweinhirt was the builder of the first saw mill. The first church built was the German Lutheran, where Pastor Stiver (Stöver?) was the preacher. There was also a German school at Tom's Run, but the name of the first schoolmaster could not be ascertained.[47] At that time, the German school and prayer books were imported from Philadelphia.

It is not known when Wayne and Van Buren Townships were first settled.[48] The latter remained unsettled due to the difficult situation, which was brought about by the Symmes' Purchase. The northern part of Van Buren Township had the settlement issues. Wayne was miles from anywhere. However, both townships were already settled in 1817 by mostly Anglo-Americans.[49]

Petition of the first setters of Dayton, Ohio, to the Senate stating the difficulties with the Symmes Purchase in 1795.

This is a short outline of the history of the original settlement of Montgomery County. In summary I need to add that the colonization of the three northern townships, east of the Miami River, was mostly done by Anglo-Americans. The land west of the Miami River and the two most southern townships east of it were predominantly settled by Germans, respectively German-Americans.[50] On the whole, the German element was predominant right from the start. Surveying the indexes of names of all public books and documents of the county, you will immediately recognize the unusually high number of German-sounding names, which today have obviously almost exclusively been Anglicized more or less by mutilation, such as Stroup instead of Straub; Newcom instead of Neukomm; Shideler instead of Scheidler; Moyer instead of Mayer; Kimmel instead of Kümmel; Shank instead of Schenk; Turner instead of Dreher. In Frybarger, Kuns, Shroyer, Waymire, Zearing and so forth one can easily recognize the German names such as Freyberger, Kuntz, Schröer, Wehmeier, Zehring and so on. Similarly, the place names provide powerful information that mostly Germans were the fathers and godfathers in these areas, such as Germantown, Göttersburg, Lambertine, New Germany, Schneidersburg (today Taylors Borough or Finchtown and Jimtown), Philippsburg, Bachmann, Pyrmont, Harschmannville and so on.)

Chapter 2
Small Town Life of Early German Settlers

Even the German national character reveals itself through the pioneers of Montgomery County: on the one hand they display diligence, domesticity, frankness and cheerfulness as positive traits and on the other hand envy, discord, quarrel and strife as negative traits. By virtue of their diligence and domesticity almost all German pioneers have achieved great wealth and their cheerfulness, which they brought with them, caused them to celebrate weddings, baptisms, outdoor festivals and the like according to old German traditions. These festivities mostly took place in Miamisburg, in the tavern of Jacob Kirchner[1] and later in the tavern of Captain Kothe[2] who relocated here from Cincinnati, in Germantown in Christopher Emerich's tavern, in Colonel Neukomm's tavern[3] in Dayton or in Scheidler's tavern at Tom's Run. There were wedding feasts and celebrations for no apparent reasons ("Kindelbier"), and violins and clarinets began playing for merry dancers who danced barn dances, waltzes, and "Dreher."[4]

During Peter Sunderland's wedding, so the story goes, it was particularly jolly.[5] Peter was a funny fellow and that he had a good fist was known from a memorandum of the first courtroom case in the county.[6] Peter had money and therefore he wanted to show the people what a wealthy German country wedding could be like. This was explained by "Uncle Abe" Weber of Liberty according to the story which he received from his mother, in the following way: The wedding took place in the house of the parents of the bride, Anna Meyer, at Big Bear Creek near the present-day town of Göttersburg.[7] All settlers within a twelve-mile radius were invited to the wedding. The wedding occurred early in the morning, it was in October in 1807, a gorgeous fall morning. All young fellows rode from Jefferson, Madison, German and Miami Townships through Miamisburg or as it was called at that time, Hole's Station, to Sunderland's house at Hole's Creek and Spring Valley Street in order to pick up the groom. There were more than one hundred riders, lead by a choir of five musicians whom Sunderland had specially brought up from Cincinnati. It goes without saying that the young men were dressed in their "finest garb;" this means they wore their best leather pants, tendon boots, jackets and hunting shirts made of home-woven half-wool materials, each wore on his head a new wide-brimmed hat decorated with a multi-colored ribbon and a feather. Sunderland purchased the hats for everyone in Cincinnati. The women of Washington and Miami Townships, who also joined the parade on horseback, were also dressed in fashionable clothes as far as their circumstances allowed because at that time there were no tailors and fashion designers in the backwoods. Nobody knew the slightest thing about "Dry Goods" and "Millinery" shops. The "ladies" of that time were dressed up in half-woolen underskirts and half-woolen or linen so-called petticoats, coarse shoes, stockings, scarves and homemade buckskin gloves. One or two might have worn a silver brooch at the bodice, a silver ring on their finger, or a pleated skirt with silver buttons, but those surely were heirlooms of their mother or grandmother who had brought those from Germany. The horses were almost exclusively without saddles and Sunderland had bought new and colorful, woolen blankets for them to serve as festive saddle blankets. All the people were accomplished riders and the pioneer ladies rode their horses astride like men. In such a manner, they rode along the forest path and where the route permitted, they rode in pairs. The rest of the time, they rode in Indian style that means one following the other. They took a break at Hole's Station in order to have an early drink and a morning snack at Kirchner's Tavern. At that time there was no bridge over the Miami River and so the cavalcade crossed the river at a shallow area, which was well passable due to its low water level. The farmers blocked the path on the other side of the river with vines that were spanned across just like a barrier. A small barrel of brandy, which was brought along, convinced the farmers, however, to open up the barrier again and the cavalcade could continue on.

About one mile from the Miami River where the path crosses the Bear Creek, the farmers had created a so-called ambush by frightening the wedding parade with an unexpected volley of gunfire, so that the horses reared up and the girls, who were good riders, screamed out loud causing the male companions, who were moved in a kind of chivalrous manner, to protect the female companions from falling. The fired volley of gunfire was at the same time the signal for the competitive ride for the bottle, a practice that was customary everywhere in the West at that time. Two of the young men raced to find out who would arrive at the house of the bride first. The worse the path, the more stumps and deep holes covered the route, the better. The start was marked by howling similar to the Indians and off they went over rough and smooth, sloughs and hills, tree stumps and shrubbery, like a wild chase, towards the house. There the brandy pitcher was ready and therefore no arbitrator was needed to decide the winner of the competitive ride. The rider, who arrived first, received the bottle with which he returned to the companions. Holding up the bottle with a cry of joy, he drank to the groom who arrived at the front of the cavalcade. He then gave the bottle to the groom. He raised his bottle to him and now the bottle circulated so that the women and the men alike drank a toast to the health of the groom.

When they arrived at the bride's home, the older neighbors were already assembled and even the preacher was present. The wedding ceremony preceded the dinner as was the tradition. After Pastor Decheron tied the matrimonial knot, the wedding feast started in the woods behind the house where six long rows of tables and benches were assembled.[8] The tables were built in the style of pioneers: the tree trunks, which were two and a half to three feet thick, were split in half, mounted to the floor onto drilled pegs, and trimmed flat at the top with an adze. The benches were constructed in a similar way. In the back woods, the tableware usually consisted of wooden bowls and plates, but Sunderland made an exception here by having only tin tableware, a luxury according to "Uncle Abe," something that was unheard of in the west. Only the pruning knives, which each of the guests brought with them, reminded us of the pioneer life of the backwoods.

"Uncle Abe" reports about the wedding meal, or rather the wedding festivities, which lasted three days. Four great fat oxen, along with pork, deer meat, bear ham, wild turkeys and other poultry and the usual vegetables, corn bread, and as a delicacy, wheat bread and cake were reported to have been consumed. The most uncommon thing, however, was the beer which the bride's parents had contracted to be brewed specially. After the wedding meal, the dance began which lasted throughout the entire night. The next morning the guests took turns having a good night's rest in the haystacks and so on, so that they could continue the festivities again around noon.

It is understood that the traditional wedding customs, which took place in the backwoods, also took place here. Around ten in the evening a number of young girls kidnapped the bride and took her to bed. As soon as this had happened, a number of young boys stole away with the groom and put him very carefully in the bed next to the young bride. Then they continued dancing. Due to the lack of seats, the young men, who were not dancing, offered the girls their knees to sit on which was never refused. The bride and groom were never forgotten amidst this cheerfulness. After midnight one or the other remembered that the young couple might want refreshments, whereupon they brought a pitcher of brandy up to them. Not always was the "Black Betty," as the moonshine bottle was called, brought up alone but rather bread, meat, cake and so on were sent up too.[9] According to custom, the groom and bride had to taste everything that was offered to them. After the wedding guests grew tired of the wedding festivities, after the third day, they all continued with their usual chores. Many years after that, they still spoke of Peter's and Anna's wedding or how they usually called it, the Sunderland Ranch, as an event in the backwoods which was one of a kind.

That was the merry, the jovial life of the Germans. But there was also the less fortunate side: resentment, envy and quarrel revealed a dark side, which was mainly preserved in the court documents. The German Justices of the Peace of the county during that period were Johannes Folkerth (Volkert? – 1804) and Christ Curtner (1806).[10] No less than 68 complaints between quarrelling neighbors were negotiated in front of Squire Folkerth in the year 1805, from which date on he kept his books in the county's court building. Germans were without exception prosecutors and defendants. The first case involved Ludwig Winter against Jacob Heck "for despiteful defamation and slanderous statements." Then one by one the names of Norbert Huey, Franz Dilts, David Rüffle, Johann Gerhard, Jacob Spittler, Heinrich Kinzer, Johannes Scheidacker (Sidicker or Scheidecker), Gebhard, Johann Gärtner and numerous others appeared before the Folkerth's Court of Justice, all accused of petty altercations, brawls and the like. Most of the charges were filed by Philipp Gunkel, the founder of Germantown, against his neighbors before both of the German Justices of the Peace.[11] Judging by this, he must have had an extremely irritable character because I have found over twenty complaints by him, even at the higher courts of the county. Among them in the year 1808 was a lawsuit for defamatory statement against Martin Erhardt and also one against Martin Schewe. In both cases Gunkel demanded $2000 in damage compensation for loss of honor. In both cases also the sheriff testified with the words: "Non est inventis," that he could not find the accused.[12]

The German pioneers of Montgomery County seemed to have had their share of problems with their women as well because it was not uncommon that they ran away as is manifested in the following ad in the "Liberty Hall and Cincinnati Mercury" newspaper published in Cincinnati on January 20, 1806:

> *Warning: Because my wife Elisabeth ran away from table and bed without giving reasons and without being provoked in the slightest, this serves as a warning to all people to lend something to said Elisabeth in my name or to shelter her. I am resolute not to pay any of her debt made after today's date.*
> *My signature as testimony,   Bernhard Speck.*
> *Please, note: It is believed that she goes by the name of Mrs. Fischer. Dayton, January 9, 1806*

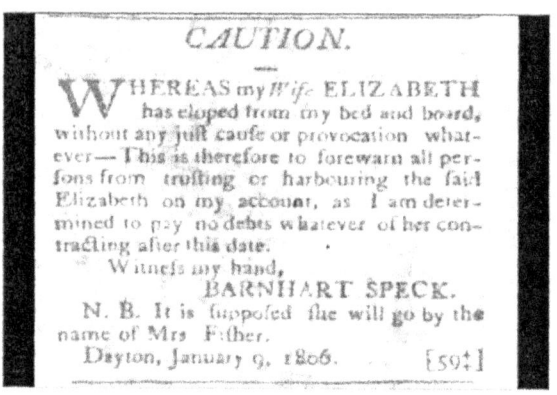

Notice by Bernhard Speck, Liberty Hall & Cincinnati Mercury, January 20, 1806, p. 3

Despite this explanation of his own good nature, our fellow countryman does not seem to have been quite as peaceable because already in the year of 1805 he was fined ten dollars and court costs during the August term of the county court because he gave a certain Adam Fischer palpable proof of the strength of his arms.[13] Might his Eva have escaped in the following winter with this Adam from the Speck-paradise?

If someone was arrested by the sheriff or constable at that time for any criminal perpetration, he was put in a safe place in a prison which was one of a kind. There was still no lodging in Montgomery County in which one could restrain prisoners. Many who were locked up in a well-barricaded barn and thought to be safe were gone the next day when they were asked to appear in front of the judge. Their recapture in the sparsely populated district was usually unsuccessful. Therefore Sheriff Neukomm came up with an original idea. He had a well next to his house, which ran dry. The prisoners were lowered into it after their arrest and were kept there until their interrogation, and then they were brought up and presented to the judge. Sheriff Neukomm acted here as a jailor at the same time.[14] The story goes that there was not one prisoner who escaped from this strange prison.

Not in all cases did the Germans act in the role of the quarrelsome neighbor. The following cases, numbers 8 and 9 in the court protocol of Montgomery County, are proof of their appreciation of freedom, their human sense of justice, and their strict opposition against slavery. Colonel Robert Patterson, the co-founder of Lexington, Cincinnati and Dayton, brought with him, when he settled in Dayton in 1801, three negroes whom he still kept in Cincinnati as his slaves, despite the ordinance of July 13, 1787. According to this ordinance, "slavery whatsoever or involuntary subservience" must not be tolerated in the areas northwest of the Ohio River, the present-day states of Ohio, Indiana, Illinois, Michigan, and Wisconsin, "except for punishment for criminal wrongdoings when the person was convicted by law."[15] He took them with him when he moved from Cincinnati to Dayton, treating them as his property and going unpunished. This very much enraged the Germans of the county against the colonel who kept slaves. Because the courts of Hamilton County, to which this territory belonged back then, were sixty to seventy miles away from Cincinnati, nothing happened initially in support of the release of the negroes. When Montgomery was elevated to an autonomous county in 1803, and when the Justices of the Peace also obtained the right to issue emancipation papers, the German settlers in particular asserted themselves to claim free land.

Colonel Robert Patterson's Signature, 1813, Dayton, Ohio

Article Six of the Northwest Ordinance of 1787 outlaws slavery

The Patterson Farm; House on left built in 1816

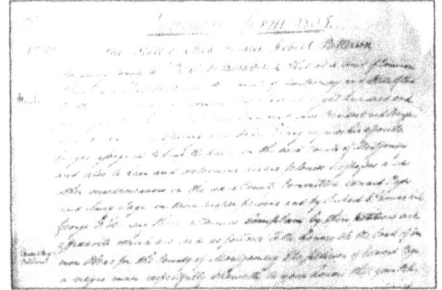

Robert Patterson Slave Case, 1805 Montgomery County Records Center, Clerk of Courts Records, Book A1, Volume 1, p. 60 ff.

The Ordinance of 1787 dealt only with the future (namely it was determined by the courts) and the question of whether the descendants of the people, that were slaves in 1787, could be held in servitude because of a right of possession and the non-retroactivity of later laws, remained undecided outside of Ohio until the year 1845. Not until this year did the Supreme Court of Illinois decide that they were free.[16] Not much confidence was being placed in the first decisions of the courts which can be demonstrated by the following: in 1804 a convention was held in Vincennes to advise on the "territorial interests" and the decision was made to send a memorandum to Congress according to which the sixth article of the Ordinance of 1787 be suspended and one should be allow to move slaves, who were born within the United States, to the territories. Congress, however, refused the request. Nevertheless, attempts were made until 1807 in Indiana and until 1816 in Illinois to legalize slavery, which was made possible in Indiana, if master and slave made a contract that the latter is willing to serve as a servant or maidservant for a certain time. After the expiration of this time period, he or she would be guaranteed his or her full-fledged freedom.[17]

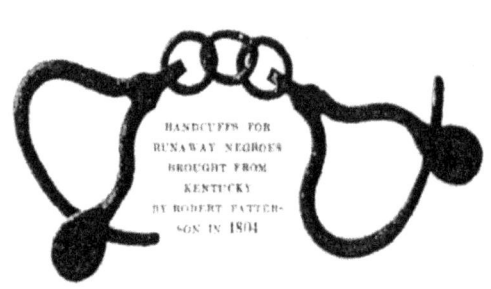

HANDCUFFS FOR
RUNAWAY NEGROES
BROUGHT FROM
KENTUCKY
BY ROBERT PATTER-
SON IN 1804

Col. Robert Patterson (1753-1827)

In Ohio the first constitution had gotten things moving through the stipulations of the second section of Article 8; however there still remained the possibility of a contractual servitude of the negroes for one year.[18] Colonel Patterson relied on the laxity of the courts and the complacency of the people and brought his slaves with him to Dayton and kept them as if he were still in Kentucky.[19] This upset the German people of the county tremendously. By the end of January of 1805 they obtained a so-called "Habeas Corpus Order" to summon Eduard Page and Lucy Page, his wife, and Moses (no further name), three negroes which "were kept contrary to the constitution and the laws of Ohio in Montgomery County in slavery" by Colonel Robert Patterson and they demanded their release. After the case was heard on February 6, 1805 by "Squire" Johannes Folkerth, it was decreed, upon having listened to the witnesses, that the negroes should be freed.[20] Colonel Patterson was beside himself with rage. He did not want to give up his human merchandise so easily. He insisted that a certain David M. Sharp, a Kentuckian, and several collaborators should kidnap the persons of African descent and bring them to Kentucky again. The Germans, however, received information about the intended human theft and uncovered the heist, just in time, at the farm of Peter Claussen in Washington as they were just trying to escape across the borders to Warren County. On this occasion one of the Germans, Hieronymus Holt, was shot at and critically wounded by Sharp. The practical Germans, however, grabbed Sharp, took him to Dayton into Colonel Neukomm's cistern-prison, where he had to stay imprisoned for a while until Colonel Patterson obtained his release by putting up bail. On January 27, 1806 the Grand Jury filed an indictment against Sharp for assault with the intention of killing a human being, but Patterson knew, by using legal sophistry, to move the case to the neighboring Warren County. I could not find out if it ever came to a trial.[21]

The following Germans were among the first settlers of the county until the year 1809 according to court books and basic property registers: Peter Felix (coming from *Elsass*), Jacob Braun, Wilhelm Diehl (Geyer or Guier and Diehl maintained already in 1808 a so-called "Wholesale Store" in Hole's Station), Adam Kugler, Georg Schaub, Jacob Philippsohn, Benjamin Lehmann, Johann Wodemann, Andreas Lack, David Müller, Johannes Flock, Bernard Keiser, Conrad Kaste, Hanns Haick, Jacob Yecki (?), Friedrich Aigenbrecht, Edmund Adam, Christian Fritz, Georg Sauerbrei (Sourbray), Jacob Schlei (Sly), Georg Kunz, Hans Banest, Samuel Beck, Fabian Engel (at one location his name is recorded as Eagle at another as Engle), Karl Tull, Wilhelm Wach, Heinrich Ledermann, Heinrich Marquard, Daniel H. Fischer, Friedrich Jordan, Jacob Harter, Peter Muselmann, Abraham Hildebrand, Johannes Weber, Christian Null, Balthasar Wilhelm (Balzel Williams), Daniel Pressel, Mathias Ringel, Abraham

Darst (who bought on July 6, 1806 the lot number 51 in Dayton) and many others. I could not find out if Edmund Mungen[22], who was one of the first county commissioners and who signed the first map of the city of Dayton together with Daniel C. Cooper[23] was a German native. The name strongly indicates this. In 1805 Wilhelm Hammer and Jacob Müller became wardens of the poor of the county and Joseph Rehbaum was elected justice of the peace. The names of Christopher Gärtner (also known as Cartner), Jobst Westphal, Daniel Kreib, Leonard Wolf, Johannes Paully, David Lammers and Johann Mickesell are recorded as members of the Grand Jury in January 1806 who filed the aforementioned accusation case against Sharp.

One of the most affluent German property owners of the county was Heinrich Mayer who died in the year 1806 in German Township. He was the grandfather of Mrs. Sunderland. After his death, his estate, 1086 acres in total, already largely farmed was divided amongst his widow Elisabeth and eight children: Johannes, Michael, Jacob, Jonas, Peter, Daniel, Anna, wife of Daniel Bauzer (the name is also written as Bowser, Bouzer and Bauzer)[24] and Christina Baumann.

With respect to the domestic life of the German pioneers, this life was just simple. Most of the people were farmers and worked their utmost on their farms carving them out of the jungle, which was truly no small task. When they arrived, they first had to build a log cabin for which all lent a helping hand. Once the house stood and they finally were secured, they faced difficulties again. A piece of land needed to be cleared out from the jungle so that the seed could be put into the ground. When cutting down trees, the German immigrants were very unskillful initially, but they soon learnt from their Pennsylvanian-German neighbors who brought the necessary experience with them from the East and who lent a helping hand and gave advice to their fellow German countrymen. Little by little they cleared the woods partially by cutting the trees down, partially by girding the trees. In a few years the German farms could compete with the farms of the Anglo-Americans.

It is easy to imagine that these men were most actively supported in their endeavor by their women. Even if the woman did not swing her ax in the woods and did not walk behind the plow, she still had to provide so much in addition to her work from morning until evening that she rightfully took an equal part in the success of the pioneers, as her male companions. In the spring she assisted in sowing and planting, in the summer and fall in harvesting the fruits and grains, and in winter, when the men chopped down the woods, built fences or stables, or hunted for rabbits, partridges, turkeys, as well as deer and bears, then the woman was occupied with her daughters at home. She provided the family with articles of all kinds of clothing, bedding and toiletries for the coming year. At that time, each house had a spinning wheel and a loom. Instead of spending their days swaying in the rocking chair, reading novels, playing piano and singing, as our ladies do today, the pioneer woman sat, sewed, and patched skirts and pants, knitted stockings and made moccasins and gloves from deer skin which was tanned by themselves. While their daughters worked at the purring spinning wheel, they sang a happy tune:

> *Turn little wheel, hum, hum hum*
> *Spin the tiny thread, buzz, buzz, buzz*
> *To fill the spool,*
> *Tomorrow comes the wooer,*

Calls me his sweetheart,
Asks me if I want to be his darling,
Fill up, fill up, canvas shrine,
in a year we should marry![25]

The brave pioneer woman sat at the loom and clapped merrily to the beat of the girls' tune. All the things that were necessary for a woman back then to learn, next to cooking, baking, knitting, mending, preparing butter and cheese, becomes apparent from the following employment letter which is recorded at the court documents of Montgomery County.[26] Georg Rüfele of German Township, whose wife died in the spring of 1807, gave his three-year-and-four-month old girl to Paul D. Buttler who adopted her. The official letter, which was drawn up on March 10, 1807 states that Maria "should serve him (Buttler) and live with him until she reaches full age and that she should labor and learn all kinds of housewifery, such as cooking, spinning, weaving, knitting, sewing, washing, and so forth." Buttler promises in turn to "provide her with sufficient food and drink, clothes suited for a girl in the common or ordinary stations of life in this country during that time." And when she reaches the legal age (which would be November 4, 1821) he promises to give her in addition: "a good duvet and bedding, two Sunday dresses" and he also promises that she will be instructed in reading and writing during the length of her service.

At that time the Germans always had an advantage over the Anglo-Americans. They made sure that their children learnt how to read, write and do math. One rarely finds an X instead of a signature even in the oldest court documents, something that was common with Anglo-Americans at that time in almost two out of three cases. Even in the religious life they were different than their Anglo-Saxon neighbors. Most Germans committed themselves to the Reformed and Lutheran Church; the Americans generally belonged to "Presbyterian," "Baptist," "Methodist" and "Episcopal." But there were also German "Methodists", the "Duncards" and the "United Brethren," two pietistic, almost ascetic sects who settled the northwest part of the county.[27] They were all Germans. However, they vastly differed from the English-speaking settlers in their liberal concept of Sunday worship. Although the Anglo-Americans attended church comparatively less frequently than their German neighbors, the Anglo-Americans, nevertheless, spent their beloved Sunday in such a dreadfully boring manner, as if it were agreeable to God to cower at home on this day, to be monosyllabic, to make a grumbling face and to be unable to utter any cheerful word, as if heaven had forbidden that man utter even one sign of joy, even a laughter on such a beautiful God-given day. The Germans behaved quite differently. They attended mass regularly on Sunday morning, listened devoutly to the pious warnings of their preachers, and when the service ended, men and women, met in the tavern or summer garden. They visited each other, probably in the afternoon, in their dwellings, and then spent the rest of the day with pleasant conversations. There usually was dancing in the taverns where young men and women of the area took part. They danced in the bowers of the summer gardens, which almost all German taverns had. The older men bowled on a primitive bowling alley for a pitcher of beer. In the winter they sat in the tavern at the card table, or in a circle by a large fire spending time in a social get-together and engaged in pleasant conversations. This annoyed the Anglo-American who could not forget the Puritan ideas of Cromwell's times and his fanatical Barebones. His intolerance, which he brought over here with the Mayflower, increased considerably, and he quickly instituted moral laws, frowning upon all merriment on the "Day of the Lord." Bowling alleys and card games, dancing music and any type of entertainment were forbidden on the Sabbath day. Finally they even invented the temperance laws. But the Germans refused to be converted into Puritan hypocrites who publicly wore their long sanctimoniously pious faces while secretly they would indulge in vices with even higher intensity. The German always remained happy cheerful people, and when the doors to his taverns were closed, due to the fanatical laws, he always knew how to find the small backdoor. Behind closed doors there still flourished the German cheerfulness and gregariousness in a quiet and familiar way.

The German preachers and clergymen did not behave at all like their English brethren. They did not prohibit the innocent amusement of the people, but rather participated often. Legend has it that old Thomas Winter, the first German Reformed preacher of Dayton, who had already gathered a German congregation in Dayton in 1810, preferred to go to Middletown or Germantown on Sunday afternoons because they led a more cheerful life there than in the more Puritan-minded Dayton. Reverend Winter, or Winters, as he is usually known today, was a German preacher in Dayton and surroundings from September 1810 until the 1840's.

St. John's Reformed Church of Germantown, Ohio

His son, David Winters, was his assistant from 1825 and later his successor as preacher of this church. The older Winter only preached in German, the younger started with German and later alternated between German and English. The present preacher of this parish, David Van Horne, uses only English. Therefore, the oldest German community in Montgomery County has changed into an English speaking community. In the year 1872, the name of the church, which stands on Ludlow between Second and Third Street, is still recorded as "German Reformed Church" on a map in Titus' Atlas. In 1876 on a map in Evert's Atlas, it is only referred to as "First Reformed Church." The following German Reformed communities existed in the county before the year 1850: in Dayton two, in Germantown two, in Middletown one, and in the townships Butler, Clay, Harrison, Madison, Jefferson, Jackson and Washington one each. The Reformed preachers of the county, as long as they applied for a general license and therefore had their names recorded in the county books (before the year 1850), were:

Name of Pastor	Date of License
Thomas Winter	September 1810
Andreas Henkel[28]	Already before 1820
Elias Nickers	July 20, 1823
Johannes Peine	July 5, 1824
David Winter[29]	August 17, 1824
Elias Kuntz[30]	October 23, 1835
Israel S. Weiß	June 29, 1843
Joseph Steiner	January 8, 1844
Hermann Schönle	April 5, 1845
Louis A. Brunner	December 17, 1846
J.R. Denis	April 15, 1848

The first German church in the county was, however, the Lutheran Church built in the year 1806 in German Township where Rev. Dechant was the first preacher. He was born in Bavaria, came to America in 1801 and then settled in Berks County where he obtained a pastorate in a Lutheran Church.[31] When in the years 1803 to 1806 the first settlement of German Township was established by a colonization company, one negotiated with the preacher to persuade him to relocate to the new homestead.

This did not happen however until the year 1806 when they had already constructed little log church and log cabin as rectory. Since the fall of this year the word of the Lord was proclaimed for the first time in the German language in Montgomery County and probably in the entire Miami area. A brother, Christoph Dechant, who was a master bricklayer in Germany also arrived here in the year 1816. He is still living as an affluent farmer in Section 16 in German Township.

Chapter 3
Small Business Endeavors in Germantown and Miamisburg

Germantown, next to Dayton the biggest town of the county, was laid out in the year 1814 by Philipp Gunkel.[1] It is a beautiful little town of about 1500 inhabitants, who are almost all of German origin. The city has seven churches, two Reformed, two Methodist, two Lutheran and one United Brethren Church. As late as 1845, the sermons in all churches, there were five at the time, were in German. Dechant was the first German Lutheran preacher (since 1806) and Andreas Henkel was the first Reformed minister (from before 1820).[2] Germantown is very beautifully designed in a magnificent valley surrounded by the most fertile land of the entire county. Until the year 1825, Germantown seemed to have equal rank with Dayton. In 1820 Germantown even threatened to displace Dayton. However, when in 1828 the canal from Dayton to Cincinnati was completed, the fate of Germantown was sealed. The first German newspaper in Montgomery County was printed in Germantown (1838): *Der Protestant (The Protestant)*, published by Walker and Espich.[3] The paper, however, only survived approximately for one year.[4] It moved with its publishers to Cincinnati, and died after a lifespan of barely two years.

Hans Georg Walker, outstanding German-American writer and theologian, was born in Urach near Reutlingen,[5] in the Kingdom of Würtemberg, around the year 1805, attended in his youth the Latin School in Reutlingen, and then the Protestant Seminary in his hometown, in order to study theology there. This was determined by his parents. After passing his exams successfully, he attended the University of Tübingen where he additionally studied theology and philosophy. In 1834 he came to America, was for a while in Maryland and Pennsylvania and was summoned to Canal Dover in Tuscarawas County, Ohio, as a Protestant preacher where he arrived in the spring of 1836.[6] In the year 1838, Walker came to Germantown to the congregation of Pastor Dechant[7] who had recently died. Here Walker and Espich (who was a book printer) founded together, as already mentioned, the "Protestant." In 1839 they also printed the statute laws of Ohio[8] which were translated into German by Walker. In doing so they lost much money. In Cincinnati, where Walker relocated in the fall of 1839, he worked for many years as publicist and died there in the summer of 1849 of cholera.[9] Walker was one of the most ingenious German writers in America. He published the following journals, one after the other: "Der Protestant" (1838-39), "Der Deutsch-Amerikaner" ("The German-American") (1839-40), "Die Volksbühne" ("The People's Theatre"), (initially in Louisville, 1840-45), "Der Hochwächter" ("The Guardian"), (1845-49).[10]

In Miamisburg, which was designed as a city in the year 1818 by Emanuel Gebhardt, Jacob Kirchner, Dr. Johannes Treon and Peter Treon, a German Protestant-Lutheran congregation was formed soon after and presided over by Reverend Decheron initially.[11]

Dr. Treon Residence, Miamisburg, Ohio

He was previously mentioned and resided in Germantown, as preacher. In 1818 the venerable Johann C. Dill became pastor of this borough where he stayed until his death in 1824.[12] In the same year he was succeeded by Christoph Heinrich Daniel Heinke as pastor. He was born on December 15, 1793 in Cuxhaven at the Weser, Hannover, emigrated to America in 1817, and arrived on September 14 of the same year in the Harbor of Baltimore. He came to Ohio soon after, in the fall. He was a merchant by trade and had received a good liberal education in Germany, but because the commercial subject did not count as scholarly craft in America, especially in the backwoods, he devoted himself in the new country to the study of theology. At that time there was no preacher seminary in the West, and therefore he had to study under the direction of Pastors Decheron, Dill and others. In the fall of 1820, Heinke applied for authorization to preach at the Protestant-Lutheran Synod of Ohio and after having passed his exams brilliantly, he was unanimously received into the ministry by the Synod.[13] In the beginning he had to work as an itinerant preacher, as did most of the pastors at this time. He visited the Lutheran congregations in Montgomery, Butler and Warren Counties and even went as far as Indiana. After Dill's death he was elected pastor of the Lutheran community in Miamisburg, which he presided over until his death on July 10, 1859. Pastor Heinke was a rather good theologian who was well versed in church doctrines, equipped with a solid knowledge, a clear head and an honest heart. At the same time he was a good preacher who knew how to talk in an easily comprehensible, short and precise and nevertheless comprehensive and exciting fashion. In his dealings with individuals he was extremely undemanding and a friend of peace and order. In the possession of such endearing qualities, it was no surprise that he was loved by all who knew and appreciated him. Heinke was said to have been a good preacher in English, although he came to America as an adult. He was fluent in spoken and written English. During Heinke's time of service, the first substantial church was built out of brick in Miamisburg, and he laid the cornerstone in the summer of 1830. Up to that point, the congregation managed with a church that was held in a barn. In 1861, however, the church, which was built under Heinke's guidance, was replaced by a more modern church, which is at the moment one of the most beautiful structures of the city. The venerable C. Albrecht has been the pastor of the congregation since April of 1860.[14]

I could not find out when the first German Lutheran or Lutheran-Evangelist church was founded in Dayton.[15] The preachers of this religious confession in Montgomery County between 1820 and 1850 were:

Name of Pastor	Date of License
Louis Markart	December 25, 1822
Jacob Gruber	January 15, 1830
Georg Walker[16]	April 11, 1836
Friedrich Reiß or Reuß	March 27, 1838
Adam S. Link	May 5, 1838
August Großkurdt	November 8, 1839
Peter Rosenmüller[17]	November 18, 1840
G. Bartels	April 30, 1842
Andreas Hardorff	January 12, 1842
G. Döpker	August 3, 1847
Andreas Hardorf	November 21, 1844

Almost at the same time as the Lutherans, the Dunkards or "Tunkers," "the United Brethren in Christ" and the German Methodists got organized in the county. The following German preachers belonged to the "Tunkers":

Name of Pastor	Date of License
Michael Etter[18]	September 12, 1822
Johannes Darst	October 28, 1833
Johann Meyer	October 24, 1836
David Schellenberger	August 10, 1840
Daniel Müller	February 6, 1842
Heinrich Rübsamen	February 1, 1845

The "United Brethren" had the following preachers:[19]

Name of Pastor	Date of License
Martin Böhm[20]	Already in 1812
Heinrich Kummler	March 29, 1823
Heinrich Joseph Frey	September 18, 1823
Georg Bonebraker (Beinbrecher)	May, --, 1827
David Baumann (Bowman)[21]	April 7, 1843

Martin Böhm (1725-1812), Co-Founder of the Church of the United Brethren in Christ

Henry Kumler, Jr., (1801- 1882) Eleventh Bishop of the United Brethren in Christ

Besides these, the following German Protestant preachers are mentioned in the license register of the county:

Heinrich Ernst Pilcher (Presbyterian), licensed	October 27, 1831
Johannes Keßling (Methodist Episcopal Church) license	August 01, 1843

Jacob Wolf and Philipp Wrampler were both licensed as preachers on April 8, 1844 without mentioning the confession they belonged to.

The first German Catholic parish in Montgomery County was founded in Dayton in 1833 by the venerable Father Emanuel Thienpont.[22] Already in 1829, the venerable father Martin Kundig came to Dayton and held church services in his private home.[23] The first mass was said, however, earlier by the well-known father Stephan Theodor Badin in Dayton.[24] Also the venerable Father Junker, who was to become Bishop of Alton, Illinois, said mass in Dayton in 1834; however the first church originated solely under Thienpont.[25] On the site, where today's Emanuel Church is located, the lot was bought by the Catholics in 1835, was a spacious barn, which was converted into a church and was dedicated by Bishop Purcell in the year 1835.[26] It received the name Emanuel Church in honor of Father Emanuel Thienpont. Pastor Thienpont, the first Catholic clergyman residing in Dayton, was a Belgian who could preach in German, Dutch, French and English. He was a highly valuable person in the backwoods where all these nations were more or less present and needed to be taken care of. Later he was transferred to Portsmouth, Ohio, where he served the French colonies at Gallipolis as a pastor and died in Portsmouth in the early fifties. Thienpont was succeeded in the pastorate by Father Junker, who had assisted him temporarily before.[27]

Fr. Martin Kundig

Archbishop John Martin Henni
1805-1881
First Bishop 1844
Archbishop of Milwaukee 1875

Fr. Henry Damian Junker

Heinrich Damian Junker, the first Catholic priest ordained in America, was born in the city of Finstingen, Lorraine, in the year 1810.[28] He arrived in America with his parents in his early youth, studied in Cincinnati where he was ordained in March 1834. He was the priest of the first German congregation in Cincinnati from where he was later transferred to Columbus, Chillicothe and Canton, Ohio. He came to Dayton in 1850 where he remained until his appointment as Bishop of Alton (1857). He died in Alton, Illinois, on October 2, 1868.[29] Junker's successor at the Emanuel Church in Dayton was Father Johann F. Hahne who has now been working over twenty-one years in the parish as pastor.[30]

The Catholic clergymen who have visited Montgomery County, specifically Dayton, in priestly functions, before the year 1850 are the following, in sequence:
Stephan Theodor Badin, before 1818
Martin Kundig, licensed in Ohio on February 16, 1829
Johann Martin Henni, now Archbishop of Milwaukee, licensed on February 16, 1829, came to Dayton in 1835.[31]
Emanuel Thienpont, licensed on March 7, 1833

J.B. Purcell, at that time Bishop, now Archbishop of Cincinnati, licensed on January 17, 1834. He performed the first confirmation in Dayton on the Sunday after Easter in the year 1834.
Heinrich Damian Junker, later Bishop of Alton, Ill., was licensed on April 2, 1834.
Mathias Wirz, licensed on July 7, 1835.

From the two German emigration waves of this century (the immigration in the thirties and the so-called immigration of the 48ers), Montgomery County received its due share, which supplied the German identity, which was threatened to fizzle out gradually next to the Anglo-Americans, with fresh and pulsating new life. The immigration in the twenties had already brought men such as Heinke, Dechant, Gruber, Peine, Kundig, Henni, Thienpont and others here, who renewed the church life among the Germans again. The German publication house, which was founded by the "United Brethren" in Dayton, contributed to a large part to the preservation of the German church life among the pietistic religious community. The strong arms of the pioneers did not get tired in their desire to provide for their material life. In order for the German character to not degenerate into uncontrolled brandy boozing, Philipp Scheick found in 1827 a practical remedy by building a beer brewery in Germantown. Scheick was a native of Lorenzen in Lower Alsace, and came to America in 1824. He was employed for a while in Philadelphia in a brewery, and in 1825 or 1826 he founded his own brewery in Germantown near Philadelphia. In 1827 he relocated to Germantown at the instigation of his cousin Christian Rohrer (a native of St. Johann by Saarbrücken) who had already settled in 1825 in Germantown, Montgomery County, Ohio.[32] He established the first true brewery of the county. Later he went as a joint partner of the Schulz Brewery[33] to Cincinnati and moved in 1836 to Madison, Indiana, where he himself operated a spacious brewery. He died approximately five years ago at a very old age. When Scheick relocated in 1832 from Germantown to Cincinnati, he transferred his brewery to his younger brother, Louis Scheick, in conjunction with his cousin Rohrer who ran the brewery later on. Louis Scheick, who was unmarried, died several years ago. Rohrer has left behind many children, who still live in Germantown even today and who are carrying on the beer brewery, brandy distillery, and farming. The brewery, located on Centre Street, is still run today by Rohrer's oldest son, Karl J. Rohrer. He was born in 1826 in Germantown. Christian Rohrer, Jr. (born in 1830) lives secluded on his farm in Section 14 near Germantown,[34] while C. Samuel Rohrer (born in 1833) owns an insurance agency on Centre Street. David Rohrer (born in 1835) operates a large brandy distillery in Section 14 and Eduard Rohrer is living, retired from business, on Walnut Street.

We may be justified to say that we nowadays praise beer as a culture-promoting drink and that beer brewers are praised as genuine benefactors of mankind, although they basically only look out for their own profit. The pioneers of the brewing trade in this country justly deserve our praise for their initial risky endeavors and we may in no way deny that. When the English local historians initially enumerated with great care the first mills and the first brandy distilleries, it is equally important that the first attempts at wine growing and beer brewing in this country should also be mentioned because milder alcoholic beverages gradually replaced the fiery, intoxicating drinks which provoke more or less brutality and are harmful to your health if consumed in larger quantities. In this context it is necessary to report that the above-mentioned brewery was established. Yet another special event is tied to the history of this brewery: in the year 1830 the first "low-fermentation" beer (*Lagerbier*) in America was brewed here by

Friedrich Germann, who had died many years ago in Louisville, Kentucky, better known by the name of "Bierfritz." Germann was a son of Scheick's sister and a native of St. Johann.[35] After his father's death he continued to run the brewery with Louis Scheick, for his mother, but when she remarried in 1829, Philipp Scheick invited both to come to America. Also Karl Geisbauer, who died last year in Covington and who also was a son of Philipp Scheick's sister, came along with the two to America and to the brewery in Germantown. He remained there for many years as a brewery assistant.

Chapter 4
German Pioneers bring Musical Entertainment to Ohio

The immigration of the 1830's introduced yet another factor for the preservation and renewal of the German identity in the county, instrumental music. Naturally, the German hymns could already be heard in the churches of the county during church services. It is not known to me when the first organ was introduced; however, it was reported that there already was an organ in the German church in Miamisburg at the beginning of the thirties.[1] The first instrumental music, besides church music, was introduced in 1832 in Dayton by the Teltow family.

Wilhelm Teltow, a native of Hannover or Braunschweig by birth, came to America in the year 1817 and soon settled in Cincinnati, where he was employed as a technician and mechanic and acquired quite a fortune. Approximately around the year 1828, he relocated with his family to the town of Hamilton where he oversaw the building of the bridge across the Miami River and became its principal shareholder.[2] The bridge was not profitable later and Teltow almost lost his entire fortune. He then moved in 1832 to Dayton where he established himself as the first music teacher in Montgomery County. He played different instruments, such as: piano, violin, flute, clarinet, horn, trumpet and so on. His family members too were all musically educated. When they settled in Dayton, they arranged for musical entertainment in the home of the Teltow family where Mrs. Teltow played the piano, Mr. Teltow himself played the violin, and the children Edwin second violin and viola, Herman flute, Otto (at that time almost still a child) clarinet and Emeline guitar. Thereby the Teltow family drew the attention of the distinguished inhabitants of Dayton, especially the Americans, and soon Teltow had found sufficient employment giving music lessons. Also the musical soirées of the Teltow family were now becoming more common and they were one after another transplanted into the parlors of the most respectable families such as the Clegg's, Smith's, Kneisly's, Rodefer's, Steele's and others. Among Teltow's students were the brothers John, Samuel and Josias Clegg, Dr. Kneisly, Jacob Boyer, Amor Smith, Josias Eversole, Wm. Bourne (since then pianoforte builder in Boston) and others. After the Teltow family had established themselves in this way, they undertook concert tours every now and then in the vicinity, played in Yellow Springs, Springfield, Xenia, Miamisburg, Germantown, Hamilton, and so forth. During the bathing season in Yellow Springs, the Teltow's gave yearly concert series, which were well received. Later the family expanded their tours further. They gave concerts in Cincinnati, Louisville, St. Louis and New Orleans, and they were then known as a famous artist family. During one of these concert tours, Wilhelm Teltow died in New Orleans from yellow fever (amaryllic typhus), whereupon the family moved to Cincinnati from where they gradually scattered all over the place. The old widow Teltow died in Cincinnati in 1849; Edwin Teltow remained in Cincinnati where he lived in the fifties as musician and maker of musical instruments.[3] He died around the year 1855. Hermann Teltow went to New York, where he found employment at the theater as musician; and Emiline married in the south, but returned however with her spouse during the yellow fever epidemic in 1839 to Cincinnati. It is said that they still live today near Westwood or Cheviot. I could not find out anything more about Otto, the youngest son. The old Teltow, according to my source of information, Mr. Amor Smith, Senior, who informed me about the Teltow family, was a noble person who was followed by disaster wherever he went and finally died in the south of this dreadful disease, yellow fever.

After Teltow's departure from Dayton, a Mr. Reuß - I could not find out his first name- became his successor. He came to Dayton in the year 1834, got acquainted with Dr. Kneisly who heard that he was a musician and who brought him one evening into the Teltow family when they were just performing a musical evening entertainment with their students. Reuß now played the following instruments one after the other: violin, flute, clarinet, horn and so forth, whereby he proved himself to be a highly accomplished musician. Because he could master both, brass instruments and woodwinds, they soon afterwards created a music school in order to create a choral music choir for Dayton. That is to say, Reuß committed himself to remain in Dayton to rehearse with such an organization, if ten students could be found, who would each pay him ten dollars per quarter. The number of dilettantes was soon accumulated and Reuß began rehearsing with them. The first students of Reuß were: Josias Clegg, E-flat clarinet; Samuel Clegg, piccolo; John Clegg, flute; Wm. Bourne, B-flat clarinet; Wilhelm Westermann, first trumpet; Dr. Kneisly, second trumpet; Josias Eversole, bassoon; Amor Smith, Senior, first horn; Richard Jacob, second horn; Jacob Boyer, trumpet; John Rodefer, little drum; and Dr. Gans, great drum.

In order to acquire the necessary instruments, that is to say the most expensive ones, the city council of Dayton approved the money for the purchase of "one bassoon, two French horns, and one big drum." Both horns were imported from Philadelphia and both together cost $36.00. The great drum and bassoon were found in Cincinnati. In exchange, the young music corps first played on July 4th, 1834 at the occasion of a public celebration of this day. The music enthusiasm, which Reuß had lent lively momentum, lasted for a while and then again dropped off. As legend has it, the number of students soon diminished and one part of them later refused to pay the teacher the promised fee. It is a fact that Reuß sued Dr. Gans for the money that was owed to him, which Justice of the Peace Folkerth granted him by law in spite of Dr. Gans' claim that he was not actually a student when he handled the big drum. Dr. Gans soon moved away to Cincinnati where he was well-known and played an important part among the German Whigs of the forties. Reuß, on the other hand, shook the dust of the city of Dayton off his feet and looked somewhere else for a more rewarding home for his talents.

After this first attempt to create a music choir in Dayton, the idea dropped off for a while until coincidence evoked it again in the year 1842. In 1840 the first German military company was created in Dayton, the "Deutsche Nationalgarde" ("National Guard of Germans"). The first captain of this company was Louis Hormel, who signed up in 1847 with a German voluntary company for the service of the United States and participated in the Mexican War.[4] After his return from Mexico, Captain Hormel settled in Springfield, Ohio. The German National Guard, however, which undoubtedly was one of the first German societies in Dayton, had to be satisfied initially during their parades which they celebrated on January 8th, February 22nd, July 4th, and so forth, with simple drum and pipe music. Around that time, Wilhelm Gemünn came as teacher to the first German Reformed Church. He then created a new music organization, the "Deutsche National Garde Bande" ("German National Guard Band"). Gemünn, who was from the Rhineland Palatinate, arrived in the year 1834 or 1835 in America. Five other of his fellow countrymen came with him: C.P. Leonhard, Adam and Johann Klein, Christ Knecht, and Jacob Scheu. They earned the necessary money for their crossing by making music during their trip through France. They continued their cheerful musicians' tour from Philadelphia through Pennsylvania, West Virginia and Ohio. While travelling, they played for weddings and played dance music everywhere. To the remote farmers they brought amusement, which was both an unexpected and pleasant treat. They always received a friendly reception and money until they arrived in Dayton, Ohio, where they separated. Gemünn, who was the soul of the entire group, remained behind for a while in Miamisburg where he and Jacob Scheu found employment in a light factory. In the evenings and on Sundays they made music in the tavern of Captain A. Kothe. Mr. Euchenhofer reported that he first learnt how to dance here. Later Gemünn received a position as teacher and organist for the German Reformed community at Ludlow Street, behind the courthouse in Dayton (Pastor Winter's Church) where he has been working for many years. Since the German militia company arranged the only German folk festivals of Dayton and surroundings then, the desire was soon felt to combine a musical choir with the company. As a result, Gemünn organized the "Deutsche National Garde Bande" ("German National Guard Band") of thirteen men. This band existed for many years and provided the Germans of Dayton with their entertainment music. All aforementioned people belonged to this music choir, including the Clegg's brothers, Westermann, Eversole and others. Of these, Scheu died later in Miamisburg and Adam Klein in Troy, Ohio; Gemünn drowned roughly six years ago in the Mad River. Johann Klein, who was elected one and a half years ago as coroner of Montgomery County, had to resign for health reasons, and is today in the hospital of the county.

This band played during the first important German ball, which was ever held in Dayton on February 22, 1842. The German National Guard organized the festivities in the market hall and almost the entire German population of Dayton took part in it. The net profit was intended for the purchase of instruments and the uniforms for the music choir. The ball made $128 in profit. At that time, the folk festivals of the National Guard were held in a lovely forest at the Mad River. The Mexican War dissolved the National Guard for a while. They rebuilt it in 1848 with Johann Valentin Nauerth as captain and then existed until 1853.

Johann Valentin Nauerth, born 1811 in Steinweiler in Rhineland Palatinate, came to Cincinnati in 1832 where he first worked for Johann Hehr at Deercreek in a slaughterhouse. Later he was working in all kinds of trades, whatever presented itself: in the quarry, building streets, digging basements and so forth. One could not afford to be choosy at that time. Later he became a waiter in Leo Zimmer's tavern on Main Street. There he met around the New Year of 1835 the well-known innkeeper Heinrich Franz who took him to Dayton where he served him as barkeeper. Franz, a native of Hannover, owned his tavern at the north side at the market, which was at that time the most prominent tavern in Dayton. Before him, in the twenties, Conrad Schmidt ran a tavern on Main and Second Street, the "Franklin House." Nauerth later started his own tavern, which he managed until around 1867 when he operated a spice and grocery store, which he still continues to run with his sons.

Another German military organization, the "German Riflemen Company," was established at the beginning of the fifties with Ferdinand Söhner as captain. In 1854 Captain Egry commanded a third German company, which existed until the year 1860. Philipp Walz was their First Lieutenant. Captain Söhner is currently a German teacher in the public schools in the city of Hamilton, Ohio.[5] Dr. Egry is still living today as a pioneer of the German doctors in Dayton.

I reported a little while ago that the first large German ball on Washington's birthday was held in 1842 at the market house. However, this was not the first dance which the Germans organized in Dayton. The old pioneer, Heinrich Sauter, reports that on Easter Sunday of the year 1835, Wilhelm Trebein, who later became such a popular innkeeper in Dayton, had already held a dance event in the new house of another German at Main Street and the Miami River. Later Trebein offered dancing in his tavern along the canal every Sunday. Heinrich Sauter, who was born in the year 1840 in Achem by Rehstatt, Baden, arrived in America in 1831. After having stayed one year in New York, he came to Elizabethtown by Lancaster, Pennsylvania where he remained again for two years and worked in his trade as shoemaker. From there he went in the year 1834 to Cincinnati and shortly thereafter to Dayton where he settled down now nearly forty-five years ago as shoemaker. Among the few Germans who lived in Dayton at that time were Schellhammer, who died approximately five years ago, Johann Dietz, Schiffermann, Johann Bohlender, Conrad Schmidt, H. Best, and Heinrich Hermann. Hermann was an Israelite who resided in Dayton since 1826 and died in 1877. He played an important role back then. There was also Rutz, the old blacksmith, Philipp Weber and Trebein. The Germans all knew each other during that period, and in a strange way, they agreed about everything among themselves. Neither religion nor politics separated them; and despite the meager existence with which all German pioneers at that time started their career, they were said to have been cheerful and in good spirits. During the above-mentioned Easter Sunday, Christ Knecht was the only musician playing the fiddle for dancing and it was reported that they had a jolly good time. Although Sauter brought the fever to Dayton and was not really in the mood for dancing, the women forced him to dance. It helped him so much, because he got rid of the fever. He later met Trebein and his wife, nee Catharina Wegemann, a native of Laer at Iburg in Westphalia, who had worked for the innkeeper Conrad Schmidt. The old pioneer shoemaker of Dayton is still in good health and told me, with visible pleasure, his memories of the pioneer life which they spent at that time between the hazel bushes and frog swamps, which surrounded the few Dayton houses everywhere.

The barkeeper, Wilhelm Trebein, who mostly hosted the dances, was born on June 4, 1800 in the Hessian Oldendorf.[6] He came to America in the spring of 1832 and has been living in Dayton since September of 1832 as one the pioneer innkeepers of this city. He died approximately five years ago.

The remaining social life of the Germans in Dayton developed later and then only gradually. In the year 1842, a general German social support society was formed with Johann Werner as the first president.[7] The society held their meetings in the classrooms of the German Reformed Church on Ludlow Street. It existed until the previous year and was dissolved due to lack of participation. The first president of the club, Werner, went as major to Mexico and did not return. The successor of Werner and president of the society for many years, Ludwig Huesmann, moved away to the north of Dayton.[8]

Arranged by age, the German singing societies of Dayton came first. They mainly owed their existence to the influence of the immigration of the Forty-Eighters. The first attempt to establish a singing society was already made in the year 1848. Among the inspirers were Daniel Leonhard, Wilhelm Haberstich[9], F.W. Bert and Jacob Linxweiler.[10] The first song they sang was

Werner's "Sah ein Knab ein Röslein stehn" ("Once a Boy a Rosebud Spied"). Since they, however, could not find a conductor, the society soon after collapsed.

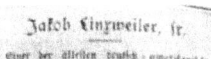

Jacob Linxweiler, Sr. (1813-1889) born in Rhenish-Bavaria, Germany, came to America in 1840; Baker, Grocer and Horticulturist in Dayton, Ohio

Jacob Linxweiler, Sr., one of the oldest German-American Pioneers of Dayton, Ohio Original obituary entry in a German newspaper in Dayton of Jacob Linxweiler, Sr., stating that he emigrated from Glan-Münchweiler, Kingdom of Bavaria, to Dayton in 1840, after a short stop in Canada. Dayton was a city with only 6000 inhabitants at that time. For an entire year he worked for only 75 Dollars and free food. In 1841 he married Carolina Heinz, also a native of Rhenish-Bavaria (*Rheinbayern*) who came over with her father in 1841. He was employed in the baking business and established his own bakery and grocery store in 1845 on the south side of Market Street in Dayton, Ohio. Later he made a name for himself as a leading member of the horticultural society in Dayton. He retired in 1870. His wife died in June 1869. He had two children: Jacob Linxweiler, Jr., who was mayor of Dayton, and a daughter, Mary L. Linxweiler who died in 1877. He was a member of the *Sociale Sängerbund*. Obituary, *Dayton Gedenkblätter*, 1889, Vol. 5. Iss. 22, p. 2-3.

The first regularly organized singing society was the *Sociale Sängerbund* (*Social Singing Society*), which was created on March 18, 1852.[11] The conductor of the society was Wilhelm Tisch who presided over the club as musical leader for many years. The first president of the club was Friedrich Wilhelm Berk.[12] From the first club members (besides the one's mentioned before) the following names have been preserved: Daniel Leonhard, Wilhelm Haberstich, Philipp Haberstich, Johannes Krehe, Wilhelm Leonhard, Jacob Linxweiler, Ludwig Huesmann, Capt. Louis Kuhlmann and Joseph Deschler. The young club participated, two months after it had been established, in the Fourth Singing Festival of the *Deutschen Sängerbund von Nord Amerika* (*German Singing Society of North America*) in Columbus, Ohio (Pentecost 1852).

Columbus Männerchor
won this ribbon in 1852

Columbus Männerchor, founded in 1848,
attends Sängerfest in Louisville, KY, in 1866

The trip to Columbus was not as simple as it is today because the railroads were still not connected everywhere. People from Dayton first had to drive by coach to Xenia from where they could take the railroad to Columbus. Of the people in Columbus at this concert, the ones from Dayton were the most cheerful of all festival companions, and therefore the next (fifth) federal singing festival was relocated to Dayton in 1853. During the individual singing in Columbus, the people from Dayton sang Conrad Kreutzer's "Glaube, Hoffnung und Liebe. – Was ist das göttlichste auf dieser Welt?" ("Faith, Hope and Love - What is the most Divine in this World?").

Type of the first Railway train running into Dayton, 1851.
Courtesy of the Dayton Metro Library
Lutzenberger Picture Collection

Conradin Kreutzer (1780-1849)
German Composer and Conductor

Stamp to commemorate Kreutzer's
100th anniversary of his death

In Columbus, the jovial singers from Dayton did not think about the great responsibility that was placed on their shoulders by hosting the singing festival. When, however, fall was approaching, they slowly thought about how the festival could be organized. The somewhat lax organization of the *Social Singing Society* was standing in the way of a successful festival. Therefore, at the beginning of December, a committee was appointed which should conceptualize a new constitution and recruit new members for the club. A new constitution was accepted on December 18, 1852 and was signed by the following 22 active members: I. Tenor: Rupert Ruß, Lazarus Schold, Jacob Schwab, Joseph Straub (now in Tippecanoe), Lorenz Rack and Philipp Beck. II. Tenor: Karl Gutheil (now in Winchester, Indiana, where he runs a tannery), Jacob Schönberg, Karl Wolf (currently in Indianapolis), H. Kreher (died) and H.W. Moß (he owns a clothing store today in Yellow Springs). I. Bass: Philipp Haberstich (died), Wilhelm Hergenröther (now in Tippecanoe), Jacob Löb, J. Ch. Höfer (died in 1879), Xaver Müller (died) and Joseph Müller. II. Bass: Daniel Leonhardt, Friedrich Ziegler, Jacob Linxweiler, Fr. Wilhelm Berk[12] (he was the owner of a horse barn and also is presently the undertaker in Dayton) and Wilhelm Haberstich. Also on this day, the following officials were elected: President: F. W. Berk; Vice-President: Philipp Haberstich; Secretary: Daniel Leonhardt; Treasurer: Jacob Linxweiler; Conductor: Karl Th. Tisch. Then, by the spring of 1853, the following new members joined the club which became one of the strongest of the societies: I. Tenor: J. Ach, Jacob Braunschweiger (died), Philipp Löb, Peter Moses and Joseph Deschler (presently innkeeper in Indianapolis). II. Tenor: G. Englert, J. Adler, Johann Ritter, Jacob Gaisser, S. Schönberg (rabbi) and Isaac Block. I. Bass: Val. Nold, H. Wollenhaupt, Georg Schweizer, August Lumpp, Fritz Greter and Peter Jahrling. II. Bass: J. Lauer (now in Indianapolis), Jacob Rundstock (died), Peter Theobald, M. Cohn, L. Huesmann, Wilhelm Leonhard, N. Raßmussen (fresco painter, now policeman in Chicago), Georg Hoffmann, Heinrich Roser and Franz Fritsch (died).

The singing festival that took place in Dayton on June 4-6, 1853 was one of the most significant events in the history of the German population of Dayton, even though the organizers of the festival suffered a considerable financial deficit due to bad weather. This had a detrimental effect on the singing society. It destroyed their enthusiasm.[13] The Society, however, did not die Säimmediately, but internal disputes, which were brought about by the singing festival, triggered the establishment of a new society, the *Dayton Harmonie* (*Dayton Harmony*). It still exists today and was ultimately absorbed by the *Sociale Sängerbund* (*Social Singing Club*). I am not informed about the exact date of the foundation of the *Harmonie* (*Harmony*), but it seems that it was created not long after the singing festival in 1853. The first clerks of this society were: President: Louis Seebohm; Secretary: P. Leonhardt; Treasurer: Wilhelm Sander; Conductor: August Ebel. The *Harmonie* was not only a singing society, but was also established with the purpose of social amusement. Under its guidance, the first German amateur theatre was developed in Dayton, which continued for years and contributed enormously to the preservation of the German culture and the promotion of German education in this city. Furthermore, the *Harmonie* had its own clubroom, a cozy sanctuary of refuge during the earlier days of the fanatical temperance movement, with which Dayton too was punished in its time. It goes without saying that the *Harmonie* also cultivated song and music. The *Daytoner Harmonie* was for many years one of the most prominent singing societies of the west, which acquired everywhere, and especially in Cincinnati, the warmest friends. During the opening ceremony of the newly renovated club house (the *Beckel's Hall*) ten years ago, the great opera *Gustav III.* was performed with exceptional instrumentation. It was written by Auber, Cincinnati's *Orpheus* and was perhaps the best opera presentation Dayton had ever seen.

Friedrich von Flotow (1812-1883)

Huston Hall (1864) as a music hall; Beckel Hall was a German theatre built in 1852.

    The most brilliant conductor of the *Harmonie* and one of the most excellent musicians of Dayton was undoubtedly Carl Rex.[14] He was born in the year 1828 in the city of Pyrmont, in the principality of Walddeck, and came to Dayton in the year 1855 where he settled as a music teacher and organist. For many years he was the organist of the Presbyterian Church and during his lifetime he was one of the most prominent music directors of Dayton. Under Rex's guidance, the *Harmonie* performed the opera *Stradella* by Flotow. He died approximately three years ago, much bemoaned by all who knew him.[15]

    The year 1853, motivated by the singing festival, which I have already mentioned, was a huge stimulus for Dayton's cultural boom. Another dramatic club was created, the "Frohsinn" ("Joviality"), which however soon thereafter was absorbed by the "Harmonie" ("Harmonia Society"). The founders of this club were: Joseph Wollinger, Louis Kuhlmann, Ludwig Markgraf and others.

    At the same time (March 18, 1853), the "Daytoner Turnverein" ("Dayton Turner Society") was formed. The head of the club was Peter Moses. Among the main supporters of the Turners were Ludwig Huesmann, Dr. Langstedt, Johann Bettelon, Daniel Leonhardt and Philipp Walz.[16]

Chapter 5
German Social Clubs, Singing Societies and Early Newspapers

The druid society, *Franklin Hain No. 2* (*Franklin Grove, No. 2*), founded in the year 1848 by Philipp Walz, Franz Schiebele, Wilhelm Kronemann, Kistner, Philipp Dein, Schweger and Niehaus, preceded the singing societies and Turners.[1] The chief officer of this lodge was Kistner, the first Lower Arch was Philipp Walz. Walz was later the founder of the *Fritz Loge* of the Druids and then served in both societies in different positions. He was also the representative of the Great Lodge of the United States. Later, in 1853, he became the co-founder of the first German Odd-Fellows Lodge, the *Schiller Loge* (Schiller Lodge) in Dayton.[2] Walz was born in 1818 in Brinzlach, Oberamt Lahr, Baden.[3] He was a bricklayer by trade, which he later continued in Dayton for many years. In 1848 he came to the New World to improve his situation, worked in New York for five years in a tea packing company and then came to Dayton in 1847 where he is still running a saloon on the corner of Wayne and Richard Street. A German Harugari Lodge, the *Ohio Lodge No. 57*, was already established in 1852, but I could not find out who was participating in the foundation of it.[4]

German Charity Order of *Harugari*, established in New York in 1847   *Unabhängige Orden der Rothmänner*, 1870

In the year 1869 (March 25) a *Deutsche Rothmänner Loge* (*German Order of Red Men*) was created in Dayton, whose main leader was Johann Bettelon.[5] Besides these there is a German *Loge der Pythias-Ritter*[6] (*Humboldt Loge No. 58*)[7], which was founded in 1873 and a German *Loge der Vereinigten Arbeiter* (*Lodge of the United Workmen*)[8], the *Teutonia Loge No. 21*[9] (*Teutonia Lodge No. 21*), which was founded in 1874. In the year 1863, the marksmen guild of Ludwig Markgraf (President), Johann Bettelon (Secretary), Heinrich Müller (Treasurer), Cölestin Schwind (Master Rifleman) and others was founded. The club has its own marvelous shooting range and presently celebrates twice a year its marksmen festivals: in the spring the

May Festival and in the fall the *Königsschiessen* (*King's Shoot*), which ranks among the main attractions of the Dayton Germans.

Johann Bettelon, presently the Secretary of the *German Pioneer Society of Dayton*, was born in the year 1829 in Steinweiler in the Bavarian Rhineland Palatinate and came with his parents in 1839 to America and Dayton.[10] In his youth he learned pastry baking from the famous Lamarche in Cincinnati. Bettelon later ran a pastry shop in Dayton. From 1860 he was in the liquor business for a length of time, and now he has been for many years a cashier at the "People's Bank" on East Third Street. Bettelon has assumed public offices numerous times: in 1870-71 he was the representative of the county in the state legislation and for four years a member of the police of the city of Dayton. This past spring he refused re-election to this office. Bettelon's parents who belong to the German pioneers of Darke County, Ohio, where they were farming, both died there.

When I have just remarked that the first German religious[11] newspaper in Ohio was published in Germantown, I still have to add to this that in November 1826, the first German political newspaper of the county originated in Germantown as well. Eduard Schäffer published it, but it did not appear to have succeeded because Schäffer moved away with his paper in 1828 or 1829 to the east. This paper bore the exalted name, *National Zeitung der Deutschen* (*National Newspaper of the Germans*).[12] The *Westliche Beobachter*, which is presently published in Canton, Ohio, wrote about the release of the first issue on November 15, 1826:

> "We have received the first issue of a German paper entitled: *Die National Zeitung der Deutschen*, published by Mr.Eduard Schäffer in Germantown, Montgomery County, Ohio. His reputation is respectable and we wish the best encouragement for the publisher in this difficult endeavor."[13]

The publisher of this pioneer of the German press in Montgomery County, Eduard Schäffer, was born in Frankfurt am Main, and was a typographer by trade, who came to America in 1817. He worked for a while in a printing shop in Philadelphia and in Reading, Pennsylvania. In the year 1821 he published in Canton, Ohio, the second oldest German newspaper northwest of the Ohio River.[14] In 1826 he moved with his print shop to Germantown and established there the *National Zeitung*. Later Schäffer published in Pennsylvania yet another German newspaper. I do not know where.

The first German newspaper in Dayton was published in the year 1851 by Johann Bittmann, the *Deutsche Journal* (*German Journal*).[15] Bittmann was once a typesetter for the *Deutsche Republikaner* (*The German Republican*) in Cincinnati and he thought to have found in Dayton a good location for a German weekly. However, he was badly mistaken because even after a two-year attempt, the *Journal* perished again. Bittmann then went to Washington where he received government employment, which he still held in 1861. At the beginning of the fifties, probably as the successor of Bittmann, Johann Peter Dietz published a small daily German newspaper in Dayton. It came about that Dietz got caught up in a dispute with the *Cincinnatier Volksblatt* which called Dietz an "odd fish." Dietz was not idle either and answered the editor of the *Volksblatt* in the following drastic manner: "N.N. from the *Cincinnatier Volksblatt* calls the editor of this paper an "odd fish," which we can accept considering that this wretched scribbler is probably a "dirty pig." Dietz later worked as co-editor for the *Cincinnatier Volksfreund* and wrote for the *Sonntagmorgen* in the year 1867-68 the *Bummelreisen eines Lunch-Reporters* (*Travel Spree of a Lunch Reporter*) in doggerel verse. In it one can find now and then some thoughts that are not too bad, which however disappeared among the lunch cacophony. Dietz, who was a native of Sigmaringen, and formerly participated in the "Forty-Eighter"[16] movement, died several years ago in Hamilton, Ohio. He was for a short time the assistant editor for Mr. Delacourt, who published the *National-Zeitung* there. Shortly after that, when Dietz' paper went under again, Hermann Rauh published a new paper, a Democratic weekly which was quickly followed by a Republican opposition paper by C.R. Bauer. Both newspapers were in existence until the summer of 1861 when both publishers, who each prided themselves on being fervent patriots and possessing committed love for the union, challenged each other to join the war, which both did. They sold their inventory and the bitter "ink squirters" became equally bitter rebel fighters. I could not find out if they had spilt much enemy blood during their military career. It also remained unknown to me what became of the inventory. For the time being, the *Daytoner Volkszeitung* (*Dayton People Gazette*) was created. The first issue appeared on Thursday, February 6, 1865. It was published for many years weekly and then three times a week. For about two years now it appears daily and weekly. Georg Neder published and edited it. In addition to the *Volkszeitung*, the *Dayton Anzeiger* has been published for two years daily and weekly.[17] The business brothers Mosbrugger and Schenk are publishing and editing it.

The oldest German newspaper, however, which is still in existence in Montgomery County, that is to say until today, is the *Fröhliche Botschafter* (*The Joyful Messenger*) edited by Reverend Wilhelm Mittendorf and published by W.J. Shuey, on behalf of the United Brethren community.[18] It is the organ of the United Brethren Church and has been their paper for 34 years already. In addition to the *Fröhliche Botschafter* there is the publication of a youth paper with the same publishers and appearing bi-monthly, the *Jugend-Pilger* (*Youth Pilgrim*), which is also published by the United Brethren.[19] These four German journals currently represent the literary life of the Germans in Dayton and surroundings.[20]

Germans always took active part in the political life of the county and the city of Dayton. Lorenz Butz, junior is presently the mayor of the city of Dayton, and the son of the old pioneer Lorenz Butz, who came to Dayton in 1835.[21] Although he was not born in Germany, he can be counted in every respect as belonging to the Germans. Previously C. L. Baumann, the current president of the school inspectors, was the civic leader of the city of Dayton. The following municipal offices are still in German hands: City Clerk, Nikolaus Metz, a native of Lorsch at the Bergstrasse in Hesse-Darmstadt; City Treasurer, H. H. Laubach; Street Superintendent, Julius Wehner; Police Superintendent, Michael Nippen; Meat Inspector, Franz Baumheckel (a native of Alsace-Lorraine); City Councilmen: J. Bohlender, P. Johantgen, H. Söhner, Johann Meyer, Wilhelm Knaub, Adam Schantz[22] (a native of Baden), F. Unger, H. F. Weil. Here is a list of people of German descent who still speak German: W. H. Pritz, J. Sortmann, Johann Feigst, A. E. Jenner and Carl W. Canary. The following members of the board of education are German, except for the president: Jacob Stephan, Peter Lenz, Leopold Rauh, D. G. Breidenbach and Georg Deis; Johnson, Snyder and Peck are of German descent; and J. E. Viot is German-French.

The municipal poor house is almost entirely under German control.[23] Dr. Anton Scheibenzuber[24] is the President and Johann Schön[25] is a member of the commission, and

Wilhelm Nauerth is the Superintendent of the institution. Jacob Stephan is one of the directors of the public school library, Friedrich Löhninger is the Principal of the Sixth District School, and Anton Stephan is the Chief of the Fire Department.

Dr. Dagobert Anton Scheibenzuber, son of Dr. Anton Scheibenzuber, was born in Austria on December 5, 1868. His father graduated from the University of Vienna and was known as one of the best physicians in Ohio. His son returned to the University of Vienna to study medicine as well. He returned to Dayton, where he worked as a physician and surgeon.

Adam Schantz (1854-1903)

..Water..
Trademark of the "Lily Water" filed on April 17, 1905 by the Schantz Estate

Obituary of Adam Schantz, Sr., German brewer and entrepreneur in Dayton, Ohio, who emigrated to America from Hesse-Darmstadt in 1854. From New York he went to Altoona, PA, to work for his uncle in a flourmill. In Dayton he learned the butcher trade, but moved to Chicago, St. Louis, New Orleans, back to Germany, England, before he came to Dayton a second time in 1862. He is known for his patent on a "System of Water Purification and Filtration." He sold his purified "Lily Water" to brewers and delivered it to homes. Adam Schantz, Sr., also gave the *Waldruhe Park* on Springboro Pike to his community as a gift. *Gedenkblätter*, May 16, 1903, Vol. 10: Iss. 3, p. 23.

Furthermore, in order for German to be taught in municipal schools, there are the following German parochial schools in Dayton: the Catholic *Emmanuels-Schule* (*Emmanuel Catholic School*)[26] and the *Dreifaltigkeits-Schule* (*Holy Trinity School*),[27] which are both directed by the Brothers of Nazareth, and the Marian School (Catholic) where both lay teachers and the German Sisters of Notre Dame are teaching.[28] Likewise there also is the *Marien Institut* (*Saint Mary's Institute*), under the direction of the Brothers of Nazareth and the reformatory school of the sisters of Notre Dame (German).[29] Besides their three large magnificent churches (*Emmanuel Church*, *Holy Trinity Church* and *St. Mary*), the German Catholics also have the biggest and most beautiful sanatorium in Dayton, which is run by the *Little Sisters*, the Elizabeth Hospital.[30]

Holy Trinity Church in Dayton, built in 1861

Saint Mary's Catholic Church in Dayton

Emmanuel Catholic Church in Dayton, built in 1873

Jewish Temple of Jeshurun Congregation in Dayton

There are German Protestant churches in Dayton: the *Deutsche Evangelische Gemeinschaftskirche* (*German Evangelical Community Church*) with Reverend Johann Kaufmann[31] as pastor; the *Second Reformed Church* with Reverend O. J. Accola as pastor; the *German Lutheran St. Johannes Church*, with Reverend F. Born as pastor; the *German Lutheran St. Paulus Church*, with Reverend Gottfried Löwenstein as pastor; the *German St. Johannes Chapel* (Lutheran) with Reverend Albert F. Seibert, pastor; the *Second United Brethren Church*, with Reverend Eduard Lorenz, pastor; the *First German Baptist Church*, with Reverend J. D. Mentges, pastor; and a *German Methodist Church*, with Reverend Johann Schweinfurth, pastor. The following clergymen are active in the Catholic churches: Emmanuel's Church, Father J. F. Hahne; St. Mary's Church, Father H. Stuckenberg; and Holy Trinity Church, Father F. J. Götz. The Jews too have two synagogues in Dayton: the *K.K. Bene Jeschurun Temple*, where E. Fischer is Rabbi, and the *Congregation of the House of Jacob* at St. Clair Street.[32] All German churches look exemplary next to the English churches and are a part of the most beautiful adornment of the city.

Even among the county administrative officials are many Germans: Friedrich Schulte, County Auditor; H.H. Laubach, County Treasurer; J. P. Kleine, Coroner; Johann G. Getter, one of the County commissioners; and Friedrich Pansing[33], member of the county poor house. Dr. Johann Schönfeld[34] from Miamisburg was repeatedly the most competent delegate of Montgomery County in the state legislature.

Emilie Schell Schönfeld (1834-1897)
Wife of Dr. Henry Schönfeld

Obituary of Emilie Schönfeld in *Dayton Gedenkblätter*, 1897, Vol. 4: Iss. 20, p. 153.

The respectable position, which the Germans already enjoy in this city and in this county, is for the large part due to the tireless pursuit of the old pioneers. It was they who struggled through the difficult beginnings of the material as well as cultural life. They were the trailblazers who cleared the land as well as awakened spiritual happiness and the human mind in the western wilderness. Therefore, we should pay homage to those who deserve it. On this note, I would like to tell the short story of a few of the oldest Germans. The life story of the remaining equally worthy German pioneers of the local area will hopefully find a more enthusiastic pen, with which to write a more fitting account of them than I can do.

Friedrich Euchenhöfer (1811)

Henry Ferneding Brewery, Dayton

Friedrich Euchenhöfer, the President of the *Deutsche Pionier-Verein*, was born in the year 1811 in Nördigen, Würtemberg.[35] He came to America in 1832 and first worked as a baker in Philadelphia for two years and about the same time he also had a bakery in Pittsburgh. Later he worked two years on a farm, which he bought near Pittsburg. In the year 1838, Euchenhöfer came to Montgomery County. He first settled as baker in Miamisburg, later adding a general store and even later a tavern to the bakery. During this time, Euchenhöfer also ran a cigar factory in Miamisburg, where he employed six to seven workers. In addition to all of this, even though he was a widower at the time, he also operated a tenement house for workers in Miamisburg. He took this business over from a German, Franz Mettauer, who came to Miamisburg in the early thirties. Euchenhöfer had a speculative, enterprising mind. In the year 1850 he came to Dayton where he operated a hotel, the *Columbus-Haus*, and continued to do so for many years.[36] Since 1861 Euchenhöfer has been in the brewery business.[37] In the meantime he also worked as flour grinder and finally solely returned to the beer brewery trade exclusively. Euchenhöfer was first married in Philadelphia with Alexandrine Renz from Schorndorf, who died however in Miamisburg in 1844. He has gotten married for the second time in 1849. His wife, Katharina Discher, is the daughter of an old German pioneer in Dayton.[38] Euchenhöfer is one of those fortunately disposed people, who always actively participate in all mental endeavors. This is a feature he has preserved to this day.

Heinrich Ferneding was born in the year 1812 in Dinklage, Oldenburg and emigrated to America in 1833.[39] He first ran a dairy business in Cincinnati. Then he came to Dayton in 1840 where he worked in a brandy distillery in the vicinity of the city. Later Ferneding founded a brewery and a malt house. He is presently the owner of one of the largest flourmills in Dayton. He grinds about 40,000 drums of flour per year. Ferneding was one of the co-founders of the German Catholic orphan society of Dayton (1849), and served as the first treasurer.[40] Joseph Zwisler was its first president.[41]

Franz Ohmer was born on June 19, 1796 in Müsbach (le Moyen) in the present-day Alsace-Lorraine.[42] He was a tailor by trade and traveled as a journeyman for many years during his youth in Europe, according to custom. After he had settled in his hometown as a master tailor, he married and with the expansion of his family, his earthly worries increased. Therefore, Ohmer decided in the fall of 1831 to emigrate to America. He landed with his family, wife and five children, after a journey of 55 days originating from Havre, in New York on January 8, 1832. The following spring they arrived in Cincinnati from where they moved to Trenton by Hamilton, in Butler County, Ohio, where Ohmer settled as master tailor and saved some money through diligence and thriftiness. However, in 1837 he moved on to Dayton and began a pastry shop on Second Street with the help of his oldest son, Nikolaus, who worked awhile for a French confectioner, Girardey[43], in Hamilton, as apprentice. Thereby Ohmer acquired a considerable fortune so that he was able to build the Dayton Hotel over the years. His son Nikolaus Ohmer, born in Müsbach in 1823, is one of the most affluent and most enterprising citizen of Dayton.[44] He is a practical horticulturist and owns a vast fruit orchard in the south-eastern part of the city. Furthermore Nikolaus Ohmer has a most entrepreneurial mind. He owns many hundreds of railway restaurants in all parts of the country, even as far as Colorado. The Ohmers, however, would like to be considered French rather than German.

Even the Anglo-Americans can no longer deny the fact that the Germans of the county as well as of the city of Dayton, rank among the first in industrial and commercial endeavors. The "Bromwell and Kielmeier Manufacturing Company[45]," established in 1872 with C.H. Kielmeier as President, and the "Herrmann und Herchelrode Manufacturing Company," established in 1893 with Christian Herchelrode as President, belong to the most prominent ironworks and engine plants in Dayton and southwest Ohio. In reality, the businesses of the Germans are counted among the best, in any respect, which is attested by the German *Teutonia Versicherungs-Gesellschaft (Teutonia Insurance Company)*[46] whose secretary and manager is Jacob Linxweiler.

Only in one respect did the Germans trail behind seriously until now: they did not assert themselves enough but rather found themselves too readily in the subservient role compared with their English-speaking neighbors. Only he who appreciates himself is treasured. He who does not make something of himself, how can he expect that others think highly of him? Hopefully it will soon get better in this respect. The *Deutsche Pionier-Verein (German Pioneer Society)*, which was organized here the year before attests to that.[47] It will lead, if properly directed, to the awakening of pride among the Germans of Dayton and the surrounding areas. Once this self-confidence, this notion that the Germans are counted among the best citizens of this country, enlivens the Germans, then they will not stoop down due to false modesty or imagined opinion about the superiority of their English-speaking neighbors, who will then gain a higher opinion of the Germans and will no longer denounce them as "*Dötschmen*"[48], but rather will feel elevated in the company of their "German fellow-citizens."

Chapter 6
Jakob Köhne's Pioneer Memoirs of Germantown, Ohio

After the preceding draft appeared in print, Mr. Jakob Köhne, one of the oldest German pioneers of Montgomery County, told us the following interesting memories, mostly with reference to Germantown.[1] In the twenties, Germantown was for the Germans a more important place than Dayton, which also had as smaller population. Such a flourishing German life, which prevailed here at that time, could not even be found in Cincinnati where the Germans disappeared among the larger number of Americans. In Germantown, however, everything was German. If you came here, you would feel as if you had been transported back to Germany because of the original German customs that prevailed here. The little town had as many inhabitants, if not more, than today. Customs and traditions were German with a slight tinge of the American nature. People simply met in the evenings in Johann Wagener's tavern for a glass of beer or wine as they were accustomed to do in Germany. And oddly enough, even the class segregation, which was customary in the old fatherland, was present: at one table sat the academic gentlemen at a table called the *Herrentisch* ("Gentlemen's Table"), at another table sat the common townsfolk. The Pennsylvanian Germans huddled around the fire, drank their whiskey and spat their tobacco waste into the fire, as if they were genuine Yankees. Not a single word of English was heard, however. Everybody spoke German although a part of them spoke in the Pennsylvanian dialect.

We would like to take a closer look at the guests of Wagener's tavern. Among the companions, who "hung around" the fire place, were old Jacob Kuntz, who was a personal friend of General James Findlay, and whose house he often visited. He was a wisecracker similar to what is called in English, a "wag," who was always quick to reply and knew how to tell many funny stories. He was called *Sau-Kuntz* ("Pig-Kuntz") because he was formerly accused of having slaughtered other people's pigs, which ran free in the huge forest to fatten them up. Then there was the old Wilhelm Bummerschein, a tall, husky person, whose father was one of the Hessian soldiers. His sons are still affluent citizens of German Township. Heinrich Bär, who settled in 1810 in Germantown, the Catrows (Zebulon and Michael), Theodor Marschall, old Oblinger, Peter Zehring, Louis Puffenberger and others belonged to this group, and whenever old Kummler of Lewisburg in Preble County came to Germantown, he too could be found there as well. He had a tannery near Lewisburg and also preached the gospel according to the Dunkards. He moved here from Ephrata, Pennsylvania, and belonged to the *Beisselites*.[2] It is told that he initially held the preacher position free of charge. Later on, however, he also requested payment, and therefore another preacher replaced him. The following refers to an excerpt from the sermon in which he requested a salary from his congregation: "I have long enough preached to you for nothing, but I do not do this any more. I should also get something for it because I am wasting my time. The preacher must be lubricated the same way as my old bark mill. If I do not lubricate it all the time, it screams grease! grease! grease! on and on."

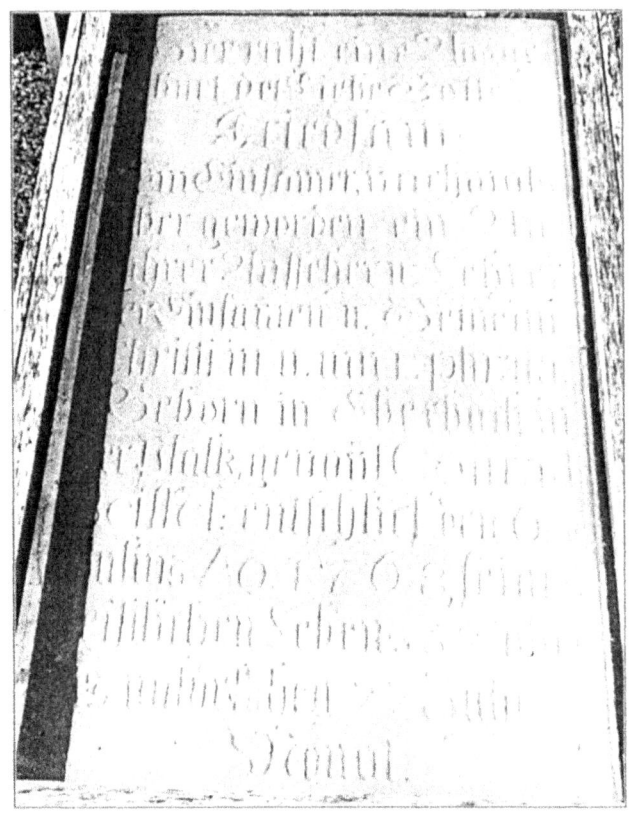
Gravestone of Conrad Beissel (1690-1768), Courtesy of the Ephrata Cloister, PA

At the middle-class table, they drank beer and at times played a game of cards. Among the guests who congregated there were: Jacob Stiehl, whose descendants have since then turned themselves into Steele; Christoph Emmerich[3], Daniel Schreiber (brewing laborer for Rohrer), native of Uchte, Hannover; Biechler, Jakob Tschudi[4] (a Swiss); Michael Schuey[5]; Wilhelm Stutzmann; the beer brewer Friedrich Dechant and others. Dechant, a native of Würzburg, brewed the first German beer in Germantown, namely from corn, before 1825.

The guests at the gentlemen table, who drank the bad swill of beer and sour wine because nothing better was available, deserve a closer look because many, not insignificant, characters were among those. Let us begin with the gentleman to whom we owe this information:

Jakob Köhne, born in Diepholz by Hannover in the year 1808, emigrated to America in the summer of 1824 after having attended High School in Bremen, and having been educated as a merchant.⁶ He immediately headed out to the West because he brought the notion from Europe to do trade with the Indians. He arrived, in the same fall, in Cincinnati on a keelboat from Wheeling, going down the Ohio River. In Cincinnati he was taken in by the Swiss family Agniel at Sycamore, between New Market (8.) and Wayne (9.) streets. In order to satisfy his desire to get acquainted with the Indians, he went on horseback to Wapaghkonetta, which was then still an Indian village known under the same name.⁷ From there he made a small detour to Fort Wayne by following an Indian trail through the jungle. The ideal, which he imagined in Germany about the Indians, was destroyed when he saw the filthy hordes of Wyandots and Pottawatamies. On his return he came through Germantown, and upon finding an educated German society, which pleased him very much, he decided to settle there as well. He soon started a grocery store with another young German, Franz Arenz from Remscheid, Dutchy of Berg, whom he met here and who also was a merchant. Arenz intended to settle in western Illinois, but was prevented from it by the imminent signs of the Black Hawk War, which had already appeared in 1827.⁸ In the fall of 1827, Köhne and Arenz moved to Scott County, Kentucky, began a store at Eagle Creek and took turns peddling around in the state of Kentucky. In doing so, they earned fairly good money. In the summer of 1829, Köhne returned to Germantown and continued managing his grocery store while his friend Arenz moved to St. Louis. At the conclusion of the Black Hawk War, Arenz settled in Scott County, Illinois, in present-day Beardstown, then called Beards Ferry, as one of the first settlers of that part of Illinois.⁹

Chief Black Hawk (1767-1838)

Battle of Stillman's Run during 1832 Black Hawk War, Illinois

Köhne soon became a very popular person in Germantown, especially since he had musical talent and knew how to sing numerous songs accompanied by guitar and later piano. The German folk songs appealed to most of the Americans in the surrounding areas who therefore became his most exclusive customers for miles around. In 1825, when he settled for the first time in Germantown, he was already known as a musician. At that time, a new Freemason lodge was founded in Eaton, Preble County, accompanied by appropriate festivities. People wanted to have music and because Germantown was at the time the headquarters of musicians in southwestern Ohio, a music choir was quickly formed, consisting of the Emmerich brothers, Carl Otto Wolpers, the old Captain Nägeli and others. Köhne played the bass guitar. Naturally they caused a stirring sensation in the back woods with their music. Later Köhne retired in a manor near Germantown and presently lives in Cincinnati where his daughter is a teacher in the public schools. A promising son, who was a doctor, died several years ago in Mariana, Florida. In

Germantown, Köhne held all honorary offices, which a municipality can award. He was justice of the peace, mayor of Germantown and under Van Buren's administration, postmaster. He also attained a most respectable position in other relations with the Americans in the neighborhood. What his German neighbors thought of him is apparent in a few commemorative pages that his friends wrote in his album when he moved with Ahrens to Kentucky in September 1827. Furthermore, these memory pages acquaint us with a number of witty German men who belonged to the circle at the *Herrentisch* ("Gentlemen's Table") in Germantown at that time. This is why they are printed here:

"Good luck! – Take this greeting from the fatherland, dear Köhne, with you on your journey, and if you remember your friends in Germantown in an idle moment then also think of me and believe that I deeply and sincerely share in your luck and well-being."

Germantown, Ohio, September 20, 1827.
Yours,
Carl Otto Wolpers[10]

A true man is solely revealed by his steadfast courage and decisiveness to face life. – When perusing these humble lines, remember your friend.
Germantown, September 21, 1827. Dr. Ludwig Henrich[11]

During all perils which may threaten you or are imminent, worthy friend, always remain the same and steadfast. They will all pass and the sun will shine a magnificent light on you through her rays. However until now, the light is covered by the veil of darkness.
This in memory of your trusted friend
Eduard Schäffer, from Frankfort-on-the-Main[12]
Germantown, Ohio, September 21, 1827.

The game of life is regarded as cheerful,
If one carries the treasure safe inside.
Schiller[13]

Dearest Köhne!
Even if we cannot always view life as a game according to the poet, his words still contain a truth within which gives me, in the present moment, when you and your worthy companions plan exclusively occupy my heart, the comforting conviction that your contentment and luck rest on safe ground! With innermost love, sympathy and respect, your loyal, devoted friend accompanies you in spirit.
Daniel Christian Lehmus[14]
from Rothenburg ob der Tauber
in the Kingdom of Bavaria
Germantown, Montgomery County, Ohio, September 21, 1827.

Dr. Carl Otto Wolpers, born in Braunschweig, had been a professor in Wolfenbüttel and came to America in 1824 in order to establish a freer home in the promised western land. He had intended to pursue farming in America; however this seemed, if viewed up close, to be too rough and prosaic. Therefore, he started a commercial business, mainly in draperies and clothing goods, which is continued at this time by his son Hermann (born in Germantown in 1840). He was a highly educated man, who even in America continued his philosophical studies as a hobby. He also undertook several chemistry experiments without achieving any practical success with it. Before Wolpers emigrated to America, he published a book in Germany, entitled *Kleine Schulgrammatik für gebildete Deutsche* (*Small School Grammar for Educated Germans*), Göttingen 1822.

Dr. Ludwig Henrich later moved east, where it is said, that his offspring is still living. He was a philologist who received his doctorate in Göttingen. Full particulars about him, are still missing.[15]

Eduard Schäffer[16] was a book printer from Frankfurt-on-the-Main who came to America in 1817 or 1818, settled for a while in Pennsylvania and published, as I have already mentioned, between 1821 and 1826 a German newspaper in Canton, Ohio. In 1826 he founded, as we have seen, in Germantown the *National Zeitung der Deutschen* (National Newspaper of the Germans), which continued for approximately two or three years. Köhne thought that Schäffer then moved to Greenville, Ohio, other reports, however, place him back east.

Daniel Christian Lehmus, doctor of philosophy, son of Christian Balthasar Lehmus, rector and professor of the Gymnasium Rothenburg at the Tauber[17], was born in the year 1786 in Rothenburg, graduated in Rothenburg from high school, then studied theology and philosophy in Jena. He passed his philosophical exam, and then received a position as professor at the high school in Rothenburg, a position he kept until the year 1814. In this year, the high school was abolished and reduced to a simple Latin school, whereupon Lehmus was appointed a professorship of mathematics at the university in Jena. Here he was suspected to be a demagogue and associated with the so-called *Männerbunde* (*Male Society*), which in contemporary history was back then one of the commonly referred to imaginary alliances which was said to exist among professors at universities. He was investigated because of it. The dishonorable suspicion nauseated him to such an extent that he resigned and emigrated to America. It is not quit clear in which year this happened. In 1825 he was already in Germantown, Ohio, and was employed there by Schäffer as editor of the *National Zeitung* (*National Newspaper*). Both had high hopes regarding the success of their paper, which did not materialize later. With respect to the circulation of the *National Zeitung*, it was said that the circulation was more widespread than having large numbers of paying readers. It is a fact that it spread as far as New Mexico where even then another German newspaper was published. Dr. Lehmus switched later to that paper. After the project failed in Germantown, Lehmus returned east and found employment with Franz Lieber[18] as assistant to the *Encyclopaedia Americana*, which was published by German scholars. It seems that Lehmus later returned to Germany, probably in 1834 or 1835.

Lehmus was a distinguished mathematician whose numerous mathematical professional journals appeared in print. Heinsius, *Allgemeines Bücherlexikon*, Leipzig 1812-1845, enumerates the following:

1. Lehrbuch der Zahlen-Arithmetik. Buchstaben Rechenkust und Algebra. Leipzig 1821.

2. Grundlehre der höheren Mathematik und der mechanischen Wissenschaften. Published as a guide to his lectures. Berlin, 1821, 2. edition, 1831.
3. Hydraulik, ohne Anwendung der hohen Analysis. Berlin, 1822.
4. Lehrbuch der angewandten Mathematik, 3. vols, Berlin, 1822, 2. ed. 1827.
5. Lehrbuch der Geometrie. 1. vol: enhält Elementar Geometrie, algeb. und analyt. Geometrie und Goniometrie. Berlin 123, 2. ed. 1826, 3. ed. 1840.
6. Übungs-Aufgaben zur Lehre vom Größten und Kleinsten. Berlin 1824.
7. Die ersten, einfachsten Grundbegriffe der Lehre der höheren Analysis und Curvenlehre, Berlin 1824.
8. Sammlung von aufgelösten Aufgaben auf dem Gebiete der angewandten Mathematik. 1. vol., Berlin 1828 (?).
9. Anwendungen des höheren Calcüls auf geometrische und mechanische, insbesondere ballistische Aufgaben, Leipzig 1836.
10. Aufgelöste Aufgaben aus der niedern, höheren und angewandten Mathematik, insbesondere Formbestimmungen von Flächen zu algebraischen Gleichungen vom 2., 3. und 4. Grad, auch zu transzendentalen Gleichungen. Leipzig 1838.

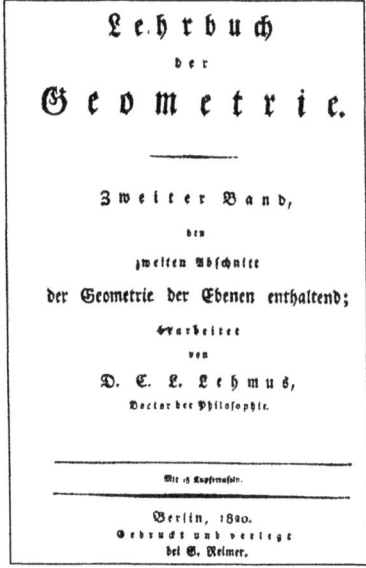
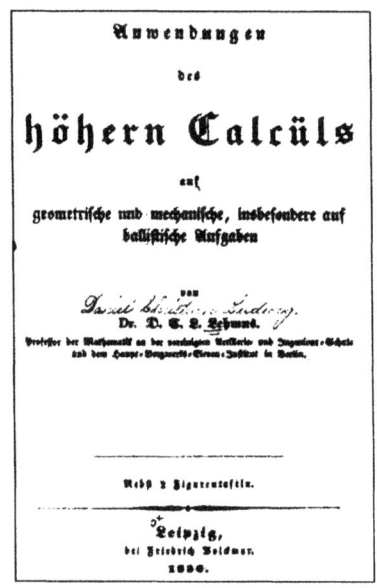

It looks like that there is a gap between the years 1824 to 1836, which is only interrupted by the small booklet, Number 8, if this is not also a second edition. The twelve years are probably the period of his stay in America, where his activities took him on another course, as we have reported.

The editorial department of the *Nationalzeitung* (*National Newspaper*) in Germantown did not absorb his intellectual activity completely. During a visit to Union Village, which is approximately 15 miles away, Lehmus met the former private secretary of Prince Blücher, Christian Burkhalter from Neu-Wied, who, at that time, belonged to the Shaker community.[19] During this occasion, both men got acquainted more closely which lasted for many years and was even later continued through correspondence when their paths separated. Burkhalter introduced Lehmus to the family of the famous statesman, Thomas Corwin.[20]

Hon. Thomas Corwin (1794-1865), also referred to as "Wagon Boy"

Thomas Corwin Estate, 210 W. Main St., Lebanon, Ohio

They formed a close relationship between each other, which may not be overlooked here. Corwin, from a German family, was born in Hinkston Creek in Bourbon County, Kentucky, settled later in Ohio, excelled at politics in his county and was already a congressman in the states legislation of Ohio. In achieving that, his striving ambition was awakened. Equipped with a sonorous voice and an inherent eloquence, he immediately, upon entering, caused a sensation in the legislative branch. With ease did the "Wagon-boy"[21] of the war of 1812 advance to become the leader of the Clay wing of the Democratic Party of Dayton, during the campaign of the year 1824. His ambition showed him the way to national politics. He gained access to it in the year 1830 and not undeservedly, because Corwin had prepared for it with untiring zeal. His acquaintance with Lehmus was of great use for him in his acquirement of in-depth knowledge. Lehmus was namely not only an excellent mathematician but also a fine linguist who mastered most of the modern European languages besides the classical ones. Corwin, who was raised on a farm, received for many years, lessons in Latin, French, Spanish, as well as logic. Therefore, without a doubt, a large part of the scientific knowledge of the famous statesman can be accredited to the German professor who ended up somewhere in the back woods. In the Corwin family, Lehmus always remained fondly remembered and even today his portrait adorns the study room, respectfully preserved by Corwin's aging widow, of the great leader of the Whig Party of Ohio. How many American celebrities might owe their entire knowledge to such German scholars who were flung into America's backwoods because of European disparities?

Even before Köhne's time, there was quite a vibrant German life in Germantown and at Wagener's *Herrentisch*, a long pipe and a student cap, as well as a doctoral cap played a large role. Among the first Germans who lived there were also: Albert Stein, the builder of the Cincinnati Water Works and the Appomatox channel.[22] He was already here in the year 1816, and so was Dr. Christian Espich who came to Germantown around 1820.[23] Espich's offspring is presently living in Cincinnati. Stein moved away to Cincinnati in the spring of 1817 which is apparent from this ad in the *Liberty Hall* from May 1, 1817:

"Mr. Albert Stein, lately arrived from Germany, who has been employed by the "French Government," solicits the patronage of the Public for instructing young Gentlemen in following branches: Drawing and Mathematical Sciences, as Geometry, Algebra, Mechanics, Hydraulics, Architecture and Construction of Machines, on reasonable Conditions. For Terms apply to him at his Lodgings in Columbia Street. Piatts Row.- Cincinnati May 1st 1817."

Albert Stein (1785-1874), German engineer, built the first water works run by steam pumps in Cincinnati in 1822

Albert Stein, German immigrant from Düsseldorf, designed and built the Cincinnati Water Works. It was the first in the U.S. to use pumps.

In 1831 or 1832 two other interesting people settled in Montgomery County, Count Jenison[24] and Dr. Wilhelm Frank[25]. Franz Jenison-Walworth was the son of the Kurpfalz count Franz Oliver of Jenison-Walworth and - - - - - ."[26]) He had received an excellent education in his youth, was a major in the Bavarian army, and was persuaded by his highly aristocratic family to emigrate to America after having married a middle-class lady, entering in a so-called *Mesalliance*. He settled at the aforementioned time in Miamisburg, however, he later moved to the vicinity of Dayton where he had a garden in the present-day 11th ward. It is in that part of town, which is presently known as *Frenchtown*. Count Jenison was a passionate enthusiast of botany, which he shared with his friend Frank. He "botanized," as we were told by one of his former acquaintances, "with the greatest diligence the different amounts of money, which were sent to him by his rich family from Germany. Other than that he made a great appearance, had a tall and stately built, a gentleman-like behavior, and was popular in any company. In the words of one, he was a born nobleman." The offspring of Count Jenison is still living in the vicinity of Springfield and in Columbus, Ohio. A certain Mrs. Ambos in Columbus is Jenison's daughter.

Dr. Wilhelm Frank,[27] the associate and friend of Jenison, the son of the famous Johann Peter Frank,[28] one of the most prominent doctors in Germany, the founder of the medical forensic science, was born in the year 1779 in Rastatt, then the capital of Baden.[29]

Dr. Johann Peter Frank (1774-1821)
Father of Dr. Wilhelm Frank

Dr. Johann Peter Frank
Father of Forensic Science

Dr. Johann Peter Frank Honorary Medal

Urged by his famous father to study medicine, Wilhelm Frank devoted himself, after he passed his exam in 1805 in Wilna and earned a doctorate degree of medicine, specializing in botany, the science he gave himself over to with great passion in later years. After he had heard the lectures of Decandolle in 1802-03 in Geneva, Frank perambulated Switzerland and Southern France in order to perfect himself by studying the botany of the Alps. After 1805 he settled for a while in Rastatt as a practicing physician and later (in 1816) received a professorship of applied botany at the University of Heidelberg. He became acquainted there with Count Jenison, who listened to his lectures. Dr. Frank then obtained a position as doctor in Count Jenison's family, where he took a strictly confidential position. In 1830 or 1831 Frank went, accompanied by his friend and pupil, the before-mentioned Count Jenison, to America and then settled in Germantown, while Jenison resided in Miamisburg and later in Dayton.

Here Dr. Frank took up the subject of botany exclusively and collected a herbarium of many thousands of plants, which he organized, described, and then sent to the Heidelberg University. A script of *Die Pflanzen in den Vereinigten Staaten von Nordamerika* (*The Plants in the United States of North America*), which was never completed, was bequeathed in manuscript form to the Heidelberg University Library, where it can still be found today.

Dr. Frank expanded his botanical journeys throughout the United States, from Texas to Lake Superior and from the Alleghany Mountains to the remote western prairies of Iowa and Nebraska. He was accompanied by Jenison on several of these excursions. Dr. Frank died in the year 1839 from yellow fever in New Orleans where he traveled at the time of a raging epidemic as a voluntary doctor. He was a heroic victim of his profession. "The city councilmen of New Orleans," as is reported by our source of information, Mr. Köhne, "expressed their condolences regarding the death of Dr. Frank and wrote a passionate eulogy about the sacrificial heroism of this martyr of his profession.

A transcript of the eulogy, as well as a copy of similar resolutions on the part of the legislature of Louisiana were delivered to the widow of the deceased in Germantown." Also the faculty of the University of Heidelberg sent condolences regarding the death of Dr. Frank, wherein his merits for the enrichment of the scientific collection of this university were duly accentuated.

Besides the above-mentioned unpublished manuscript, Dr. Frank also wrote a book about America, which was published in the year 1839 in Cassel, in the Luckhardt bookstore, entitled *Deutschland in Amerika, das einzig rechte Ziel aller deutschen Auswanderer* (*Germany in America, the only true Destination of all German Immigrants*) in eight volumes.[30] This interesting German society existed until the fifties. In the year 1848, the famous judicial councilman, Groneweg from Bielefeld came here and made an attempt at farming near Germantown.[31] Groneweg emigrated to America with his family because of his participation in the liberal efforts of the year 1848. He returned to his hometown, however, after having received amnesty, where he is still living at this time. A nephew of Groneweg died as pharmacist and owner of a drugstore in Cincinnati.[32]

Those were the German people in Germantown as it was related to me by Mr. Köhne. It was, in one word, a model city of German life during the said period. The citizens did not want to have their lives corrupted by the intrusion of disagreeable characters, and they knew of an effective means, which they termed *Finkeln*. The word got its origin from a rough fellow, by the name of Fink, because the procedure was first used on him. This man was a Pennsylvanian-German roughneck, who had disturbed the patrons at Wagener's tavern a few times. The irritated guests decided to dispose of the fellow effectively. For this purpose, one day a small group of young people, headed by the above-mentioned Stutzmann, bound Fink's hands behind his back, put a rope around his neck, and led him so, preceded by a tambourine player, who played the *Spitzbuben Marsch* ("Rogues March"), through the little town and over the Twin River. Stutzmann, who was as strong as a horse, was leading him, submerged him a few more times under the water, loosened his ties from neck and hands and thus let him go, telling him that in the case of his return, the rope around his neck would be tied to a tree branch so that his feet could not reach the ground. The procedure of the *Finkeln* was later performed a few more times whereupon Germantown was freed from the menace of troublemakers as a consequence.

Germantown soon became, through the presence of these intellectuals, a gathering place for men of knowledge in the area, and in later years, however, it became a stronghold of a Whig free-soil, like-minded great people of Ohio.[33] The following people gathered here at the time, besides Corwin, John Johnston of Piqua, the Indian agent of the United States[34]; the historian of Ohio, Caleb Atwater[35]; John McLean[36], the future judge of the United States Supreme Court; General Harrison and others. After 1830 Salmon P. Chase[37] joined the circle, which frequently met in Germantown. They were brought together here because of the pleasant communication, which was not restricted by the inflexible Puritan customs that were everywhere else predominant. The warm spirit of the German jovial disposition was the attractive force of these prominent men who enjoyed their holidays here.

Caleb Atwater
(1778-1867)

John McLean
(1785-1861)

Salmon P. Chase
(1808-1873)

Was the influence, which the German element in Germantown at that time made on the educated class of Americans, who came in contact with them, permanent? This question must decidedly be answered in the affirmative, although the findings speak against it. Like a stone, when it is thrown into the water, initially creates deep yet narrow orbital waves, which then spread out more and more, yet also lose the depth, the transmission of cultural elements behaves likewise. The closest circles are thereby most deeply moved. In fact, these circles forward the ideas that were received, however, not with the same intensity as they have received it. However, what is then lost in depth, is replaced by width to a great extent. The world cannot be guided, all at once, into certain desired destinations, but only slowly, little by little and invisibly does it reach the point, which it navigates towards. Pessimists will, however, complain constantly that the German element in America perishes, because they are unable to perceive their influence with the naked eye. The intellectually-minded people, however, gaze over larger periods and there they see and observe the progress in its natural path. In order to view the influence, which the Germans of Germantown have exerted in this respect, we may not only look at Germantown which over the course of the years did not progress with the surroundings, but we rather have to look at the larger circle and there we observe the living proof of those intellectual pioneers of the German identity. As an example: Judge McLean in Cincinnati kept company with the Findlays,[38] Torrences,[39] Pendletons[40] and Longworths,[41] all families of pure Anglo-American antecedents with their associated way of living. These families came therefore very early into much closer contact with the Germans in Cincinnati than the general public. Their contact continued with their descendants and was beneficial because the first foundation was laid in these families. It is now frequently the custom that aristocratic families sent their children to Germany to receive a good education, although their position would allow them to be well educated here. The younger generation of the Pendletons, Longworths, and so forth, all speak German and on top of everything, have formed of habit of the best German customs and manners without descending to the lowest classes. What I have said here about Judge McLean is true for the other Americans of the educated class who resided at Germantown. Truly, the former German scholars of the now almost forgotten Germantown have sowed a culture-promoting seed into the American soil, which now has already borne hundreds of golden fruits.

Lastly, may it be mentioned here that the city Pyrmont in Montgomery County was founded by Heinrich Mundhenk, a native of Pyrmont, around the year 1840.[42] His wife, Mrs. Margaretha, was the well-known milk woman who saved General Lafayette's life at Fort Ollmütz.[43] This was reported already in the *Pionier*, volume VIII, page 125.[44]

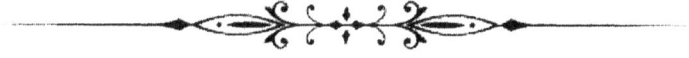

Appendix A

INDEX OF GERMAN NEWSPAPERS & PAPERS IN DAYTON, OHIO

The Appendices A, B, and C contain some supplementary materials that would interrupt the flow of the book, yet could add value to the publication. A search of early German newspapers and papers of Dayton, Germantown and Miamisburg was conducted and the findings are presented in tabular format.

Three sources were consulted:
1) Online Newspaper Databank, *Chronicling America* < http://chroniclingamerica.loc.gov/>
2) Karl J.R. Arndt and May E. Olson. *Deutsch-Amerikanische Zeitungen und Zeitschriften, 1732-1955* (Heidelberg: Quelle und Meyer, 1961).
3) Augustus Waldo Drury, *History of the City of Dayton and Montgomery County, Ohio* (Chicago-Dayton: S.J. Clarke Publishing Co., 1909). Question marks indicate missing data.

A digital search in the ***Chronicling America*** website with these search parameters (Montgomery County, Ohio; no city selection; German language) from 1690 to 2014 produced eight German newspapers. The duplications seem obvious, but sometimes papers discontinue and start again.

Name of Newspaper	Place & Date of Publication	Publisher/ Editor
Der Fröhliche Botschafter	Circleville, OH 1851-1930	R. Altmann
Deutsche Zeitung	Dayton, OH, 183?-18?	s.n.
Der Jugendpilger	Dayton, OH, 1870-1914	United Brethren Pub. House
Die Daytoner Volkszeitung	Dayton, OH, 18??-?	Geo. Neder
Gross-Daytoner Zeitung	Dayton, OH, 1914-1947	Greater Dayton German Gaz.
Deutsches Journal	Dayton, OH, 1849-1852	John Bittman
Die Daytoner Volkszeitung	Dayton, OH, 1866-1914	Geo. Neder
Dayton Volkszeitung	Dayton, OH, 186?-18?	Geo. Neder

Source: <http://tinyurl.com/k9xmpxx>

Missing in *Chronicle of America*
Eleven German newspapers or papers are missing in the list above. Drury's *History of Dayton* (1: 409-410) was consulted to fill the gap.

Name of Newspaper	Place & Date of Publication	Publisher/ Editor
Deutsche Zeitung[1]	Dayton, 1835-1835	Burghalter
Ohio Intelligencer	Dayton, 1835-?	Louis Huesmann[2]
Der Deutsch-Amerikaner	Dayton, 1839-?	?
Freiheits-Freund	Dayton, 1841-?	?
Das Deutsche Journal[3]	Dayton, 1848-1850	John Bittman
Die Stimme des Volkes[4]	Dayton, 2 years	Stierlein
Dayton Democrat[5]	Dayton, 1856-1858 ?	Haisch & Engler

Dayton Wochenblatt[6]	Dayton, 1859-1864 ?	Herman & Rauh
Dayton Abendblatt[7]	Dayton, 1859-a few weeks	Dietz & Egry
Dayton Pioneer[8]	Dayton, 1860-1862 ?	Richard Bauer
Dayton Volk Zeitung[9]	Dayton, 1866-18?	George Neder
Anzeiger[10]	Dayton, 1876-1882	Moosbrugger & Schenk
Greater Dayton German Gazette	Dayton, ?	?
Religious Telescope	Circleville, 1834-?	United Brethren of Christ

The following is a list of thirty German newspapers and papers published in Dayton located in: Karl J.R. Arndt and May E. Olson, *Deutsch-Amerikanische Zeitungen und Zeitschriften, 1732-1955* (Heidelberg: Quelle und Meyer, 1961), 478-481.

Name of Newspaper	Place & Date of Publication	Publisher/ Editor
(Lost Paper)	Dayton, 1851-????	Johann Peter Dietz
(Lost Paper)	Dayton, 1859-1861	Hermann Rau
(Lost Paper)	Dayton, 1859-1861	C.N. Bauer
Dayton Anzeiger	Dayton, 1876-1882	Moosbrugger Bros & Schenk
Wöchentlicher Dayton Anzeiger	Dayton, 1876-1882	?
Der Deutsche Teleskop	Dayton, 1846-????	Nehemia Altman
Deutsches Journal	Dayton, 1849-1852	John Bittmann
Diakonissen Bote	Dayton, 1891-1896	?
Evangel. Sonntagsschulblatt	Dayton, ?	United Brethren in Christ
Farmers' & Mechanics' German-English Almanac	Dayton, ?	?
Der Fröhliche Botschafter	Circleville, 1846-1915	United Brethren in Christ
Gedenk-Blätter	Dayton, 1894-1913	
Deutsch-Amerikanischer Bulletin	Dayton, 1933-1941	W.H. Brauckmann
Die Geschaeftigte Martha	Dayton, 1838-1841 Dayton, 1851-1853	?
Gross-Daytoner Zeitung	Dayton, 1866-1947	several
Der Jugend Pilger	Dayton, 1870-1914	United Brethren in Christ
Der Kirchenchor	Dayton, 1897-1930	several
Männerbote	Dayton, ?	?
Maria Hilf	Dayton, 1873-????	?
Medicinal Zeitung	Dayton, 1889-1890	J. Schreiber
Nützlicher Freund	Dayton, 1882-1892	Rev. M. Bussdicker
Ohio Volksfreund	Dayton, 1840-????	Rudolph von Maltitz
St. Joseph's Post	Dayton, 1896-1898	?
Sonntagschulblatt	Dayton, ?	United Brethren in Christ
Sonntagsschul-Lectionen	Dayton, 1890-1914	Rev. Wilhelm Mittendorf
Das Volksblatt	Dayton, 1891-?	Dayton Publishing Company
Dayton Volkszeitung	Dayton, 1865-?	?
Wöchentliche Dayton Volkszeitung	Dayton, 1869-1920	?
Der Wächter	Dayton, 1886-1891	M. Bussdicker
Zum Gruss	Dayton, 1890-?	?

Notes to Appendix A

1. According to Augustus Waldo Drury, *History of the City of Dayton and Montgomery County, Ohio* (Chicago-Dayton: S.J. Clark Publishing Company, 1909), the first German newspaper in Dayton, the *Deutsche Zeitung (German Gazette)*, appeared first on September 19, 1835 and "was issued from the *Dayton Journal* office, the editor being Mr. Burghalter," 1:409. This paper only survived until the end of the year 1835. Also, see *Don Heinrich Tolzmann, ed., Dayton's German Heritage: Karl Karstaedt's Golden Jubilee History of the German Pioneer Society of Dayton, Ohio* (Bowie: Heritage Books, Inc., 2001), 87, who points out that both Dayton German newspapers, *Neue Deutsche Zeitung* and the *Intelligencer* survived only for a short time.

2. Ibid, 409. Drury adds that Huesmann taught German and music classes in Dayton. Dates when the paper was discontinued are unknown. Copies of any issues of both the *Deutsche Zeitung* or the *Ohio Intelligencer* are missing, according to Drury.

3. Ibid. *Das Deutsche Journal*, a weekly newspaper, *started* in 1848 with John Bittman as publisher but was discontinued after two years, according to Drury.

4. Ibid. Die *Stimme des Volkes* existed for two years with Stierlein as the publisher. Drury provides no dates.

5. Ibid. *Dayton Democrat* was published by Haisch and Engler in 1856 and ran for about two years.

6. Ibid. *Dayton Wochenblatt*, first published in 1859 by Herman and Rauh was in existence for approximately five years.

7. Ibid, 410. *Dayton Abendblatt*, published in the same year as the *Dayton Wochenblatt* in 1859, was the first German daily paper. It survived only a few weeks. The publishers were Dietz and Egry.

8. Ibid. *Dayton Pioneer* started in 1860 by Richard Baur and lasted for approximately two years.

9. Ibid. *Dayton Volk Zeitung* was first published on April 26, 1866 by George Neder, as a "six-column, four-page paper. In June, 1866, a semi-weekly issue was published in additon to the weekly and in October the semi-weekly was displaced by a tri-weekly issue. About the 1st of September, 1876, a daily paper appeared, a weekly and daily both being published from that time." This information is listed here, although the Library of Congress, Chronicling America databank mentions that newspaper. More details are provided here.

10. Ibid. *Anzeiger*, first appeared on September 1, 1876, was a Democratic paper with initial ownership by Otto Mossbrugger and Charles Schenk. Later Schenk sold his shares to Kinno Moosbrugger and the two brothers continued the publication until April 17, 1882, when the paper merged with the *Volk Zeitung*.

Appendix B

INDEX OF GERMAN NEWSPAPERS & PAPERS IN GERMANTOWN, OHIO

A digital search in the Library of Congress, ***Chronicling America*** website with these search parameters (Montgomery County, Ohio; Germantown; German language) from 1690 to 2014 produced no German newspapers. A digital search in the *Chronicling America* website with these search parameters (Montgomery County, Ohio; Germantown; no language) from 1690 to 2014 produced no German newspapers, but 14 English newspapers.
Source: <http://tinyurl.com/l4j3xk9>

Missing in *Chronicle of America*:
The following is a list of two German newspapers and papers published in Germantown, Ohio: Karl J.R. Arndt and May E. Olson. *Deutsch-Amerikanische Zeitungen und Zeitschriften, 1732-1955* (Heidelberg: Quelle und Meyer, 1961). 482-483.

Name of Newspaper	Place & Date of Publication	Publisher/ Editor
Germantown Gazette[1]	Germantown, 1845-1857	W. Gunckel, Walker, Reeder
National Zeitung der Deutschen[2]	Germantown, 1826-1833	Eduard Schäffer

One important German newspaper in Germantown, Ohio, the *National Zeitung der Deutschen* published by Eduard Schäffer was not listed on the *Chronicling America* website. It is essential to understand that it was Germantown, Ohio, and not Cincinnati, with its very large German population, which received the second or third German newspaper in all of Ohio.[3] Germantown, as Goebel points out, was much larger than Dayton, Ohio, in 1824 and populated by German intellectuals. This was one of the reasons why Eduard Schäffer, the publisher of the German newspaper moved to Germantown, Ohio, from Canton. Goebel reports that the *National Zeitung der Deutschen* was first published on September 4, 1826 in Germantown, and ran until 1833, when Schäffer died of cholera, and the printing press went to Dr. Espich.[4]

Notes to Appendix B

1. Arndt does not list a publisher or editor for the *Germantown Gazette*. According to Drury (1:886), the *Germantown Gazette* had several editors. William Gunckel and his partner Moses B. Walker were the initial publishers. In 1849, Drury continues, the paper was sold to Joseph Reeder and Josiah Oblinger, who renamed the paper, *Western Emporium* and later to *Twin Valley Locomotive*.

2. Drury, 886. Drury reports that the first paper was published in Germantown in 1826 by Conrad (!) Schaeffer. Several other sources refer to him as Eduard (!) Schaeffer. The newspaper was half German and half English, which might be one reason why the *Chronicling America* search returned no results. Drury states that the publisher left Germantown after one year. A business idea by George Walker who came to Germantown with a printing press in 1839 to make the laws of Ohio available to all settlers by printing the translation into German, failed. Only a few issues were sold.

3. Julius Goebel, ed., *Deutsch-Amerikanische Geschichtsblätter*, (Illinois: Deutsch-Amerikanische Historische Gesellschaft von Illinois, 1912), XII: 298. It should be noted here that Goebel uses a different first name (Eduard instead of Conrad). Don Heinrich Tolzmann, ed., *Early German-American Newspapers: Daniel Miller's History*, (Bowie: Heritage Books, 2001), 101, also mentions *Edward Schäffer* as the publisher of the *National Zeitung der Deutschen*.

4. Ibid., 301. It is not clear how long this paper was published after 1833. Goebel mentions that not a single issue is still available. The same year when Germantown got its first German paper, Cincinnati published their first German newspaper, the *Ohio Chronik*. 302.

Appendix C

INDEX OF GERMAN NEWSPAPERS & PAPERS IN
MIAMISBURG, OHIO

A digital search in the Library of Congress, *Chronicling America* website with these search parameters (Montgomery County, Ohio; Miamisburg; German language) from 1690 to 2014 produced no German newspapers. When selecting English as a search parameter, the following four English newspapers are listed. No German newspapers are listed.

Name of Newspaper	Place & Date of Publication	Publisher/ Editor
Miamisburg Bulletin	Miamisburg, 1867-1895	Blossom Brothers - English
The Miamisburg Union	Miamisburg, 1856-18??	Isaac Pepper - English
Gridiron Revivdus	Miamisburg, 1839-1839	John Anderson - English
The Miamisburg News	Miamisburg, 1880-current	Chas. E. Kinder - English

Source: <http://tinyurl.com/lhrfslb>

Arndt and Olson:
Karl J.R. Arndt and May E. Olson, *Deutsch-Amerikanische Zeitungen und Zeitschriften, 1732-1955* (Heidelberg: Quelle und Meyer, 1961) do not list any German papers or newspapers for Miamisburg, Ohio.

Drury:
He only mentions that the *Gridiron* was the first published newspaper in Miamisburg, but no German newspapers are recorded.

Images

Image of the Cincinnati German Pioneer Society Composite Picture used with permission from the Campbell County Historical & Genealogical Society (CCH&GS). The original is the property and in the possession of The Campbell County, KY Historical & Genealogical Society, 8352 East Main St., Alexandria, KY 41006.

Map of Montgomery County, Ohio, 1875. Everts, L. H. Combination Atlas Map of MontgomeryCounty, Ohio / Compiled, Drawn and Published from Personal Examinations and Surveys by L.H. Everts. Philadelphia : L.H. Everts, 1875, p. 15.

Miamisburg Images (Images by Nicole Dona)

Daniel Gebhart Tavern opened in 1811 as a place for food, entertainment, news, and rest for travelers, boatmen and pioneers. The tavern together with the Treons' medical practice (1811) belonged to the first structures in Hole's Station (now Miamisburg). The tavern was closed in 1840 when it was turned into the first boarding house. In 1981 it was restored and is now managed by the Miamisburg Historical Society.

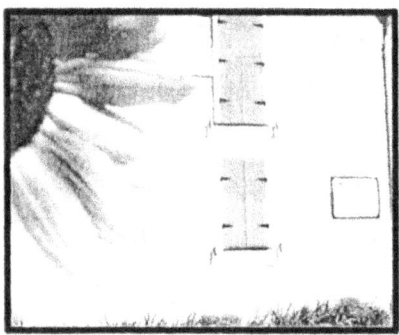 

Jacob Kercher Home (1808-1810). The early pioneer and co-founder of Miamisburg came to Ohio in 1806 with his wife, Margaret Gebhart. The log cabin was discovered under siding, which was added later. The Miamisburg Historical Society oversaw the restoration efforts and in August 2009 it was dedicated in Miamisburg during their 200th anniversary.

George Hoff Home (1872). He was the son of William Hoff, whose grandfather was born in Westerburg, Germany. Georg Hoff worked with his father in the dry goods business in Miamisburg. The house was later also the home of the singing McGuire sisters, famous as a trio in American popular music.

William Hoff Home (early 1800's) was built in the Pennsylvanian German , a stone building with two floors. Two physicians (Dr. John Treon , Dr. Wiliam Shuler) worked in this house.

St. John's Evangelical Lutheran Church
Miamisburg, Montgomery County, Ohio

St. John's Cemetery (early burial
site in Montgomery County, Ohio)

German inscription on gravestones in the St. John's Evangelical Lutheran Church Cemetery

Germantown Images (By Nicole Dona)

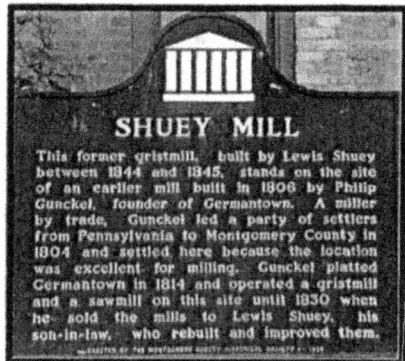

Koeppel Building, 1886, Germantown, Ohio   Koeppel Building, 2014

Town Hall, Germantown, 1873   Town Hall, Germantown, 2014

Florentine Hotel, Germantown, Ohio, 2014

Residence of David Rohrer, 1865

Residence of David Rohrer, 2014

View of Germantown, Ohio, in 1885. Philip Gunckel, who came in 1804 with German-speaking settlers from Berks County, Pennsylvania, platted the town in 1814. German was widely spoken.

German Township Oldest House, 1798. Courtesy of the Germantown Public Library.

On October 4th, 1814, a clerk dipped his pen into an inkstand, and made a boldly scripted entry in the Records of Montgomery County. His entry showed that one Philip Gunckel had filed a plat plan for the Village of Germantown.

It was a unique design, laid off in eight blocks which were twenty perches (330 feet) square, running from Mulberry Street to Walnut Street, and from Market Street to Back (Warren) Street.

Each block was divided by a diagonal alley system, the hub of which was a central open space some 66 feet square.

While the clerk failed to set down Philip Gunckel's rationale for the plan, it seems clear that the village's precise and methodical German settlers wanted their building fronts close to uncluttered streets, with buggies parked and horses stabled in the rear. The central square not only served as a turn-around space, but also as a beckoning place where children gathered to play.

Front Page of the First Issue of *Der Westliche Beobachter*, a German Newspaper from Nov. 15, 1826. Courtesy of the Stark County District Library, Canton, Ohio.

The Greeneville Treaty was signed August 3, 1795. Treaty line went through Shelby County. Indian tribes surrendered to the United States large parts of their land (present-day Ohio). The Indians could still hunt on the land they have given up. <www.remarkableohio.org>
Used with Permission from Ohio History Connection, Columbus, OH. No copyright restrictions.
Source:

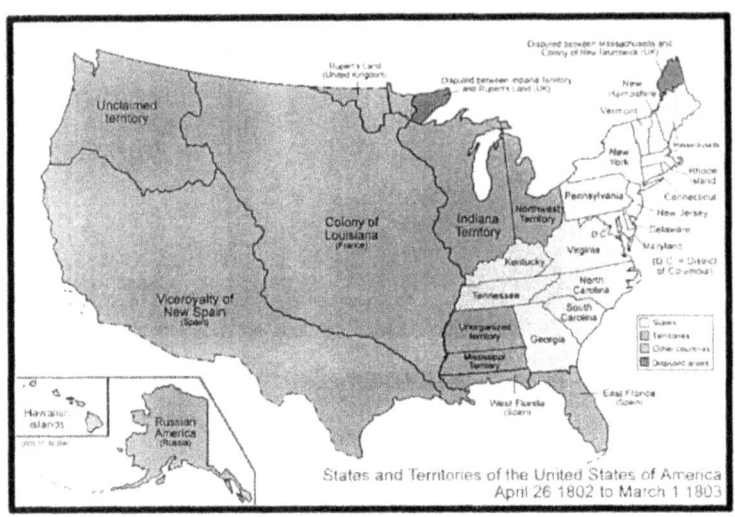

Subject	Ohio Estimate	Margin of Error	Percent	Percent Margin of Error
ANCESTRY				
Total population	11,544,225	*****	11,544,225	(X)
American	1,014,096	+/-20,874	8.8%	+/-0.2
Arab	73,884	+/-6,876	0.6%	+/-0.1
Czech	57,515	+/-4,246	0.5%	+/-0.1
Danish	20,420	+/-3,232	0.2%	+/-0.1
Dutch	180,853	+/-7,576	1.6%	+/-0.1
English	1,036,346	+/-21,816	9.0%	+/-0.2
French (except Basque)	265,841	+/-11,367	2.3%	+/-0.1
French Canadian	28,606	+/-3,246	0.2%	+/-0.1
German	3,033,395	+/-29,229	26.3%	+/-0.3
Greek	59,128	+/-5,494	0.5%	+/-0.1
Hungarian	195,424	+/-8,573	1.7%	+/-0.1
Irish	1,591,069	+/-22,482	13.8%	+/-0.2
Italian	738,471	+/-18,189	6.4%	+/-0.1
Lithuanian	25,584	+/-3,953	0.2%	+/-0.1
Norwegian	37,056	+/-3,701	0.3%	+/-0.1
Polish	428,034	+/-12,026	3.7%	+/-0.1
Portuguese	9,834	+/-2,006	0.1%	+/-0.1
Russian	78,230	+/-5,992	0.7%	+/-0.1
Scotch-Irish	111,976	+/-6,576	1.0%	+/-0.1
Scottish	210,593	+/-9,320	1.8%	+/-0.1
Slovak	133,997	+/-7,482	1.2%	+/-0.1
Subsaharan African	109,928	+/-9,100	1.0%	+/-0.1
Swedish	76,800	+/-5,967	0.7%	+/-0.1
Swiss	76,717	+/-7,063	0.7%	+/-0.1
Ukrainian	40,612	+/-3,574	0.4%	+/-0.1
Welsh	122,265	+/-6,517	1.1%	+/-0.1
West Indian (excluding Hispanic origin groups)	14,942	+/-2,747	0.1%	+/-0.1

Source: U.S. Census Bureau, 2012 American Community Survey

According to the U.S. Census 2012 American Community Survey, 16.3% or 3,033.395 Ohioans claim German heritage, making German the largest ethnic group in Ohio. <http://tinyurl.com/lgvrysg>

Notes

Introduction

1. Don Heinrich Tolzmann, *The German-American Experience* (Amherst: Humanity Books, 2000), 257. Two examples of German historians who wanted to archive the contributions of the Germans were: Emil Klauprecht, *Deutsche Chronik in der Geschichte des Ohio-Thales: Und seiner Hauptstadt Cincinnati in's Besondere* (Cincinnati: G. Hof & M.A. Jacobi, 1864); and Franz Löher, *Geschichte und Zustände der Deutschen in Amerika* (Cincinnati: Eggers und Wulkop, 1847).

2. Albert Bernhardt Faust, *The German Element in the United States: With Special Reference to its Political, Moral, Social, and Educational Influence* (Boston: Houghton Mifflin Company, 1909), 1:428. Also see, Carl Wittke, ed., *The History of the State of Ohio* (Columbus: Ohio State Archeological and Historical Society, 1942): "Although statistics are lacking it is clear that the Germans were the most numerous of the foreign-language groups. 10 Germans were found in almost every county even in the first decade of statehood, but as they came in larger numbers, settlements were formed which preserved their identity for more than a generation," II:394. It is necessary to add that although many German settlers were born in Germany and came to the United States, there was also a large group of German-speaking immigrants of German descent who came to Ohio from Pennsylvania, Virginia and Maryland.

3. Faust, 1:429.

4. "U.S. Census Bureau." American Fact Finder, 2010. Web. 6. Feb. 2014. <http://factfinder2.census.gov/faces/tableservices/jsf/pages/productview.xhtml?pid=ACS_10_1Y R_DP02&prodType=table>.

5. "U.S. Census Bureau." American Community Survey, 2012. Web. 6. Feb. 2014. <http://tinyurl.com/lgvrysg>.

6. Mary Edmund Spannheimer, *Heinrich Armin Rattermann, German-American Author, Poet, and Historian, 1832-1923* (Washington: Catholic University of America, 1937).

7. Mary Edmund Spannheimer, and Don Heinrich Tolzmann, ed., *The German Pioneer Legacy: The Life and Work of Heinrich A. Ratterman* by Sister Mary Edmund Spannheimer (Oxford: Peter Lang, 2004).

8. Henry Willen, "Henry Armin Rattermann's Life and Poetical Work," Ph.D. Diss., University of Pennsylvania, 1939.

9. Marc Surminski, "Heinrich Armin Rattermann und Der Deutsche Pionier," M.A. Thesis, University of Cincinnati, 1988.

10. Don Heinrich Tolzmann, ed., *Festschrift for the German-American Tricentennial Jubilee* (Cincinnati: Historical Society, 1982), 55.

11. For more information about the German Pioneer Society, see Rainer Sell, "Der Deutsche Pionier-Verein von Cincinnati, Heinrich Armin Rattermann und Der Deutsche Pionier," *Yearbook of German-American Studies* 20 (1985): 49-60. Also, see Don Heinrich Tolzmann, *Cincinnati's German Heritage* (Bowie: Heritage Books, Inc., 1994).

12. Genealogists will find many authentic records, such as birth records; death notices and obituaries; marriage notices; dates of immigration and location of emigrants' origins in Europe; and specific locations of events. For a list of most names of immigrants appearing in *Der Deutsche Pionier* as well as references to volumes and pages in the magazines where they appear, see Clifford Neal Smith, *Early Nineteenth-Century German Settlers in Ohio (Mainly Cincinnati and Environs), Kentucky, And Other States.* (McNeal: Westland Publications, 1984). For more information about the German settlers in Dayton, see *Don Heinrich Tolzmann, ed., Dayton's German Heritage: Karl Karstaedt's Golden Jubilee History of the German Pioneer Society of Dayton, Ohio* (Bowie: Heritage Books, Inc., 2001).

13. *Der Deutsche Pionier: Erinnerungen aus dem Pionierleben der Deutschen in Amerika.* (Cincinnati: Deutsche Pionier-Verein, 1879/1880), XI:126, 170, 217, 254, 300, 344. According to Rainer Sell, "Der Deutsche Pionier-Verein von Cincinnati: Heinrich Armin Rattermann und *Der Deutsche Pionier*," *Yearbook of German-American Studies* 20 (1985), 53, Rattermann's contributions to the *Deutsche Pionier* about the history of the Germans in Ohio "are among the best contributions." For details about the German Pioneer Society of Dayton, see Don Tolzmann, ed., *Dayton German Heritage*, 12.

14. *Jahresbericht des Vorstandes des Deutschen Pionier-Vereins von Cincinnati, Ohio für das Verwaltungsjahr 1887-1888* (Cincinnati: Rosenthal, 1887-1889). Also see, Sell, 51.

15. Ibid., 52. *DPVC* is the abbreviation of *Deutscher Pionier-Verein Cincinnati.* A *Zweigsverein* is a branch club. A *Stiftungsfest* refers to a foundation celebration.

16. Mary Edmund Spannheimer, *The German Pioneer Legacy: The Life and Work of Heinrich A. Rattermann. Ed. Don Heinrich Tolzmann* (Oxford: Peter Lang, 2004), xix.

17. Tolzmann, ed., *Dayton's German Heritage*, xi.

Chapter 1: History of Original Settlement of Montgomery County, Ohio

1. Wyandots, Delawares, Miamies, Ottawas, Chippewas, Pottawatamis, Kickapoos, Weas, Ceels, Piankaschaws and Kaskaskias, - J.H. Perkins, Annals of the West, 2nd ed., pp. 445-46. HAR

2. "Following the 1795 Treaty of Greenville, the floodgate for immigration was opened and the first settlers entered the area known today as Montgomery County." *A Sense of Community: In Celebration of the Bicentennial of Centerville, Washington* Township 1796-1996 (New York: American Heritage Custom Publishing, 1996), 2. EVD

3. Several years later Johann Weber established the village at the Little Miami under the name of Weaverville. Presently the railway station Alpha is located next to the Dayton and Xenia railroad. The third settlement appears to never have been founded. HAR

4. This fact could be verified in Drury's *History of the City of Dayton and Montgomery County, Ohio* (Chicago: S.J. Clarke Publishing Company, 1909), 68: "Forty-six men had agreed in the fall of 1795, to become settlers at the mouth of Mad river in the following spring. Some of these located at intervening points. Fifteen persons kept their engagement, four others joining them, and with those dependent on them, probably not less than sixty in all, in March 1796, left Cincinnati in three parties for their new home. Two parties went by land and one by water." EVD

5. There are conflicting opinions about the true nationality of Georg Neukomm (1771-1853). Although Albert Faust in *The German Element in the United States* (Boston and New York: Houghton Mifflin Company, 1909) on page 428 insists on Georg Neukomm to be German and the son of Christian Neukomm of Zweibrücken, he tries to explain the misconception about their Irish nationality. He and Rattermann point to a marriage of the Neukomm's with Margaret McCarthy, who was Irish. Georg Neukomm, himself, also married an Irish woman later, Mary Henderson. Faust notes that the family was originally named Neukomm, but later used the names Newcomer and Newcom. Beers in his *History of Montgomery County, Ohio* (Chicago: W.H. Beers & Co., 1882), 452 lists the Newcom's with their Anglicized spelling as being of Irish origin. Edgar in *Pioneer Life in Dayton and Vicinity* (1896) adds that Colonel George Newcom was born in Ireland in 1771, arrived in America with his parents in 1775, came to Cincinnati in 1794, and left on March 21, 1796 to Dayton. Faust also mentions that Christian Neukomm used the name "Newcomer, and later Newcom" (p.428). The surname "Neukomer" is listed as a German name in: *Pennsylvania German Church Records of Births, Baptisms, Marriages, Burials, Etc. from the Pennsylvania German Society Proceedings and Addresses* (Baltimore: Genealogical Publication Company, 1983) 3:756. EVD

6. According to an oral testimony by A. Smith, who was a close friend of Colonel Neukomm or Newcom in the years 1828-1834. The opinion that the Newcom's were Irish is stated by M.C. Curwen in his *History of Dayton* which was added to the *Dayton Directory* of 1850. HAR

7. John F. Edgar, *Pioneer Life in Dayton and Vicinity: 1796-1840* (Dayton: Shuey, 1896), 22-23, using the Anglicized name, William Hamer, mentions that he was born in Maryland around 1750 and traveled west in 1792. After staying in Cincinnati for a while, he moved to Dayton in March 1796. Edgar also states on page 22 and page 245 that Hamer was the first Methodist minister in

Dayton and one of his sons was born on December 9, 1796, making him the "first white boy born in the settlement." They named the child Dayton. EVD

8. When Böhm re-visited Dayton in February of 1859 on his last trip, he wrote in his diary: "I went to Dayton which formerly when I was there, was only a small city, but now it has thirty thousand inhabitants. The *United Brethren in Christ* have established a publication house here. When I entered the building and looked at the wall, I saw the picture of my father (Martin Böhm, who founded the *United Brethren* church with Otterbein and who, together with him, was one of the first bishops of this sect.) I have not seen this in fifty years." – Wakeley, *The Patriarch of One Hundred Years*, New York, 1875, p. 488. – At another location Böhm writes: "Fifty-two years later when I visited this part of Ohio, I met many Germans, who could have heard me preach in German in 1809." – Ibid. p. 259. HAR

9. Most Dayton history books of the time agree that little is known about Salomon Goß (Solomon Goss), but Drury in the *History of the City of Dayton* mentions that Solomon Goss resided in Dayton in 1799, but "probably soon afterward moved further up the Miami." I:92. EVD

10. Robert W. Steele, *Early Dayton: With Important Facts and Incidents from the Founding of the City of Dayton, Ohio, to the Hundredth Anniversary, 1796-1896* (Dayton: Shuey, 1896), 23, points out that Abraham Glaßmeier (Anglicized spelling, Glassmire) was a German bachelor and "a very useful member of the little community, making looms and showing much ingenuity in contriving conveniences not easily obtained by pioneer housekeepers." Later he refers to him as an "ingenious pioneer weaver." 33. For further information about living conditions of early pioneer life in Dayton, Ohio, see Steele, *Early Dayton*, 17ff. EVD

11. Howard R. Houser writes in *A Sense of Place in Centerville and Washington Township* (Centerville: The Society, 1977), 6: "The original proposal presented to Congress on August 29, 1787, was to purchase two million acres, using in part his certificates of indebtedness received for his financial aid to the army." When Symmes could not come up with the money, he made a petition to Congress for a smaller lot. Congress answered his petition by offering to sell Symmes a million acres with a frontage of 27 miles extending eastward from the mouth of the Great Miami River." Rattermann mentions, however, that Symmes owned 20 miles. When the U.S. government passed the Northwest Ordinance of 1787, allowing surveying and selling of land north of the Ohio River, Judge John Cleves Symmes (1742-1814) of New Jersey, recognized the potential for future settlement and bought a large portion of the land. The land was incorrectly surveyed and since Symmes sold more land than he owned, he left many of the early settlers without a valid land deed. For more information, see Peter Onuf, *Statehood and Union: A History of the Northwest Ordinance* (Bloomington: Indiana University Press, 1987). EVD

12. Ellen T. Berry in *Early Ohio Settlers: Purchasers of Land in Southwestern Ohio, 1800-1840* (Baltimore: Genealogical Publication Company, 1986), ix, mentions that Symmes and his business partners were unable to pay even for the 311, 682 acres that were granted in the end. This real estate disaster had severe consequences for the early pioneers who bought land from Symmes. Houser also writes that Symmes received a patent for 311,682 acres: "In 1794, President Washington issued a patent for the amount of land actually paid for – 311,682 acres –

for a purchase price of sixty seven cents per acre." 6. This fact is interesting since the government tried to charge the early Dayton settlers two dollars per acre because of Symmes mistake: "Everybody who wanted it owned land. It was so superabundant it was not much prized. A few years later the government of the United States, owing to Judge Symmes' failure to complete the terms of his contract of purchase, tried to make the Dayton settlers pay $2.00 an acre for the land they held. But our worthy sires drew up resolutions in the schoolmaster's best handwriting to inform the government they had worked harder reclaiming the land from the wilderness and making it taxable, than the land was worth." Joseph Sharts, *Biography of Dayton* (Dayton: Miami Valley, 1922), 7. EVD

13. When history books refer to the *Symmes Purchase* they are pointing out the sad fact that the early settlers of Montgomery County, Ohio, had to re-purchased their land from the Federal Government, because Judge John Cleves Symmes sold more land than was assigned to him. EVD

14. M.E. Curwen, *History of Dayton* in L.H. Ever's *Historical Map of Montgomery County*, p. 22. – Perkins', 403, 494. – Howe, *Historical Collection of Ohio* (Edition of 1861), p. 370. HAR

15. According to Houser, "Only James Byers and William Wells, a land speculator who had acquired large tracts of land from John Cleves Symmes, exercised their right of preemption." (6). EVD

16. Western Spy", April 26, 1800. – Cist, "Cincinnati in 1841", p. 170, - Klauprecht, *Deutsche Chronik*, p. 143. – „Deutsche Pionier", I. 41. HAR

17. According to Edgar in *Pioneer Life in Dayton and Vicinity*: "The first school in Dayton was taught by Benjamin Van Cleve in the blockhouse during the winter of 1799-1800. The second was held in 1804, in a cabin on Main Street, by Cornelius Westfall, of Kentucky, and in 1805 by Chauncy Whiting, of Pennsylvania. In 1807 the Dayton Academy was incorporated by James Welsh, Daniel C. Cooper, William McClure, David Reid, Benjamin Van Cleve, George F. Tennery, John Folkerth, and James Hanna, Mr. Cooper donating two lots, numbers 139 and 140, to the trustees, at the corner of Third and St. Clair streets, on part of which a two-story brick house, with belfry, was built." (249) This fact was confirmed in the *History of Dayton*: "As early as 1799 a school was taught in a block house located near the river batik, at the head of Main Street, which had been built for protection against Indians. Benjamin Van Cleve, so prominent in the early history of Dayton, was the teacher, and the school was continued through parts of the years 1799 and 1800. It is probable that Dayton was at no time without a school, but the names of only a few of the teachers have come down to us. Cornelius Westfall, a Kentuckian, opened a school in the fall of 1804 and taught a year in a cabin on Main Street, south of First. He was succeeded in 1805 by Chauncey Whiting, of Pennsylvania." (219) This was also confirmed in the *Biography of Dayton*. (7) Early pioneer schools were subscription schools where parents were asked to pay a certain amount of money for each child that wanted an education. The first schools were usually held in a log cabin of one of the early settlers. EVD

18. Court transcript of Montgomery County, O., Volume A, pages 106-108. HAR

19. Steele in *Early Dayton* describes the landscape, sounds, and smells of Dayton around 1800 (24-26). EVD

20. According to Edgar in *Pioneer Life in Dayton and Vicinity* (57-58), Montgomery County was named after General Richard Montgomery (1738-1755) who was a an officer in the Revolutionary War. EVD

21. Ibid., 26. Neukomm's home served many functions in early Dayton history: it was the first store, first court, the first jail, the first tavern and also served as the home of the Georg Neukomm and his family. On page 84, Edgar describes the first court hearing in Dayton, Ohio, on July 27, 1803, which was opened by Honorary Judge Francis Dunlevy. EVD

22. The Daniel Gebhart Tavern (built in 1811) is still in existence and is a museum in Miamisburg with Pioneer furniture, and historical information about the tavern. Unfortunately, Daniel Gebhart is not indicated as being German. http://www.miamisburg.org/daniel_gebhart_tavern_museum.htm. EVD

23. The Jacob Kercher pioneer home (built between 1808-1810) was restored through the initiative of the Miamisburg Genealogical Society and is now serving as a historic visitation site. EVD

24. According to Augustus W. Drury, *History of the City of Dayton and Montgomery County, Ohio* (Chicago: S.J. Clarke Publication Company, 1909), 1:829, Anthony Chevalier was a Revolutionary soldier and an early settler of Miamisburg. Beers (III:132) points out that Anthony Chevalier was a "native of France, one, of those intrepid bands of patriots who left their native land under the leadership of the gallant Lafayette, to fight for American independence. He served throughout that struggle against English oppression, and at its triumphant close settled in Virginia, where he married Rachel Scott, a cousin of Gen. Winfield Scott; lived subsequently in Kentucky, and from there came to this county. He settled at Hole's Station, from whence, after a few years' residence, he removed to Section 15, and is yet well-remembered by many old citizens." EVD

25. Howe writes in1847: "The early settlers were of Dutch origin, most of whom emigrated to Berks County, Pa. The German is yet much spoken and two of the churches worship in that language." Ohio Hist. Coll. p. 374. -- The churches in Miamisburg in 1847 were the German Reformed Church, the German Lutheran Church, and the Methodist Church, in the latter German and English sermons were given alternately. HAR

26. I agree with Rattermann here after consulting the *History of Montgomery County, Ohio* (III: 132) where much information can be found about Col. William Dodds, born in Pennsylvania, William Lamme (Lamb), who arrived from Kentucky and built the first grist mill, and Maj. George Adams, who received many battle scars because of his activities in the War of 1812 while defending the pioneer settlers. Not too much is known, however, about William Van Arsdale (Vernosdell), who resided with his family "southwest of the mouth of Holes Creek." EVD.

27. According to Edgar, *Pioneer Life in Dayton and Vicinity* (57), Dr. John Hole was born in 1754 in Virginia, married on August 4, 1778, moved in 1796 to Cincinnati, and in 1797 to the Miami Valley. Because he was an officer in the Revolutionary War, he received "military land bounty warrants" with which he could pay his land. For more information about this surgeon, see 57-58. EVD

28. According to Drury (I:773) Peter Sunderland filed the first common pleas court case against Benjamin Scott accusing him of assault and battery. EVD

29. For additional information about the life of Dr. Hole also see: Howard R. Houser, *Wilderness Doctor: The Life and Times of Dr. John Hole* (Centerville: Centerville Historical Society, 1980). It is interesting to note here that Houser mentions that Dr. Hole received his medical education in Germany: "After receiving some preliminary medical training under his preceptor, John Hole was sent by the good doctor to Germany in 1770 to complete his education at the University of Berlin. History does not firmly establish the name of his benefactor (although a Dr. Fullerton has been mentioned); nor is there any information available about John Hole's studies or his life in Germany." 4. EVD

30. Everts, 27. HAR.
L.H. Everts, *Combination Atlas Map of Montgomery County, Ohio* (Philadelphia: Hunter Press, 1875), 27: Everts does not refer to Dr. Hole's home as "Cincinnati" as is quoted in Rattermann, but rather as "...made my way to my cabin near Fort Washington." EVD

31. A confirmation of the first schoolteacher in Mad River Township, a Mr. Beck, was found in *Reed's Illustrated History of Montgomery County: From its Earliest Recollections to the Present Time: Complete Compilation of the Present Most Important Business Interests, With Faithful Illustrations* (Dayton: H.S. Reed, 1995), 16. EVD

32. More on Butler Township, which was formed on October 7, 1817, can be found in John C. Hover's *Memoirs of the Miami Valley* (Chicago: Robert O. Law Company, 1919), II:31-32. The names and accomplishments of some early settlers are recorded here. It is also mentioned that Andrew Waymire (*Andreas Wehmeier*) platted Little York, the first settlement town (31). John Quillian (*Johannes Quillian*) had a son by the name of William. This child was the first white child born in Butler Township (31). No mention was made of the German background of the early settlers, and all of their names were Anglicized. Drury in his *History of The City of Dayton and Montgomery County*, Ohio (910) states that Butler Township was first settled by pioneers from the Carolinas. He also mentions that Martin Davenport and David Hoover, Sr. were the first land prospectors who came around 1800. When they saw how fertile the area was, they returned with their own families and several others. Drury also informs us that Daniel Waymire and Phillip Hummer arrived with their families from North Carolina in 1805. He provides more background to Waymire (*Wehmeier*) including his German background: "The parents of Daniel Waymire came from Germany about the year 1735. The mother died on the voyage. The father's sisters were sold for their passage and never afterward heard of. The father settled in North Carolina and again married. From the two unions there was a large family of children, all of whom came to Ohio, and they became the ancestors of a large progeny. Many of the

descendants of the founder of this family in America reside in Butler Township and the surrounding territory, a due proportion of them bearing the name Waymire," (911) EVD

33. The construction of flourmills and sawmills provided bread and shelter for the early settlers. Once these mills were established many more pioneers arrived. Interestingly enough, the next construction that would follow, would be a distillery. *Joseph Küfer* appears as Joseph Cooper in Drury's *History of the City of Dayton and Montgomery County, Ohio* (920). EVD

34. Drury (911) writes that Abijah Jones, who came from North Carolina, belonged to the Society of Friends and settled in Butler Township in 1805. The *Centennial Anniversary Of West Branch Monthly Meeting Of Friends* (West Milton: n.p., 1907), 24 mentions that Abijah Jones, whose parents were Richard and Jemima Jones, was born in 1767 and married Rachel Harris in 1791. He and his family of eight children lived in Montgomery County, Ohio and he was a registered minister. EVD

35. Drury (1:901) points out that many of the early pioneers of Madison Township were German settlers and one of the earliest schools built there educated students using German and English (903). Dunkards also called Tunkers were German Baptists who built their first church in Madison Township in 1832 (904). Beers in his *History of Montgomery County* explains: "*German Baptists* - The Dunkers, or Dunkards, as they are commonly called, were the next to organize a church inside of the present limits of Randolph Township. In the year 1800, Jacob Miller came from Flat Rock Valley, Va., and settled on the west side of the Miami River, near Dayton, Ohio. He was born in Pennsylvania in 1735; was a man of ability and labored earnestly for his church. He was much revered by the red sons of the forest, who said that he was "the good man the Great Spirit sent from the East. He raised a family of nine sons and three daughters, three of the former becoming able ministers in the Dunker Church. The earliest pioneer Dunker preacher in Randolph Township was Emanuel Flory, who, in 1810, organized a congregation of his co-religionists." (III:60). EVD

36. The Daniel Miller house is still standing today (3525 Dandridge Avenue, Dayton, OH) and is registered as historic site on the National Register of Historic Places. Daniel Miller, who arrived from Huntingdon County, PA, erected both, a saw and a gristmill on the Wolf Creek (*Montgomery County Ohio 1990: A History Written by the People of Montgomery County, Ohio* (Dallas: Taylor Pub. Co., 1990), 188. EVD

37. Colonel Robert Patterson was an important citizen of Montgomery County and intrinsically connected with the growth of the county. Patterson founded Lexington, KY, and was one of three co-founders of Cincinnati (Drury, 1:638). He had Scottish ancestors and was born on March 15, 1753 in Bedford County, PA. According to Drury (I:36), Colonel Patterson, along with John Filson and Israel Ludlow, was one of the early explorers and assistants of Symmes. In 1803, after buying land by the Little Miami River, he built a mill. "Colonel Patterson was a man of deep religious convictions and was actively connected with the Presbyterian Church, first at Lexington and then at Dayton. He died at the Rubicon home November 9, 1827." (Drury, 121-122). Patterson, however, was a slave owner and moved the slaves he owned in Kentucky with him to Dayton. In 1805, a case was brought against Patterson to free some of his black slaves, since

slavery was not allowed in the state of Ohio. The court decided in favor of the slaves and set them free. (Drury, 122-123).

Although Colonel Robert Patterson was a Revolutionary and Indian War hero, Conover did not include him in her book with the lofty title, *Some Dayton Saints and Prophets* (1907) as one of Dayton's twenty-four honorable citizens. She included Julia J. Patterson (79-87), the wife of his youngest son. Conover published in 1902 the personal letters and stories of Colonel Robert Patterson and Colonel John Johnston in her book *Concerning the Forefathers*. The Patterson Homestead, located at 1815 Brown Street in Dayton, Ohio, built by Colonel Patterson is a museum today and listed on the National Register of Historic Places. There is also a Patterson log cabin, which was built around 1778-1780 on the campus of Transylvania University, KY. Wright State University's Dunbar Library *Special Collections and Archives* houses a collection of the *Patterson Family Papers* containing letters, legal papers, financial records, photographs, and newspaper clippings from 1780-1970. EVD

38. According to Reed's *Illustrated History of Montgomery County* (19), the county received its name in honor of President Jefferson, the third President of the United States and one of the people who signed the Declaration of Independence. The early settlers arrived in 1804 and Fulcus surveyed the township. He also mentions that Jacob Gripe (*Jakob Gripe*) built the first log cabin on Bear Creek, followed by Peter Weaver's (*Peter Weber*) second log cabin. EVD

39. Ibid., 19. The first schoolteacher is listed as Oblinger, not Oehlinger: "The name of the first schoolmaster was — Oblinger, who taught both German and English in a log cabin which had been abandoned by one of the pioneers for a better one. Their reading-books were the Bible and Testament. Webster's *Spelling-book* was authority for hard words, and Talbot's *Arithmetic* completed the "course." (19). Beers (III:72) mentions that Oblinger held classes in the log cabin, where Peter Weaver moved out. EVD

40. According to John C. Hover, ed., *Memoirs of the Miami Valley* (Chicago: Robert O. Law Company, 1919), II:44, German Township was formed in the Spring of 1803 and was one of the first four townships of Montgomery County, Ohio. The vast majority were Germans "either by birth or descent," 45. Hover describes the scene when the first settlers arrived there: "The coming of the first residents of German township vary in no essential particulars from the early settlements of the other townships of Montgomery county. The wigwams of some of the Shawnee tribe still stood on the banks of the stream that preserves their name, and it was with reluctant, saddened hearts that the poor red men saw their beloved forests fall before the relentless ax of the encroaching pioneers." 44. EVD

41. He and his brother-in-law Leonhard Stumpe bought on July 20, 1805 land "adjacent to Philipp Gunkel." Emerich bought 100 acres for $1600 and Stumpe 60 acres for $150. -- Deed-book B pp. 117, sq. HAR

42. Beers, III:60: "The earliest pioneer Dunker preacher in Randolph Township was Emanuel Flory, who, in 1810, organized a congregation of his co-religionists. For many years, they had no house to worship in, and held service every alternate Sabbath at the dwelling-house of some one of its members. Every member that was able to have meeting would take his or her turn, "so to speak," in having the meeting at his or her residence." Beers explains the nature of the Dunkers: "The Dunkers are an agricultural people, quiet, inoffensive and unostentatious, making no

display in wearing apparel, and living strict, temperate, industrious lives, taking little or no interest in Governmental affairs and few of them, especially among the older members, casting a vote. A great many strictly oppose a collegiate education, or even a higher education of the masses, on religious grounds, and are, therefore, looked upon as out of harmony with the spirit of this age; yet they are model farmers, good neighbors and honest and conscientious to a fault. They have three colleges in the United States, under the control of the church--one in Illinois, one in Pennsylvania and one in Ohio, where a higher education may be obtained and where students are welcomed regardless of creed, so long as they conform to the moral standard required and enforced in these institutions," 60. EVD

43. According to Beers (III:62), John Leatherman (*Johannes Ledermann*) laid out the town of Salem on January 15, 1816 dividing it into seventy-five lots. The town is now called Clayton. Hover (II:27) mentions that Leatherman platted the town of Salem in 1816. EVD

44. Everts in his *Combination Atlas Map Of Montgomery County, Ohio* (24) mentions that Joseph Miksell, Sr., coined the name for the township referring to its soil. Jacob Gripe erected the first sawmill and Joseph Miksell, Jr. (*Joseph Mickesell*) ran the first store. EVD

45. Ibid., 24: Perry Township was settled in 1819. EVD.

46. Ibid. Reverend Beenbrieck (*Beinbrecht*) was the first minister of Perry Township. Andrew Cleener (*Clemer*), built the first grist mill, Miller (*Müller*) is listed as the first teacher, Toby was introduced as an influential man, and the school house was built one mile away from John King's (*Joseph König*). EVD

47. Ibid. Jackson Township was named in honor of General Jackson. The first pioneers arrived in 1813, according to Everts. In 1816 Stephen Miller (*Stephan Müller*) erected the first "frame house" and in the same year Adam Swineheart (*Adam Schweinehirt*) built the first saw mill. A simple Lutheran church was constructed and referred to as Stiver's Church. A primitive schoolhouse was also present. EVD

48. According to *Memoirs of the Miami Valley* (II), Montgomery County, Ohio, was made up of fourteen townships. Wayne Township became a township on January 1, 1810 and was named after the hero of the American Revolutionary War, General Anthony Wayne (1745-1796), who is also known as "Mad Anthony," 50. General Wayne was one of the idols of the Ohio pioneers. Van Buren became a township in 1841 (17). In Evert's *Combination Atlas Map of Montgomery County* one can also find a reference to the lack of details about the Van Buren township history: "This Township is situated immediately south of Dayton, and is one of the most productive in the County. It is impossible to get the time of the original settlement, or who were the first settlers, or, in fact, anything pertaining to the early history of the Township, owing to the fact that all the oldest inhabitants are dead. The name gets its origin from President Van Buren," 27. EVD

49. Ibid., 44: " The first Shakers appeared as settlers in Van Buren township in the year 1805. A few years later, more people of the same faith arrived, until there was quite a settlement, to which was given the name of *Shakertown*. The chief industries of this peculiar people, were the raising of fine garden seed, improvement of live stock, and wool growing, but naturally the

singular beliefs of the Shakers, in time, tended to diminish their number, and now they are scarcely more than a name and a remembrance in the township." EVD

50. References to German ancestry or German-Pennsylvanian descent are rarely made in the history books of Montgomery County, Ohio, which makes Heinrich Armin Rattermann's account so important for local historians and people interested in German pioneer history. EVD

Chapter 2: Small Town Life of Early German Settlers

1. Jacob Kercher (*Jakob Kirchner*) together with Philip and Daniel Gephart, was one of the founders of Miamisburg, which was initially called Hole's Station (Everts, 29). According to Howe's *Historical Collections of Ohio*, Miamisburg was platted in 1818 and Jacob Kercher, Emanuel Gebhart, Drs. John and Peter Treon are listed as "original proprietors," II:299. Kercher moved from Pennsylvania to Ohio in 1806, where he died in 1855 (Everts, 36). He is buried at Hillgrove Cemetery in Miamisburg, Ohio. Miamisburg, which was named after the river, became a thriving city when the Miami and Erie Canal was built and passengers and goods were shipped via Miamisburg on their way between Dayton and Cincinnati (Hover, III:33). A plat map of Miamisburg can be found in Everts' *Combination Atlas Map of Montgomery, County, Ohio* (1875, 160). The Kercher House, which was built in 1806, was preserved through the efforts of the Miamisburg Historical Society and the city of Miamisburg. It is now used for educational purposes. <http://tinyurl.com/l5de34o>. For further information about Miamisburg, see Esther Light, *Miamisburg, Ohio, The Story of Our Town: A Collection of Historical Essays from 1818 to 1993* (Miamisburg: Miamisburg Lions Club, 1993). EVD

2. Political debates were common among the Germans. Many of those discussions took place in the coffeehouse of Captain Kothe. In Clifford N. Smith, *Early Nineteenth-Century German Settlers in Ohio* (McNeal: Westland Publications, 1984), Kothe is described as a well-educated gentleman who died at age 74 in Miamisburg on May 25th, 1852. 51. EVD

3. Colonel Newcom's Tavern (*Neukomm*) had many uses over time: it was a home and it served as a courtroom after 1803 (Everts, 23). The first court case was held on the second floor of the cabin. The dry well of Colonel Newcom even served as the first jail. Prisoners were lowered into the well until their cases were heard (Everts, 22). For more information about the tavern, see *Newcom Tavern at Carillon Historical Park* (Dayton: Carillon Historical Park, 1996).
The Coat of Arms of the City of Dayton, which was designed in 1935, presents a golden image of the Newcom Tavern symbolizing the pioneer settlers of Dayton. EVD

4. A *Dreher* is a typical pair dance from Lower Franconia. EVD

5. For more information about Peter Sunderland and his large family, see Howard R. Houser, *The Royal Rebels: The Sunderlands In America* (Centerville: Centerville Historical Society, 1992). EVD

6. Rattermann has mentioned before that the first court case in Dayton was between Peter Sunderland and Benjamin Scott and was heard on the upper floor of George Newcom's Tavern, which served as a courtroom at that time. Drury (I:773) confirms that "the first case tried in the court of common pleas, as the record show, was the charge of assault and battery against one Benjamin Scott, on complaint of one Peter Sunderland, to which the defendant plead guilty." It is interesting to note that the fine was $6.00 and court costs and both parties were in court again the following year. EVD

7. Gettersburg (*Göttersburg*), which was created between 1800-1803, is now renamed to Ellerton. <http://tinyurl.com/l6zzbes>. EVD

8. According to Reed's *Illustrated History, Montgomery County, Ohio* (19), the first church in Gettersburg was a Lutheran church with the first minister by the name of Decheron. EVD

9. Richard Thornton in *An American Glossary; Being an Attempt to Illustrate Certain Americanisms Upon Historical Principles* (New York: F. Ungar, 1962), 1:66, writes that *Black Betty* was a *spirit-bottle*. This usage was also confirmed by looking at anecdotes of the time. Lewis Collins, *Historical Sketches of Kentucky: Embracing its History, Antiquities, and Natural Curiosities, Geographical, Statistical, and Geological Descriptions with Anecdotes of Pioneer Life, and more than One Hundred Biographical Sketches of Distinguished Pioneers, Soldiers, Statesmen, Jurists, Lawyers, Divines, Etc.* (Maysville: L. Collins, 1848), 163, describes a similar early pioneer wedding ceremony where *Black Betty* refers to a whiskey bottle that is being sent to the newlyweds. EVD

10. Edgar, *Pioneer Life in Dayton and Vicinity*, 133 mentions that John Folkerth (*Johannes Folkerth*) came from Pennsylvania to Ohio before 1804. He was elected Justice of the Peace, a position, which he held for 52 years, and also became the first Mayor of Dayton. Folkerth was instrumental in the incorporation of the *Dayton Academy School* in Dayton in 1807. EVD

11. Ibid., 100-103. Philip Gunckel (*Philipp Gunkel*), born in Berks County, PA, April 7, 1766, was a miller by trade, who moved in 1804 with twenty-four other families west. He was their leader and Edgar mentions that he might have been the only one who knew the English language. On June 20, 1804, the Gunckel party, which took all their belongings with them on the flatboats in Pittsburg, arrived in Cincinnati. They did not stay long there, but went north towards Hole's station. "All the desirable locations on the east side of the river had been taken, but at the forks of the Great and Little Twin creeks Mr. Gunckel finally found the mill site he was in search of, together with good land for farming purposes. The few squatters were soon bought out, and the settlers bought from the government all the land the new settlers wanted. This was a strong colony, both as to numbers and money. They built good, warm cabins, and hunting parties were kept out during the winter, all sharing in the supplies brought in, while those at home were kept busy clearing the land and building cabins. Mr. Gunckel built a two-story log house the first winter, and had the best house in the settlement." The close-knit community soon elected Philip Gunckel justice of the peace for German Township. In 1805 Gunckel started to build a saw and gristmill and laid out Germantown in 1806 "donating lots for school, church, and graveyard purposes on his plat." Gunckel had eight children, married twice, and died on May 24, 1848, at age 82. One can visit his grave in the Germantown Cemetery, which was founded in 1849. <http://tinyurl.com/lw8vqeg>. Gunckel also built the second oldest inn in Ohio, the Florentine Hotel, two years after he and some German settlers came to Germantown in 1804. For more information on the hotel and pioneer cooking, see Debbie Nunley, *A Taste of Ohio History: A Guide to Historic Eateries and their Recipes* (Winston-Salem: John F. Blair, 2007) 48. For more information about the origin of names for Ohio's cities, see Willian D. Overman, *Ohio Place Names: The Origin of the Names of Over 500 Ohio Cities, Towns, and Villages* (Ann Arbor: Edwards Bros., 1951). EVD

12. Court Records "A," pp. 163 and 219. HAR

13. Ibid., p. 162. HAR

14. Edgar in *Pioneer Life in Dayton and Vicinity* attributes the idea to use a dry well as a jail to Newcom's Irish wit: "After the county was erected, and Dayton made the seat of justice, George Newcom, as sheriff, had to provide in some way for the prisoners who were by the court committed to jail, no jail having at that time been built. Newcom was an Irishman, of ready wit, and immediately put to such use a dry well at the rear of his house for white prisoners. The Indians he would buck and chain to his corncrib," 79. Newcom's Tavern, Dayton's oldest structure, was moved in 1965 to Carillon Historical Park, where it serves as a museum today. EVD

15. *Land Laws of the United States*, Washington, 1828, pp. 356 sq. – Albach, *Annals of the West*, pp. 466-472. – Atwater, *History of the State of Ohio*, (Cincinnati 1838) pp. 372. HAR

16. Albach, *Western Anals*, pp. 949-950. HAR

17. Ibid., 950-951. – It is easily comprehensible that this was abused, because the slave owners always knew to make arrangements to send their human commodity back to a slave state before the end of that term. HAR
The actual title and complete information of Rattermann's quote is: James Perkins, James H., John Mason Peck, and James R. Albach, *Annals Of The West* (Pittsburgh: Haven Book and Job Printer, 1837). EVD

18. The Northwest Territory prohibited slavery according to the Northwest Ordinance of 1787. The question was what will be done with the slaves that were already owned by the settlers in that territory or slaves that would run away. According to Marcus D. Pohlmann, *Student's Guide to Landmark Congressional Law on Civil Rights* (Westport: Greenwood Press, 2002), 15, the Ordinance created six articles of agreement between the original United States and the newly created territory. Article 6 "prohibited slavery or involuntary servitude, except in the case of convicted criminals. The law specifically provided, however, that any enslaved person escaping into the new territory from one of the original United States could be reclaimed by the owner." 15. Pohlmann also mentions that although Ohio was a free state, the 1830 census shows 16,000 blacks still living in Ohio, Indiana, Illinois, and Michigan. "Yet, despite the Northwest Ordinance, there were also 788 officially listed "*slaves*."14. EVD

19. For more information about Colonel Robert Patterson as slave owner and the Ohio incident with the two slaves in 1806, see the article by Emil Pocock entitled "Slavery and Freedom in the Early Republic: Robert Patterson's Slaves in Kentucky and Ohio 1804-1819," *Ohio Valley History* 6 (Spring 2006): 3-26. Pocock states that Ned Page and Lucy Page were brought from Kentucky illegally to work on his farm as slaves (6) and that eventually the Dayton residents in Colonel Newcom's Tavern stopped the slave catcher, David Sharp, from taking the two slaves by force (16). The Lucy and Ed(ward) case was said to be the first fugitive slave case recorded in Ohio. EVD

20. Court Records, Vol. "A," pp. 46-47. – The following Germans served as jurors: Nicolaus Horner, Johanes Devor, Martin Ruple or Rüffle, Georg Westfahl, Friedrich Nutz, Thomas Claussen (Clawson), David Mayer and Benjamin Wallings. HAR

21. Pocock, 18: In a jury trial, David Sharp was found not guilty for assaulting Jerome Holt (*Hieronymus Holt*) with a weapon and the Patterson case was also dismissed (17). To read more about the first run-away slave case in Ohio, see William Henry Smith, *The First Fugitive Slave Case of Record in Ohio* (Washington: Government Printing Office, 1894). EVD

22. There is a historical marker in Centerville, OH, on 9955 Yankee Street, stating that Brigadier General Edmund Munger (*Edmund Mungen*), was a Norfolk, Connecticut, a New England native. "In 1799, his wife Eunice Kellogg and five children traveled by wagon and flat-bottomed boat to claim land in Washington Township. A blacksmith by trade, Munger was deeply interested in community affairs."
< http://tinyurl.com/p64rfbs>. For additional information, see Howard Houser, *From Blacksmith to General: General Edmund Munger and the War of 1812 in Ohio* (Centerville: Centerville Historical Society, 1985). Also, Patrick R. Carstens, *Searching for the Forgotten War - 1812 United States of America* (n.p.: Patrick Richard Carstens, 2011). The grave of Edmund Munger (Sept 30th, 1763 - April 14, 1840) can be visited in the old Centerville Cemetery. EVD

23. The layout is recorded in Volume B on page 8 of the basic property books of Montgomery County. HAR

24. A record of the marriage between Anna Myers (*Anna Mayer*) and Daniel Bowser (*Daniel Bauzer*) on December 11, 1804 in German Township exists. "Ohio, County Marriages, 1789-1994," index and images, FamilySearch (http://tinyurl.com/pkub6oo: accessed 04 Nov 2013), Montgomery > Marriage records 1803-1827 vol A1. EVD

25. The song, which was sung while spinning was called *Dreh dich, dreh dich*. An arrangement by Thomas Grundlach can be listened to here <http://tinyurl.com/na6mvae>. EVD

26. Records, Vol. B, pp. 37-38. HAR

27. According to Tannehill, *Ohio Interrogation Points* (Columbus: Heer, 1917), 55-56, Dunkards are German Baptists, who originally came from Germany in 1700. They get their name from their baptismal ritual, since they "believe in triple immersion." Tannehill also adds that Dunkards settled at Germantown, PA, in 1719, and are plainly dressed. Hanna in *Historical Collections of Harrison County, in the State of Ohio* (New York: Privately printed, 1900), 37, mentions that of the 435,000 total population in Pennsylvania in 1700, there were 145,000 Germans. Among the German immigrants were Hessian soldiers, the Dunkards, German Calvinists, Moravians, Schwenkenfelders, Omishites, Mennonites, and Separatists (also called Seventh Day Baptists). For a more in depth reading, see Carl Bowman, *Brethren Society: The Cultural Transformation of a "Peculiar People"* (Baltimore: Johns Hopkins, 1995). EVD

28. He was the first Reformed preacher in Germantown. HAR

29. J. Peine and D. Winter call themselves preachers of the *High German Reformed Church*, as opposed to the others, who call themselves *German Reformed* preachers. HAR

30. Kuntz was a Reformed preacher in the year 1835 in Germantown. HAR

31. According to *History of Jerusalem Lutheran and Reformed Church of Western Salisbury* (Allentown: Haas & Co., 1911), 20, Reverent Jacob William Dechant was born in Kreutznach in the Palatinate on February 18, 1784, and was the son of John Peter Dechant and Jacobina Dechant came to Baltimore in 1805 where he studied theology under Rev. C.L. Becker. In 1815 he went as a missionary to Ohio, where he stayed three and one-half years before he returned to Pennsylvania. He died on October 5, 1832 in Berks County, PA, at age forty-eight. EVD

Chapter 3: Small Business Endeavors in Germantown and Miamisburg

1. Two important published sources about Germantown, Ohio, are: J. P. Hentz, *Twin Valley: Its Settlement and Subsequent History, 1798-1882* (Dayton: Christian Publishing House, 1883) and Carl M. Becker, *The Village: A History of Germantown, Ohio, 1804-1976* (Germantown: Germantown Historical Society, 1980). Both describe two waves of settlement to Germantown. According to Becker, the first white pioneers who were natives of Pennsylvania, Maryland, or Virginia first emigrated to Kentucky and then moved intermittently to the Germantown area, mostly squatting on the land between 1798 and 1804 (4). They were not interested in building a community and according to Becker, "they laid down no roads, established no institutions for community, created no history for their successors." (4). Pioneers of the second wave, however, in 1804, shared their own German language, culture, traditions, and religious beliefs. Their forefathers were born in the Palatinate and had originally belonged to the large German migration to Pennsylvania in the 1720s (4). Philip Gunkel, George Kern, Christopher Emerick, and David Miller were some of the leaders that brought families from Berks County, PA, to Ohio. Becker also points out that this group came by boat from Pittsburg to Cincinnati and stayed on their quest to find land up north at Hole's Station where the German farmer, Alexander Nutz, welcomed them and let them stay for a while (5). On August 1, 1804, they arrived in what is now Germantown. The area grew quickly because by 1806, three or four hundred German-speaking pioneers lived there (Becker, 6). EVD

2. Andrew Henkel (*Andreas Henkel*) came from a family of preachers and he was even related to the first Lutheran minister in America, Rev. Mulenberg (Hentz, 39) and since he could preach in German and English, was well received in Germantown, although some were against preaching in English (Hentz, 45-46). Henkel moved to Germantown in 1819 to be the preacher for the pioneers and he later built a brick church. He died in 1873 at age eighty (Frank Conover, *Centennial Portrait And Biographical Record Of The City Of Dayton And Of Montgomery County, Ohio* (Logansport: Bowen, 1897), 1128-1129. For more on Rev. Andrew Henkel, see Hentz, 39-67. EVD

3. According to Beers, *The History of Montgomery County*, (III:48), the first newspaper published in Germantown was called the Germantown *Gazette*, and "was started in 1826 by Conrad Schaeffer, a German, from Alsace, France. He was a pioneer newspaperman, and, previous to his advent here, had published papers in Lancaster and Canton, Ohio. One-half of the *Gazette* was printed in German, and one-half in the English language. He remained here but one year, after which he went to Hamilton, Ohio, and, in partnership with John Woods, established the Hamilton *Intelligencer*. In 1839, George Walker, a German, came to Germantown, and, in partnership with Dr. Espich, began printing *The Laws of Ohio in the German language*. They issued several volumes, but found few purchasers, and the enterprise proved a failure, and their labor and investment a total loss. This was the only attempt at the publication of books in Germantown." A search of the Library of Congress Digital Archives, confirmed an Edward Shaeffer published *The Germantown Gazette, and Montgomery County Weekly Advertiser* in Germantown (http://chroniclingamerica.loc.gov/lccn/sn90068987/).
For more information about Georg Walker, see Gustav Philipp Körner in *The German Element In The Ohio Valley: Ohio, Kentucky & Indiana / By Gustav Koerner; Translated and Edited by*

Don Heinrich Tolzmann (Baltimore: Clearfield, 2011) who mentions that Georg Walker, who was closely connected to "the German press of Cincinnati" (29), was born around 1808 in Urach near Reutlingen in Würtemberg, and relocated to Germantown, Ohio, in 1838 where he established the *Protestant* in cooperation with Dr. Christian Espich (30). Körner emphasizes that besides in Cincinnati, a flourishing German settlement was also established in Dayton, Ohio, where Georg Walker founded the German paper, *Der Deutsch-Amerikaner*, in 1839, which was followed by another German newspaper, *Der Freiheitsfreund*, in 1841 (59-60.) EVD

4. Rümelin is totally incorrect in his biography of Walker, regarding dates as well as names of geographic locations. See "Pionier" IV, p. 141 ff. HAR
Carl Rümelin was one of the editors of *Der Deutsche Pionier*. EVD

5. Rümelin says Plörach near Tübingen. However, where is Plörach? HAR
When investigating the source, which Rattermann provided, it turns out that *Der Deutsche Pionier: Erinnerungen aus dem Pionierleben* (VI:142) lists indeed "Plörach bei Tübingen" as his parent's town. Henry A. Ford in *Every Name Index, History Of Cincinnati, Ohio: With Illustrations and Biographical Sketches* (*Cleveland*: Williams, & Co., 1881), 136, mentions that George Walker was born in Urach near Reutlingen, Würtemberg. EVD

6. His license, which a preacher had to have according to Ohio's laws of that time, is dated as New Philadelphia April 11, 1836. HAR

7. Rümelin let him arrive in Miamisburg rather than Germantown. HAR

8. The title of the book is: *Deutsches Gesetzbuch: enthaltend, nebst der Unabhängigkeits-Erklärung und Verfassung der Vereinigten Staaten, die Verfassung und allgemeinen Gesetze des Staates Ohio. – Gesammelt und übersetzt von Georg Walker.* – Germantown, OH, Gedruckt bei Walker u. Espich. 1839." (8 vol. 314 pages).
(*German Code of Law: Containing, next to the Declaration of Independence, the Constitution and General Laws of the Ohio States. – Collected and Translated by Georg Walker*). HAR

9. According to Walter J. Daly's article "The Black Cholera Comes to the Central Valley of America In the 19th Century - 1832, 1849, and Later" in *Transactions of the American Clinical and Climatological Association* 119 (2008): 143-152, there were four cholera epidemics in North America in the early 19th century: 1832, 1849, 1866, and the late 1870s. He argues that in 1849 (the year Walker died) the population was larger and cholera was spread faster. He lists the death toll of cholera in 1849 in Cincinnati as 5,969, which was much larger than Detroit or St. Louis, for example. EVD

10. It seems like George Walker is unsuccessful in many of his paper publications: *Der Protestant*, *Der Deutsch-Amerikaner*, and now *Die Volksbühne* in Louisville barely survived one year. When he concentrated on a "religio-political paper" in Cincinnati, *Der Hochwächter*, he sold more subscriptions and remained the publisher of this paper until his death in 1849 (Ford, 137). EVD

11. For additional information about the beginning of Miamisburg, formerly known as Hole's Station, see Henry Howe, *Historical Collections of* Ohio (Cincinnati: Krehbiel, 1908), II: 299. Howe states that the first settlers were Dutch, probably because many settlers came from Berks County, PA. Although he correctly writes in the next few sentences that German was the prevalent language: "The German is yet much spoken, and two of the churches worship in that language." EVD

12. Reverend John Caspar Dill was the first pastor who started the Evangelical Lutheran community in Miamisburg in 1821 until his death on August 24, 1824, when he was succeeded by Rev. Christopher Henry Daniel Heinke (Everts, 27). Also see, J.P. Hentz, *History of the Evangelical Lutheran Congregation in Germantown, Ohio and Biographies of its Pastors and Founders* (Dayton: Christian Pub. House, 1882), 29-38, for more information about Rev. John Caspar Dill, a German born in Wertheim, Grand Duchy of Baden, on February 2, 1758. He studied at the renowned University of Giessen, yet he decided to go to America. He arrived on September 4, 1792 in Baltimore, MD, went to Philadelphia and later moved to Ohio persuaded by Reverent William Dechant. Dill arrived in Germantown, OH, in 1815. He preached in up to ten towns, but mostly in Germantown and Miamisburg. EVD

13. Reverend Heinke became a respected minister who applied his knowledge as itinerant theologian. Everts describes him: "Notwithstanding this brother was a German by birth, and had arrived at the years of maturity before he studied the English language, be yet acquired sufficient to enable him to write it correctly and speak it fluently. He served the Lutheran congregation of Miamisburg from 1826 to the end of his laborious life, July 10, 1859, a term of thirty-three years." 27. EVD

14. According to Conover, *Centennial Portrait And Biographical Record Of The City Of Dayton And Of Montgomery County, Ohio* (Logansport: Bowen, 1897), 928, Reverend Christopher Albrecht was born in Baden, Germany, on March 10, 1824, who emigrated with his parents to Baltimore, MD, in 1833. They later came to Ohio, where he studied Theology at the Capital University in Columbus, Ohio. Between August 1, 1860 and April 1, 1883, he served in Miamisburg. EVD

15. According to Drury (I:327), the first German Lutheran church in Dayton, OH, was the *St. John's German Evangelical Church*. It was established on July 18, 1840. He also points out that the German immigrant settlers of the area organized the church. Drury (319) observes that Dayton only had about four thousand citizens, but two Lutheran churches were established almost at the same time: *Zion Church*, later called *First Lutheran Church* and the *St. John's German Evangelical Church*. Prior to that, in 1834, the few German families worshipped with Rev. David Winters of the *First Reformed Church*, who could preach in German and English, in a small church on Ludlow Street (327). The Germans prayed later in the courthouse, between Third and Main Street, from 1836 to 1840, when the *St. John's German Evangelical Church* was created (319). Although the German church was faced with two disasters, a tornado damaged the church in 1871, and in 1899 a fire burnt down the church, the congregation was not discouraged, but made plans to erect a brick church. Finally, it is interesting to note that Dayton's *Deaconess Hospital*, later called *Miami Valley Hospital*, was founded by Pastor Carl Mueller (*Karl Müller*) of the *St. John's German Evangelical Church* in 1890 (Drury, p. 327) with the Protestant Deaconess Society of Dayton (266). Two assistants from Bielefeld, Germany, Sister Anna Von

Ditfurth and Louise Goerke helped Pastor Mueller (269). The German Protestant community offered important services to Dayton. EVD

16. Walker registered his license in Montgomery County on February 11, 1839. HAR

17. The church, in which Pastor Rosenmüller preached, stood where today's post office is. HAR

18. M. Etter was the only one who called himself *"Tunker"* (Dunkard), the others called themselves *"Deutsche Baptisten"* (German Baptists). HAR

19. For more information about the United Brethren and the beginning of their church, see Paul R. Fetters, *Trials and Triumphs: A History of the Church of the United Brethren in Christ.* (Huntington: Church of the United Brethren in Christ, Dept. of Church Services, 1984). Philip William Otterbein (June 3, 1726- November 17, 1813), a native of Dillenberg, Germany who came initially to Pennsylvania to do missionary work, founded the United Brethren in Christ (53-85). Otterbein was praised for establishing a spiritual bridge "connecting the German colonists with their spiritual heritage in Europe." 17. Fetters also points out that since the "spiritual life of the German immigrants was disorganized and weak," the Church of the United Brethren in Christ contributed to "the organization of religious life among the colonists and upon new denominations born on American soil." 27. Augustus W. Drury wrote a biography about Philip Otterbein: *The Life of the Rev. Philip William Otterbein* (Dayton: United Brethren Pub. House, 1884). EVD

20. Martin Böhm was a nephew of the before-mentioned Heinrich Böhm. He already settled in 1812 in Montgomery County, Ohio. Bishop Otterbein sent him there as a preacher. HAR

21. David Baumann called himself a preacher of the *"German Brother"* congregation. HAR

22. According to Drury (I:357- 364), the Catholic Church in Dayton was established late. His reasoning is plausible: since there were no Catholic Germans among the first settlers to Dayton and the first German Catholic families did not arrive in Dayton until 1832, the numbers needed to establish a Catholic Church was too small. Soon, between 1832 and 1833, many Irish and German Catholics arrived, and Fathers Thienpont, Junker, and Stephen Theodore Badin visited Dayton from Cincinnati. Around 1829 there were already eighty-seven German Catholic families in Cincinnati (Roger Fortin, *Faith and Action: A History of the Catholic Archdiocese of Cincinnati, 1821-1996* (Columbus: Ohio State University Press, 2002), 40.
Emanuel Church was established where German was the language of worship with Father Thienpont as the first Catholic pastor in 1836. Drury says that of 89% of the people arriving in Dayton were American-born, 11% were foreign-born, two-thirds of which were German and "the majority of the last named being Lutheran or Reformed. (357) EVD

23. Father Martin Kundig was a travelling Catholic missionary who visited many early Catholic settlers to preach to them. Itinerant missionaries in Ohio usually travelled many miles on horseback subjected to the extreme elements of heat and cold. In order to receive an appreciation what these early missionaries did, John Lamot in his *History of The Archdiocese of Cincinnati, 1821-1921.* (New York: F. Pustet Co., 1921), 168, records the few possession that were given to Father Kundig when going on a mission: eight plates, 4 forks and knives, 4 tablespoons, 2 bowls,

2 saucers, 2 teaspoons, 4 sheets, 2 pillow cases, 3 towels, 1 small pot, 1 chalice, 2 chasubles, 1 albe, 2 matresses, 2 cots, 2 beds, 1 drawer, 4 chairs, 1 oil stock and two chairs. For more information about struggles and stories of this busy pioneer priest, Martin Kundig, see Peter Leo Johnson, *Stuffed Saddlebags: The Life of Martin Kundig, Priest, 1805-1879* (Milwaukee: Bruce Publishing Company, 1942). EVD

24. According to Drury (1:357), Reverend Stephen Theodore Badin (July 17, 1768 - April 21, 1853) was the first Catholic priest ordained in the United States. EVD

25. Drury (1:850) says that Reverend Henry Damian Junker of Dayton held mass at the home of Peter Hart and Mr. Swisler. Before the establishment of church buildings, it was common to celebrate mass at the homes of various Catholic members of the church. EVD

26. Ibid., 357. While Rattermann says that the *Emanuel Church* was dedicated in 1835, Drury writes that Bishop Purcell dedicated the church on November 26, 1837. It is rare that Rattermann makes an error. EVD

27. Ibid., 357. Father D. Juncker (*Heinrich Damian Junker*) was the successor of Father Thienpont in 1844. Reverend Junker left the congregation in 1857 when he became the Bishop of Alton, Illinois, where he stayed until his death on October 2, 1868. He is buried under his cathedral in Alton. EVD

28. Ibid., 357. Father Stephen Theodore Badin (and not Henry Juncker) was "the first priest ordained in the United States." According to John Shea, *The Hierarchy of the Catholic Church in the United States Embracing Sketches of all the Archbishops and Bishops* (New York: Office of Catholic Publications, 1886), Reverend Henry Damian Juncker "was ordained priest March 16, 1834, being the first one who received holy orders from the hands of Bishop Purcell." 184.

29. Roger Fortin, *Faith and Action: A History of the Catholic Archdiocese of Cincinnati, 1821-1996* (Columbus: Ohio State University Press, 2002), 420, points out that Father Henry Juncker also travelled to Springfield, Ohio, to serve the growing German Catholic population there. After the Emmanuel Church was formed, the second German Catholic church, St. Mary, was created in 1859, followed by the Holy Trinity Church. EVD

30. Frank Conover, *Centennial Portrait and Biographical Record of the City of Dayton* (Logansport:Bowen, 1897): Rev. John F. Hahne (*Johann F. Hahne*) was born on April 19, 1815 in Schleswig, Germany, studied theology in Freyburg, Switzerland, was ordained priest on December 23, 1848 in Osnabrück, Germany, emigrated to Cincinnati, Ohio, in 1851 and relocated to Dayton, Ohio, in 1857. *Emanuel's Catholic Church* on Franklin Street in Dayton, was built through the effort of Rev. John F. Hahne. Conover paints a picture of Hahne as coming from a poor family, but he reached his goal to become a minister with much dedication, hard work and ingenuity. EVD

31. John Martin Henni (*Johann Martin Henni*) was born in Misanenga, Switzerland on June 15, 1805. After having studied in St. Gallen, Lucerne, Rome, and Bardstown, KY, he came to the Diocese of Cincinnati, Ohio, when invited by Bishop Edward Fenwick. He ordained Reverend

Henni as a priest on February 2, 1829. To find out more about the fifty years Rev. Henni, who worked for the German immigrants as a Catholic priest in Ohio, as bishop and as first archbishop of Milwaukee, read Peter Leo Johnson, *Crosier on the Frontier: A Life of John Martin Henni, Archbishop of Milwaukee* (Madison: State Historical Society of Wisconsin, 1959). According to Johnson, Rev. Henni was particularly concerned about the struggling German immigrants: "His preoccupation with problems attendant upon immigration could have centered in any national group, but his work in Cincinnati placed him in the midst of the German immigrants still struggling for recognition in a strange land. As a priest he sensed the threat to their traditional faith." vii. Father Henni earned his title "Apostle of the Germans" while at the same time trying to foster a better understanding of the new United States as editor of the first German Catholic newspaper in America, *Der Wahrheitsfreund* (*The Friend of Truth*), viii. Heinrich Rattermann considered Father Henni "as the most prominent of the German-American leaders in a wide range of activities." 173. Also see Rattermann, *Gesammelte Ausgewählte Werke* (Cincinnati: H. A. Rattermann, 1906-1912). Rattermann, who divides the German immigration into two parts (1800 to 1817 and 1817 to 1832), explains that most German immigrants were craftsmen or farmers, however, some educated Germans such as teachers and preachers were among them, who helped all to retain their German customs and language. (XVI:223-224). Among others, Rattermann listed Dr. Johann Martin Henni and Father Martin Kundig. Finally, Dr. Henni was also Professor of German in St. Xavier's College for three years, starting in 1841 (*Records of the American Catholic Historical Society of Philadelphia* (Philadelphia: American Catholic Historical Society of Philadelphia, 1886), XX: 112. EVD

32. Conover in *Centennial Portrait* mentions that Christian Rohrer, born in Lancaster County, PA, one of the early settlers of Germantown, Ohio, bought a flourmill there and rebuilt a distillery on his property, where he made "the first Bourbon whiskey distilled in Montgomery County." 104. Later, his son, David Rohrer, took over the distillery in 1864 and created the famous "Mud Lick" whiskey, named after the river the distillery was on. For more information about the brewery history in the Dayton area, see Curt Dalton, *The Breweries of Dayton: An Illustrated History* (Dayton: Dalton, 1995). EVD

33. For more information about the Schultz Brewery, see Timothy J. Holian, *Over the Barrel: The Brewing History and Beer Culture of Cincinnati* (St. Joseph: Sudhaus Press, 2000), 1:21. Dalton in *The Breweries of Dayton* does not mention Philipp Scheick or the Schulz Brewery, but adds that "in 1852 lager beer was introduced to Dayton by John and Michael Schiml." i. EVD

34. Everts states erroneously that he was born in Pennsylvania. HAR
Rattermann did not provide the complete source for his statement above. It is L.H. Everts, L. H. Everts, *Combination Atlas Map of Montgomery County, Ohio: Compiled, Drawn and Published from Personal Examinations and Surveys* (Philadelphia: Hunter Press, 1875). Everts writes about Christian Rohrer: "This gentleman is the son of Christian and Ann Marie Rohrer, of Lancaster County, Pa. He was born on December 21, 1804, and lived in Pennsylvania till the year 1830, when he moved to Dayton, Ohio." 30. EVD

35. Julius Goebel, ed., *Deutsch-Amerikanische Geschichtsblätter: Jahrbuch der Deutsch-Amerikanischen Historischen Gesellschaft von Illinois* (Chicago: Gesellschaft, 1912), XII:300, writes that the first *Lagerbier* in the United States was brewed by Friedrich German

in 1828. Friedrich German, also known as *Bier-Fritz* was born in St. Johann, near Saarbrücken and died in 1849. Dalton in *The Breweries of Dayton*, notes that John and Michael Schiml opened the J. & M. Schiml Brewery in Dayton in 1852. He continues: "The first lager beer of Montgomery County was believed to have been made there on December 13, 1852." 65. Rattermann on the other hand informs us that the first *Lagerbier* in America was already brewed in Germantown in 1830 by the German pioneer, Friedrich Germann. Michael Schiml, a native of Reglasreuth, near Baireuth in Bavaria, Germany, was born on August 4, 1825. His older brother, John, came to America in 1845, but Michael arrived with his mother and sister in Montgomery County in 1848 (Dalton, 66). Both brewers, Germann and Schiml were Germans, but Rattermann dates the introduction of lager beer in America to 1830 and mentions Germantown, Ohio, as the place where that happened. Since other sources state a different time, Rattermann seems to indicate an earlier date, which should be further researched.

For more information about lager beer, see Don Heinrich Tolzmann, *Christian Moerlein: The Man and his Brewery* (Milford: Little Miami Publishing Company, 2012). He states that there are conflicting dates about who and when the first lager beer was brewed. Quoting Maureen Ogle, *Ambitious Brew: The Story of American Beer* (Orlando: Harcourt, 2006), 12, it seems that 1838 is the date. Timothy J. Holian in *Over The Barrel: The Brewing History and Beer Culture of Cincinnati* (St. Joseph: Sudhaus Press, 2000), 1:39, states that the first lager beer in America could have been brewed in 1834. In summary, Rattermann's dating of the brewing of lager beer to 1830 (Germantown, Ohio), pre-dates other references to it having been brewed in 1834 (Cincinnati) and 1838 (Alexandria, Virginia). EVD

Chapter 4: German Pioneers bring Musical Entertainment to Ohio

1. According to Frédéric Louis Ritter, *Music in America* (New York: Johnson Reprint Corp., 1970), it "seems even probable that *Trinity Church* [New York] possessed the first organ in America." 135. Nothing is mentioned about the first organ in Ohio. EVD

2. Several of Teltow's letters, regarding the building of this bridge, are contained in the manuscripts of James McBride, the author of *Pioneer History of Butler County, Ohio*, located in the *Historische und Philosophische Gesellschaft von Ohio* in Cincinnati. In one of them, dated Cincinnati September 15, 1818, Teltow speaks about his plans for the bridge in detail. – See McBride's *Private Letters*, Vol. II, Ms. HAR

3. He had his workshop at the west side of Sycamore, between Franklin and Webster Street. HAR

4. According to Drury (I:728), Captain Lewis Hormell (*Louis Hormel*) led his German brigade, the *Dayton National Guards*, located on Second Street, between Main and Jefferson. This German organization recruited people to enlist to fight in the Mexican War. Lewis Hormell, a native of Hesse-Darmstadt, Germany, and Captain in the Mexican War, was the commander of the First Ohio Volunteer Infantry where he worked for thirteen months, according to Newton Bateman, Paul Selby, eds., *Historical Encyclopedia of Illinois, Volume 2* (Chicago: Munsell, 1909), 668. EVD

5. Ferdinand Söhner's life ended tragically. Born in Mudau, Baden, Germany in 1821, he emigrated with his wife and children to America in 1849, at age 28. He worked in Dayton at a Catholic School for two years, then opened a photography shop in Middletown, Ohio, before working again as a teacher at a German School in Hamilton, Ohio, for twenty years. On December 28th, 1890, when travelling from Cincinnati to Hamilton by train, he slipped and died when run over by a train (*Daytoner Volks Zeitung: Gedenk-Blätter*, 1894-1904, Dayton, Ohio). EVD

6. The 1870 U.S. Census lists William Trebein (*Wilhelm Trebein*) as being born in Hesse Darmstadt. "United States Census, 1870," index and images, FamilySearch (http://tinyurl.com/nvf2k98: accessed 29 Dec 2013), Ohio > Montgomery > Mad River; citing NARA microfilm publication M593). EVD

7. This German society was called *The Dayton German Grenadiers* and John Werner was the captain. "There were one hundred enlisted men, among them thirty-five from Montgomery county. They were ordered to report at Camp Washington and on May 31, 1847, were escorted to the canal landing and after several speeches in German and English, were sent on their voyage amid the salute of the famous cannon heretofore described." (Drury, I:730). EVD

8. It looks like German pioneer musicians left an impression on early Dayton history. Charlotte Conover, *Dayton, Ohio: An Intimate History* (New York: Lewis Historical Pub. Co., 1932) states in her chapter XIX about "Music and Musicians in Dayton" that Louis Huesman (*Ludwig Huesmann*) followed John Van Cleve, the organist and choir director of Christ Church." 249.

"Toward the 'forties we find Louis Huesman, pianist-organist and teacher of both, organizing choirs and giving concerts. In the 'sixties and 'seventies' two names stand out – Charles Rex, a short, blond German and Adolph Carpe, a tall blond German, who between them, divided the music pupils that the census of Dayton then afforded." 249. Conover in *Some Dayton Saints and Prophets* (Dayton: United Brethren Publishing House, 1907), 216, points out that Prof. Huesmann was a traditional music teacher who was particularly fond of Palestrina, Bach, and Beethoven. EVD

9. In the 1880 U.S. Census, William Haberstich (*Wilhelm Haberstich*) lists his native birthplace as Germany and his profession as being a cabinetmaker. <https://familysearch.org/pal:/MM9.1.1/M8S3-C4Q> EVD

10. According to the Conover, ed., *Centennial Portrait and Biographical Record of the City of Dayton*, Jacob Linxweiler, born in Rhenish Bavaria, belonged to the early Dayton settlers. He came to the United States in 1840 and after a few weeks in Canada arrived in Dayton, Ohio, where he was 'held in highest esteem as one of the honored patriarchs of the city." 263.
Linxweiler was everything from a baker, a grocer, a farmer, and he also became a leader in the "horticultural society" in Dayton. For more information about Jacob L. Linxweiler, Jr., see *Don Heinrich Tolzmann, ed., Dayton's German Heritage: Karl Karstaedt's Golden Jubilee History of the German Pioneer Society of Dayton, Ohio* (Bowie: Heritage Books, Inc., 2001), 39. EVD

11. Charlotte Conover, *Dayton, Ohio: An Intimate History*: "Dayton has many German citizens who brought their music from the fatherland with them, as Germans always do. In a new environment they hardly wait to unpack their belongings before they begin to sing. The Lord made them that way and they can't help it. The outstanding *Liederkranz* in Dayton is the *Harmonia Society* under the leadership of Mr. Carl A. Schlaefflin. Formed by a consolidation of the *Sängerbund* and the *Frohsinn* societies, it entertained the *National Saengerbund* most successfully, as recorded in a Detroit paper dated 1853. It would be interesting to know where four hundred singers could assemble in the Dayton of that day and include an audience. Certainly Huston Hall would not have accommodated them. Our *Harmonia* is a member of the *Nord Amerikanerische Sängerbund*, which once in three years gathers in a certain city and gives forth its five-thousand-voices chorus. For precision, shading, tone volume, and beauty of rendition these German societies are preeminent." 255. Rattermann himself wrote a series of articles about the history of the first and therefore oldest German singing society of North America: Rattermann, "Die Geschichte des Ersten Deutschen Sängerbundes von Nord-Amerika," in *Der Deutsche Pionier: Erinnerungen aus dem Pionierleben der Deutschen in Amerika* (Cincinnati: Der Deutsche Pionier-Verein, 1869), XI. Rattermann starts by referring back to the oldest European music in America, the Gregorian chant, which was sung by the monks and priests who came with the Spanish conquistadors; the Puritans, arriving on the Mayflower at Plymouth Rock in 1620, brought the first Protestant church songs (24). Much later, in 1815, the *Haydn and Händel Society* was formed in Boston to sing during worship in churches. Then a German Jesuit missionary pioneer born in Austria, Villanders near Klausen, P. Antonius Sepp, introduced the first multiple-voiced form of singing in America (25). According to Rattermann, Father Sepp was the founder of the first German Singing and Music Society in America, since he created in Paraguay in 1692 a four-voice choir and an orchestra which included American Indians who sang Latin and German songs (25). The first German choral singing was established in America

by Conrad Beissel (1691-1768), the German-born religious founder of the Ephrata Community in Pennsylvania. Franz Löher in *Geschichte And Zustände der Deutschen in Amerika.* (Görringen: Wiegand, 1855), says about the German singers at Ephrata: "Es ist merkwürdig, wozu es die guten Deutschen nicht schon gebraucht haben." 122. Rattermann continues with his history by mentioning the Moravian community of the *Herrnhuter* who preserved the tradition of the cultivated German choir singing. American Indians in Pennsylvania, North Carolina, and Ohio, who were converted by the Moravians, sang these German songs during church services (25). Germans were also the leaders in secular music, exemplified by the foundation of the first German singing society in the summer of 1836 in Philadelphia, the *Männerchor* (male chorus) (26). Then in December of 1836 the formation of the Baltimore *Liederkranz* was followed by the creation of the *Deutsche Gesangverein* in Cincinnati, Ohio, in 1838 or 1839 under the musical direction of Wilhelm Schragg (26). According to Charles Theodore Greve, *Centennial History of Cincinnati and Representative Citizens* (Chicago: Biographical Pub. Co., 1904), I:922, it was not until 1846, however, that female voices were included in a choir. The first German singing society, which permitted female members to sing was the G*esang- und Bildungs-Verein Deutscher Arbeiter* established in 1846 under the musical leadership of Henry Damm (922). Greve summarizes the importance of the *German Singing Society of North America* in Cincinnati, Ohio: "To the Germans of Cincinnati must be given the credit of originating the festival idea that is now prevalent in so many different parts of the country. Away back in 1849 a small number of singing societies met together in Cincinnati for the purpose of effecting an organization similar to those already established in Bavaria and other parts of Germany, that would foster through its good fellowship the folk song of the fatherland." 922. Rattermann informs us that the first German mixed choir in America was established in1838 when the *Männerchor* of Philadelphia and the *Liederkranz* of Baltimore sang together and included the *Liederkranz Damenverein* of Baltimore (26). The first formal organization, which united singing societies of Cincinnati, Louisville, and Madison, Indiana, set up the first German *Sängerfest* (*Singing Festival*) in America in Cincinnati, Ohio, from June 1-3, 1849; during this festival, on June 2, 1849, the *German Sängerbund of North America* was established. (Greve, 923). This was the beginning of the great musical festival traditions in America. For additional information about the history of the first German singing society of North America, see Rattermann, "Die Geschichte des Ersten Deutschen Sängerbundes von Nord-Amerika," in *Der Deutsche Pionier: Erinnerungen aus dem Pionierleben der Deutschen in Amerika* (Cincinnati: Der Deutsche Pionier-Verein, 1869), XI:23-28, 50-61; 90-96; 273-278; 309-319; 438-444; 473-480. EVD

12. Drury, *History of the City of Dayton*, II:542-543) portrays Frederick W. Berk (*Friedrich William Berk*) as a successful business owner who was born in Germany on December 6, 1824 and after starting in Dayton as a cabinetmaker, soon turned his business into a funeral enterprise. As was expected of a businessman, he participated in social organizations as a member of the Schiller Lodge, the Harurgari, the *German Pioneer Society of Dayton*, and he also was a member of the *German Lutheran Church*. EVD

13. A description of this festival will be reported in the history of the "First German Singing Society of North America" in the *Pionier* at that time. HAR
The exact source of Rattermann's quote is: Rattermann, "Die Geschichte des Ersten Deutschen Sängerbundes von Nord-Amerika," in *Der Deutsche Pionier: Erinnerungen aus dem*

Pionierleben der Deutschen in Amerika (Cincinnati: Der Deutsche Pionier-Verein, 1869), XI:23-28, 50-61; 90-96; 273-278; 309-319; 438-444; 473-480. EVD.

14. According to Hover, *Memoirs of the Miami Valley* (II:107), Charles Rex (*Carl Rex*) belonged to the outstanding musicians of Dayton, who left his imprint on the city's music scene. EVD

15. Charles Rex, music teacher in Dayton, Ohio, was born in 1835 in Germany and died on November 4, 1875 in Dayton, OH, according to the Ohio Death Record ("Ohio, Deaths and Burials, 1854-1997," index, FamilySearch (https://familysearch.org/pal:/MM9.1.1/F6VL-QTG: accessed 15 Nov 2013), Charles Rex, 04 Nov 1875.) EVD

16. For more information about the *Dayton Turner Society*, see Dann Woellert, *Cincinnati Turner Societies: The Cradle of an American Movement* (Charleston: The History Press, 2012), 139-141. Woellert puts the date for the establishment of the *Dayton Ohio Turnverein* on March 18, 1853, when ten German-American citizens started the society (139). The time for such a club was ripe since breweries, industries, and a large German immigration group were present in Dayton. The building of the Cincinnati, Hamilton and Dayton Railroad provided a link between the Turner communities of those cities in the 1850s. Also, see Don Tolzmann, *German Cincinnati* (Charleston: Arcadia, 2005). Tolzmann points out that the *Cincinnati Central Turners*, founded in 1848 by Friedrich Hecker, a German immigrant leaving Germany because of the failed 1848 Revolution, "was not only the oldest, but also the largest and most influential German American society." 58. He mentions that a memorial in honor of the founder of the Turner Movement in Germany, Friedrich Ludwig Jahn (1778-1852), can be visited in Inwood Park in Cincinnati, Ohio (15). Besides in Cincinnati, OH, there is a Jahn statue in Forst Park, St. Louis, MO, other Jahn memorials are located in Groß-Gerau, Germany (a *Gedenkstein* (memorial stone) by Darmstadt), and in Leopoldsberg by Vienna, Austria (a *Gedenktafel* (plaque). EVD

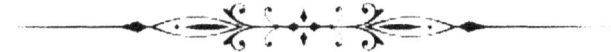

Chapter 5: German Social Clubs, Singing Societies, and Early Newspapers

1. Drury, *History of the City of Dayton* (1:500) argues that the large number of Germans in the Dayton area of the time provides on explanation of the many German societies, as well as their intention to keep their language and customs alive: "The Germans do not easily give up their use of their mother tongue, their love of the fatherland or their fellowship as Germans. There is maintained in Dayton an alliance of German-American Societies (*Deutsch-Amerikanischer Central-Verein.*) The German societies are of different classes - social and educational, musical, for physical culture, fraternal and beneficial and denominational. In all there are no fewer than forty German societies of different kinds." He also mentions that in 1850 roughly one-tenth of the Dayton inhabitants were German. EVD

2. For more information about the *Odd Fellow Society*, other U.S. fraternal societies, see Thelda Skocpol, *Civic Engagement in American* (Washington: Brookings Institution Press, 1999).

3. Philip Walz (*Philipp Walz*) appears in the Ohio Deaths Record as being born in Germany in 1818 and he died in Dayton on May 11, 1889. His profession is listed as stone maker. "Ohio, Deaths and Burials, 1854-1997," index, *FamilySearch* (https://familysearch.org/pal:/MM9.1.1/F6V2-S36 : accessed 02 Jan 2014), Philip Walz, 11 May 1889. The U.S. census record for 1870 discloses that Philip Walz was born in Baden, Germany and his wife in Oldenburg, Germany. "United States Census, 1870," index and images, FamilySearch (https://familysearch.org/pal:/MM9.3.1/TH-266-12068-80697-90?cc=1438024&wc=M94C-D2M:1403691311 : accessed 15 Nov 2013), Ohio > Montgomery > Dayton, ward 05; citing NARA microfilm publication M593. EVD

4. The *Order of Harugari*, developed with beneficial and cultural intentions and started by the German Americans in New York in the 1840s, intended to promote German culture and assist German Americans from anti-German nativist assaults (Skocpol, 42). Conover, ed., of *Centennial Portrait* lists Dr. Schoenfeld as having been a member of the Order of Harugari for forty years and he has been an *ober grosse barde*, chief officer of the United States." 1046. EVD

5. Skocpol describes the *Improved Order of Red Men*, founded in 1834, as being "racially and ethically exclusive...consisted of white Christians who dressed up like Native Americans and dated their order from 1492, when Columbus arrived in America." 41. According to Skocpol, the German Americans "launched their own *'Independent' Order of Red Men* in 1850, a fraternal that met in federated *'stamms'* rather than *tribes*." 42. EVD

6. Drury (1:495) writes: "*The Knights of Pythias* hold a large and influential place in the city of Dayton, especially so for an organization of recent establishment, the order of *Knights of Pythias* having been formed at Washington, D.C., February 19, 1864." The Humboldt Lodge No. 58" was established in Dayton on September 23, 1873. EVD

7. Harvey Crew, *History of Dayton, Ohio: With Portraits and Biographical Sketches of Some of its Pioneer and Prominent Citizens* (Dayton: United Brethren Pub. House, 1889), 678-679, writes that the *Humboldt Lodge No. 58, Knights of Pythias*, was established by Peter Reinhardt, Peter Weidner, and Robert George on August 26, 1873. EVD

8. Ibid., 681: The *Ancient Order of United Workmen, Miami Lodge No. 16*, was established on February 9, 1874 with twenty-three members. EVD

9. Ibid: *The Teutonia Lodge No. 21* was established on April 15, 1874 with thirty-two members. EVD

10. Beers, *The History of Montgomery County, Ohio* (III:190-191), mentions that John Bettelon, born January 13, 1829 in Germany, was a saloon and restaurant owner in Dayton, where he arrived with his father from Germany. He was a both a baker and confectioner apprentice. Before he opened a saloon and restaurant in 1852, he worked as a pastry chef on the river. In 1858 he started yet another enterprise, his "wholesale liquor business." From 1871 to 1876 he changed to the banking business and was employed by the People's and Savings Bank. At that time he returned to the wholesale liquor business and later ran a successful saloon and restaurant. Bettelon married Mary Ann Mouter from Dayton and raised seven children with her. EVD

11. Through a misprint on page 217 of this volume of the *Pionier*, they say "first German newspaper" instead of "first German religious newspaper." HAR

12. According to Becker, *The Village: A History of Germantown, Ohio, 1804-1976*. (Germantown: Historical Society of Germantown, 1981),10, Edward Shaeffer (*Eduard Schäffer*) began publishing the first newspaper, *Die National-Zeitung der Deutschen* in 1826. Soon after he began publication of the Germantown *Gazette* in English. EVD

13. The original newspaper entry was in German. The passage was translated by EVD.

14. The first German newspaper, which was printed in the state of Ohio and in the entire northwest of the time, was *Der Westliche Adler von Lancaster*, published in Lancaster, Ohio. The first issue already appeared in the year 1807. HAR
According to Rattermann, *Abhandlungen* (225), Schäffer published in Canton, Ohio, in 1821, yet another German paper, *Der Deutsche Beobachter*. EVD

15. According to the Library of Congress, *Chronicling America*, the *Deutsches Journal* was published in Dayton, Ohio, from 1849-1852 by John Bittmann. <http://chroniclingamerica.loc.gov/lccn/sn85026001/> EVD
Drury in *History of the City of Dayton* (Vol 1, p. 409) says that the first German paper that was published in Dayton, Ohio, was the *German Gazette* or *Deutsche Zeitung* on September 19, 1835. A second source confirms that fact: <http://chroniclingamerica.loc.gov/lccn/sn90068180/> EVD

16. According to Christian B. Keller and Thomas Adam, Ed., *Germany and the Americas: Culture, Politics, and History* (Santa Barbara: ABC-CLIO, Inc., 2005), the "Forty-Eighters were political refugees from the failed democratic revolutions of 1848-1849 in Germany. Realizing that true popular reform would never take root after the crushing of those revolutions and aware of the danger posed to their persons and careers by remaining in German-speaking Europe," many settled around the 1850s in the United States, attracted by personal freedom, democracy, and equality among people. (369). Although their numbers were only a few thousand, the Forty-

Eighters, who came to the Midwest, influenced the social and political scene of the German Americans in this area. Keller mentions that the formation of the Republican Party "remained their most enduring legacy" (369) because the Republican notions of "economic freedom, empowerment of the average citizen, resistance to aristocratic pretensions (in Republican parlance, the 'slaveocracy' of the South), and a hatred of African slavery " appealed to the Forty-Eighters. (370). Since most of the Forty-Eighters were educated at German universities, they were attracted to the German American press and the intellectual German societies, but not all German immigrants invited them with open arms, since the Forty-Eighters' beliefs "conflicted with the more conservative - and Americanized - values of earlier German immigrants." 370. Forty-Eighters insisted that all German immigrants should assimilate to American society by becoming more Americanized. These educated and revolutionary Germans were not the typical German immigrant. Forty-Eighters were anti-slavery and signed up in the Civil War to fight on the side of the Union Army, and continued after the war as leaders in the German American communities (371). Besides having leading positions in politics, the German Forty-Eighters were also successful in education, business, and the arts. Keller mentions the introduction of the *kindergarten* into American society, the establishment of private institutes of learning, the support of both German- and English-language schools (371). Forty-Eighters also made a mark in business by "establishing the most successful (and most long-lived breweries, piano factories, and German language newspapers; and publishing hundreds of volumes of books on subjects as diverse as history, medicine, physics, and German literature." 371. For additional information on the Forty-Eighters, see Charlotte Brancaforte, ed., *The German Forty-Eighters in the United States* (New York: Peter Lang, 1989). Also see: Don Heinrich Tolzmann , ed., *The German-American Forty-Eighters, 1848-1998* (Indianapolis: Max Kade German-American Center, Indiana University-Purdue University at Indianapolis: Indiana German Heritage Society, 1998). EVD

17. The dates of publication of the German *Daytoner Volkszeitung* are listed from 1866-1914. <http://chroniclingamerica.loc.gov/lccn/sn85034432/>. A second source, Drury (Vol I, p. 409), mentions that George Neder began the *Dayton Volkszeitung* on April 26, 1866. The *Dayton Anzeiger* was first published on September 1, 1876 by the owners Otto Moosbrugger and Charles Schenk (p. 410). EVD

18. *Der Fröhliche Botschafter* was published from 1851 to 1930 in Circleville, Ohio, the location of the United Brethren Publishing House. <http://chroniclingamerica.loc.gov/lccn/sn89077206/>. EVD

19. *Der Jugend-Pilger*, published by the United Brethren in Christ from 1870-1914, was a German-language youth periodical with religious lessons. <http://chroniclingamerica.loc.gov/lccn/sn92063756/>.
Daniel Berger in *History of the United Brethren in Christ* (New York: Christian Literature Co., 1894) writes: "*Der Jugend Pilger* (*The Youth's Pilgrim*), established in 1870. In size and general character it is like the Children's Friend. For four years it was issued as a monthly. Since then it has been a semimonthly. The publication of a Sunday-school quarterly, called *Sonntagschul-Lectionen* started in 1890. It contains twenty-four pages, with cover. These periodicals have always been under the same editorial care as *Der Fröhliche Botschafter*. All of these papers are edited with much ability, and all deserve much larger circulation than is possible with the

limited German membership of the Church. Relatively the German portion of the Church gives a far better support to its publications than the English membership does, and for this the Germans are worthy of all praise." 415. EVD

20. For additional information about the German-language press in America, see Stephen L. Vaughn, ed., *Encyclopedia of American Journalism* (New York: Routledge, 2008), 196-198. EVD

21. Lorenz Butz, senior, was born in 1811 in Oberschopfheim, Lahr, Baden, Germany and came to Dayton in 1840 after he stayed in Auglaize County, according to Curt Dalton, *The Breweries of Dayton* (Dayton: Dalton, 1995), 21. Butz started many enterprises, from a candle manufacturing plant to a grocery and feed store, to becoming a partner in the City Brewery with Henry Ferneding. Butz died on September 24, 1900. EVD

22. Ibid., 55-58: Adam Schantz, born in Mittel-Kinzig, Hessen, Darmstadt, Germany on September 7, 1839, was a well-known German citizen in Dayton. All five Schantz brothers emigrated to America from Germany to escape military service. Although he suffered many set backs in America, opened a small meat shop, built a meat packing plant, started with his brother, George Schatz the brewery *Riverside* in 1882, and was actively involved in Dayton's civic life. He died in his winter residence in Florida from pneumonia on April 20, 1903. According to Dalton, Adam Schantz had the "dubious distinction of being the largest individual tax-payer in both Montgomery County, Ohio and Volusia County, Florida." 56. At the time of his death, he was worth a million and a half dollars. EVD

23. Beers, ed., *History of Montgomery County* (518-519), states that the Montgomery County Infirmary was established in 1826 when seven inmates were admitted. Later a building for the insane was built as well. The buildings were heated; physicians cared for the patients and provided medicines to the poor. However, although Beers mentions (519) that the infirmary staff provides excellent care of the "inmates," an article, written to the editor of the paper, appearing a few years later in the *Dayton Journal* on January 21, 1889 paints a different picture: <http://www.rootsweb.ancestry.com/~ohmontgs/infirmary/1889_news.html>. EVD

24. According to Drury (II:592), Dr. Dagobert Anthony Scheibenzuber, born in Austria on December 5, 1868, came with his family in 1870 to the United States. His father studied medicine at the University of Vienna and many years later, his son would return to Vienna to study medicine as well. Upon his return, Dr. Scheibenzuber practiced in Dayton. He also was physician of the *St. Joseph's Orphans Home* in Dayton. He died at age forty-nine on August 11, 1891. EVD

25. According to Drury (I:550), in 1868 John Schoen (*Johann Schön*) was the Vice-President of the *Dayton Building Association No. 1*, which was founded on March 23, 1867. The members of this first business enterprise of this sort met in the basement of the *German Reformed Church* in Dayton. EVD

26. Ibid., 462: The Catholic school was associated with the *Emanuel Church* and was established in 1832. A brick two-floor brick school building with six schoolrooms was built in 1865. EVD

27. Ibid., 359: Reverend Francis Joseph Goetz, the first pastor of the *Trinity Catholic Church*, built the *Trinity School* in 1860. Hover, ed., *Memoirs of the Miami Valley* (II:157) states that Reverend Joseph F. Goetz created the *Holy Trinity Parochial School* in 1862. EVD

28. Ibid., p. 462: The Sisters of Notre Dame used to teach both, the girls and boys, until 1875, at which time the Brothers educated the boys. EVD

29. Ibid., 463-464: The Catholic *St. Mary's Institute* was designed as a "boarding and day college for young men and boys, under the direction of the Society of St. Mary." Students were admitted from different states and from abroad into four courses of study, "preparatory, high school, business and collegiate." For more information about the remarkable history of the school, see Drury (1:464). EVD

30. Ibid., 261: *St. Elizabeth Hospital*, Dayton's first real hospital, was established by the Sisters of the Poor of St. Francis on August 15, 1878 and had twelve beds. The enlarged *St. Elizabeth Hospital*, with two hundred beds, goes back to 1882. A third enlargement was added in 1903. For more information about the opening ceremony of the St. Elizabeth Hospital, see an article by Howard Burba, "The Opening of the St. Elizabeth Hospital," which appeared in the Dayton Daily News on April 1, 1934, fifty-six years after the opening. The Austrian Infirmary Board Director, Dr. Scheibenzuber, and the German Infirmary Board Director, Dr. Schön, were also present at the ceremony. EVD

31. Frank Conover, ed., *Centennial Portrait*, 616-617, points out that Rev. John Kaufmann (*Johann Kaufmann*), pastor of the *Emanuel Evangelical Church*, was a native of Fluorn, Oberamt Oberndorf, Würtemberg, Germany, where he was born on August 13, 1834. After having been educated in Germany, he came to America in 1854. The *Emanuel Evangelical Church* was established in 1840 with Rev. A.B. Schaefer as its first minister.

32. Drury (1:364-365) speaks of "three Jewish congregations in Dayton of which one is the *Reformed* and the other two the so-called orthodox congregations." German immigrants who came to America in the late 1840s and 1850s formed the *Reformed Jewish Congregation*. In 1854 the congregation was incorporated and known as *Kehillath Kodesh B'nain Yeshurun*. After meeting in the Dayton Bank building to worship, they bought the Baptist church building in 1863, and in 1892 they built a new temple on Jefferson Street. Rev. E. Fisher (*Fischer*) was their first rabbi in 1875. According to Drury, the two orthodox congregations "are composed of the families that emigrated from Russia and Poland during the religious persecutions in those countries in the early eighties of the Nineteenth Century and since that time." *The House of Jacob Congregation* was established in 1886, but their first synagogue was not built until 1893. Rabbi Finkelstein is listed as their pastor. Rattermann does not mention the second orthodox Jewish congregation, *The House of Abraham*, which was established in 1902 with Rabbi Burick. EVD

33. R.E. Lowry, *History of Preble County, Ohio: Her People, Industries and Institutions* (Indianapolis: B.F. Bowen, 1915), 455, describes Frederick B. Pansing, born on October 25, 1839 in Hannover, Germany, as a farmer and land owner from Montgomery County, Ohio. He then became the county infirmary director, township trustee in Clay Township, and bank director

in Verona, Ohio. According to his gravestone in Verona Cemetery, Ohio, he died on September 27, 1926. EVD

34. If Rattermann is referring to Dr. Henry Schönfeld, physician in Miamisburg, see Drury (II: 632-634). Dr. Schönfeld was born in Hanau Hessen, Kassel, Germany in 1829. His father left Germany because of his political views. Dr. Henry Schönfeld started his medical practice in Miamisburg in 1853, but he also served areas in Kentucky, Michigan, Indiana, Minnesota, Wisconsin, Florida, Kansas, and Kanda. Dr. Schönfeld, an active community leader, was also a member of the *Independent Order of Odd Fellows*, *Knights of Pythias*, *German Order of Harugari*, and belonged to the *German Reform Church*. EVD

35. For more biographical information about Frederick Gottlieb Euchenhofer (*Friedrich Euchenhöfer*) and his son, see Drury (Vol. II, pp. 432-436). Frank Conover, ed., *Centennial Portrait* (p. 339) says that Frederick H. Euchenhofer was born in Switzerland about 1812. This is an error, since the death records indicate that he was born in Germany. Conover also adds that Euchenhofer was director of the *Teutonia Insurance Company of Dayton*. Euchenhofer also belonged to the *Odd Fellows* and the *Harugari*. For additional information about Euchenhofer's brewery business, see Curt Dalton, *The Breweries of Dayton* (Dayton: C. Dalton, 1995), 68-69. EVD

36. Drury reports that Frederick Euchenhofer took over the *Columbus House*, "one of the oldest hotels in the city, where the utmost cordiality was shown to citizens and strangers, and he continued in this business until 1864." (II:435). EVD

37. Ibid.,435: Euchenhofer also ran the *Third Street Brewery* from 1858 to 1867 as an owner of the business. After he sold the brewery, he bought the Tate flourmill and ran it until he sold it in 1873, when he returned to the brewery business. EVD

38. Ibid., 438: Catherine Discher, Euchenhofer's second wife, bore him ten children; he also had one child, Albert, who was born in Miamisburg in 1844, with his first wife. Frederick Euchenhofer died February 3, 1891, at age 80, only four months after going into retirement. EVD

39. Ibid., 819: Henry Ferneding (*Heinrich Ferneding*, 1812-1905) belonged to the early pioneers in Montgomery county. He was also known for the H. Ferneding & Sons flour and milling business. For additional biographical information, see Dalton, *The Breweries of Dayton*, 18-21. Dalton mentions that Henry Ferneding, born on November 10, 1812 in Matinus, Dinklage, Grand Duchy of Oldenburg, Germany, came to Baltimore on June 4, 1833, at the age of 20. Ferneding then actually walked from Baltimore to Pittsburgh. He then took a boat to Cincinnati, where he found employment as a driver of a milk wagon. Once he arrived in Dayton, he carried the water to the workers who were digging the Miami and Erie Canal. After many setbacks due to illness and injuries, he, his brother, John Casper Ferneding, and Frank Otten bought a malt house in 1845 (18). According to Dalton, Henry Ferneding built in 1859 a two-story brick building which housed his new brewery located between Brown and Warren Street, called the City Brewery (20). In 1861 Ferneding started a flour manufacturing business under the name of Ferneding,

Mause and Co. He retired in 1898, at the age of eighty-six. He died on November 16, 1905, at the age of ninety-three. EVD

A relationship betweem Henry Ferneding and the German pioneer Catholic priest Joseph Ferneding (1802-1872) of Cincinnati could not be established, but is likely, since both were born in Oldenburg, Germany and took a similar route to America. For biographical information about Rev. Joseph Ferneding, see *Der Deutsche Pionier*, 1872, (III:353-362). Rev. Jospeh Ferneding was born on February 18, 1802 in Ihorst, Oldenburg, Germany, studied theology in Germany, and came in 1832 to America, as one of the first German pioneers from that area in Germany (354). Joseph Ferneding took the same route as Henry Ferneding: from Bremen to Baltimore to Cincinnati. Father Ferneding was a missionary priest for German and Irish Catholic immigrants in the wilderness in Kentucky and Southern Indiana. In Cincinnati he preached to large numbers of immigrants, built churches and schools and also worked in the *St. Aloysius Orphanage*. After many years of service, Father Ferneding died on February 1, 1872. Regarding the Cincinnati Germans, see Don Heinrich Tolzmann, *Cincinnati's German Heritage* (Bowie: Heritage Books, Inc., 1994). EVD

40. John Armstrong reports in *St. Joseph's Orphan Society: Children's Treatment Center Records, 1849-2004* (Dayton: *Wright State University Library Catalog, 2007-2008*), 4, that the *St. Joseph Aid Society* was initiated in 1840 by the Catholic citizens of Dayton for the goal to assist poor and forgotten families. In 1849 a cholera outbreak killed many parents and the organization renamed itself to *St. Joseph Orphan Society* on August 5, 1849 to represent their new scope of providing an education to orphaned children. The organization was incorporated in 1857 under the name *German Roman Catholic St. Joseph Orphan Society*. "The very early minutes, 1849 to 1890, are in old German script." 7. EVD

41. In *Portrait and Biographical Album of Fulton County* (Chicago: Biographical Publishing, 1890), 425, one can read that Joseph Zwisler, born in Bavaria, Germany, on March 1, 1834, was also educated there before he came to Dayton where his uncle lived and ran a hotel. Zwisler also worked as a carpenter in Miamisburg. The book adds that Zwisler "comes from a nation that has contributed most generously to the population of the United States, and among the many nationalities found in this country, none are more steady, enterprising and respected citizens than are the Germans." 426. EVD

42. It seems that Francis Ohmer (*Franz Ohmer*) wanted to be regarded as French. In the U.S. Census of 1850, he listed his nationality as French and his profession as "hotel keeper."
< https://familysearch.org/pal:/MM9.1.1/MX37-X9H>. Edgar, *Pioneer Life in Dayton and Vicinity*, (1840, p. 229), confirms that Francis Ohmer was born in Lorain in 1796, married Margaret Floquet in 1882, came to New York in 1832 and to Dayton in 1837. Edgar also mentions that he worked as a tailor as well. There is a ten-page diary, written by Michael Ohmer, Francis Ohmer's son, entitled *A Boy's Impression of Dayton 64 Years Ago (1901)*, where Michael Ohmer provides a description of Dayton around 1840. EVD

43. Giradey wrote a German cookbook in 1842, entitled *Höchst Nützliches Handbuch über Kochkunst*, in Dayton, which was later translated into English. A French version, which he promised, was never published. George Girardey, *Manual of Domestic Economy, or, House-Keeper's Guide: Comprising a Very Large Collection of Original Receipts, Derived from the Practical Experience of the Author (*Dayton, OH: John Wilson, 1841). EVD

44. A plaque in the Calvary Cemetery, Dayton, Ohio, where Nicholas Ohmer (1823-1903), designer of that cemetery, lies buried, states that Ohmer was on the board of trustees and had a talent for horticulture. He was the founder of the *Montgomery County Horticultural Society* in 1867. His frequent trips back to Europe influenced his "Victorian garden style" cemetery. Nicholas Ohmer's house, located on 1350 Creighton Street, Dayton, Ohio, is listed as a National Historical Place (October 16, 1974). There is also an Ohmer Park in Dayton, Ohio, celebrating that civic leader and successful citizen of Dayton.
<http://www.findagrave.com/cgibin/fg.cgi?page=pv&GRid=102173400&PIpi=92972396>
For more information on Nicholas Ohmer and his father, Francis Ohmer, Sr., see Beers, ed., *History of Montgomery County* (III:441-442). Regarding the *Montgomery County Horticultural Society*, see the special collections at Wright State: Elli Bambakidis, *Montgomery County Horticultural Society: A Special Collection Of Historical Materials At The Dayton & Montgomery County Public Library* (Dayton: Dayton and Montgomery County Public Library, 1996). EVD

45. According to Conover, *Centennial Portrait and Biographical Record* (391, 339), the *Brownell & Kielmeier Manufacturing Company* was an engines plant. It was reorganized from the *Brownell Company* in 1867 when it changed its name to *Brownell, Roberts and Company*. In 1871 the company name changed again to *Brownell and Kielmeier Manufacturing Company* and was incorporated. The first president of the business was C.H. Kielmeier. EVD

46. The Germans are also connected to Dayton's financial history. The *Teutonia Insurance Company* was established in Dayton, Ohio, in 1865 and was viable until 1918. Harvey Crew, *History of Dayton, Ohio* (Dayton: United Brethren Publishing House, 1889), 659. According to the *Cyclopedia of Insurance in the United States*, (Part 2, 1890), 603, the *Teutonia Fire and Marine Insurance Company* in Dayton, Ohio, was established in 1865 with E. Pape as as the President and J. Linxweiler, Jr., Secretary. Conover, ed., *Centennial Portrait* (339) mentions Edward E. Euchenhofer as one of the founding members of the *Teutonia Insurance Company*. EVD

47. Drury (1:818) writes that the *German Pioneer Society of Dayton* was established on July 2, 1878: "By frequently meeting together immigrants who came from the same parts of Germany kept alive the memory of the earlier years. Later, pioneer associations were formed to keep alive and review the memories of early experiences in their new American home." 500-501. The *German Pioneer Society* was created to foster friendship, preserve memories, and collect historical pioneer information. The opening of the Dayton branch of the *Pioneer Society* was described in *Der Deutsche Pionier: Vereinsangelegenheiten*, (1878-1879), X:253-256. The German settlers should be brought together by the formation of this club, which has social and supportive functions. The article continues that it was the Germans who created the foundation for the social and political development of the country and through their hard work they will enjoy the benefits of civilization. Many left their overpopulated and tyrannical homeland in order to find a new home here for themselves and their families. In order for the founding members to have been selected for the foundation of the society, they needed to have been in America for twenty-five years. The first elected president was Andreas Weingärtner (in America since 1832), vice president was Cölestin Schwind (in America since 1850), and secretary was F. Hussong (in America since 1850). For more information about the history of the *German Pioneer Society of*

Dayton, see Don Heinrich Tolzmann, ed., *Dayton's German Heritage: Karl Karstaedt's Golden Jubilee History of the German Pioneer Society Of Dayton, Ohio* (Bowie: Heritage Books, Inc., 2001), 5,10, 59. EVD

48. Joseph Kleiber in his book *Amerika wie es ist als: Städte, Land, Verkehr, Eisenbahnen, Schiffahrt* (München: Finsterlin, 1877), 2, explains that because in 1626 the Dutch East India Company bought the island of Manhattan from the Indians, the first settlers in New Amsterdam were Dutch. In English they were called *Dötschmen* and later this mocking name was used for the Germans who generally did not like that word. For more information about *Dötschmen*, see, Joseph Salzbacher, *Meine Reise nach Nordamerika im Jahr 1842* (Wien: Wimmer, Schmidt & Leo, 1845), 366, who points out that the disrespectful term *Dötschmen* (actually the pronunciation of *Dutschman*) was wrongly applied to the German immigrants to show disdain and disrespect. EVD

Chapter 6: Jakob Köhne's Pioneer Memoirs of Germantown, Ohio

1. Beers, ed., *History of Montgomery County, Ohio* (III:46-47) lists Jacob Koehne (*Jakob Köhne*) as the first treasurer of the *Germantown Academy*, an institution of higher learning, which was established on October 11, 1841. Jacob Koehne is also mentioned as an officer of the *Germantown Cemetery Association*, which was founded on July 1, 1849. Drury (I:874) states that in 1842 Jacob Koehne was the Mayor of Germantown, Ohio, which was incorporated on March 16, 1833.
The *Ohio Historic Places Dictionary* (St. Clair Shores: Somerset Publishers, 1999), II:1046, describes the Koehne-Poast farm as an "excellent example of Greek Revival Ohio farmhouse, the Koehne-Poast Farm is a complex in a rural environment on forty-two acres just west of the village of Germantown." The Koehne-Poast Farm was added to the National Register of Historic Places on April 11, 1977. The farm owner, Jacob Koehne, purchased the land in 1839 and constructed the house in 1853. The *Dictionary* lists the incorrect date of the formation of the *Germantown Cemetery Association* as 1841, but the association was formed on July 1, 1849. Carl Becker, *The Village: The History of Germantown, Ohio* (11) counts Jacob Köhne to the early German immigrants who came to this town about 1825 and brought his love for music, considered a German tradition, with him. Jacob Köhne, who played guitar and piano, attracted many people to the area who wanted to be entertained by German folk songs. Heinrich Rattermann in *Die Deutschen Pioniere von Montgomery County, Ohio* (1880-1881), XII: 488, writes that Jacob Köhne was born on January 10, 1803, in Diepholz, Hannover, Germany, and arrived in America in the summer of 1824. Köhne died on August 10, 1880. Beers, ed., *History of Montgomery County* (III:51-53) ranks Jacob Köhne among the prominent men of German Township and one of the "citizens who have done much toward the growth and development of its best interests." 51. He lists him as one of the "men who did their share in building up the moral as well as the material interests of Germantown." 52-53. EVD

2. According to Jeff Bach, *Voices of the Turtledoves: The Sacred World of Ephrata* (University Park: Pennsylvania State University Press, 2003): "The *Ephrata community*, or *Ephrata Cloister*, was called by its own members *der [sic] Lager der Einsamen*, or Camp of Solitaries. German-speaking contemporaries often called them *Beisselianer* (Beisselites) or *Siebentäger* (Sabbatarians)." 4. For information about Conrad Beissel (1690-1768), who was born in April 1690 in Eberbach, Germany, and became a leader in the Ephrata community, see *History of the Church of the Brethren of the Eastern District of Pennsylvania* (Lancaster: The New Era Printing Company, 1915), 32-43. EVD

3. Beers, ed., *The History of Montgomery County* (III:28), counts Christopher Emerick (*Christoph Emmerich*) to the first settlers of Germantown, Ohio, who came in 1803 with Philip Gunckel, David Miller, and George Kern from Berks County, PA, to find an area for a new settlement in Ohio. According to *Montgomery County, Ohio, Deed Book 9-W 604*, Christopher and Catharine Emerick donated land on November 26, 1836, on which *Sunbury Hill Graveyard*, the oldest in Germantown, Ohio, was established. For more information about Christopher Emerick, see J. P. Hentz, *History of the Evangelical Lutheran Congregation in Germantown, Ohio, and Biographies of its Pastors and Founders* (Dayton: Christian Pub. House, 1882). EVD

4. According to P. C. Croll, *The Pennsylvania-German; A Popular Magazine of Biography, History, Genealogy, Folklore, Literature* (Lititz: Express Printing Company, 1910), XI: No. 1, 347, Jacob Tschudi and Joseph Ulrich founded in 1802, the town Uhrichsdorf, which is now called Uhrichsville, in Tuscarawas County, Ohio. However, John Brandt Mansfield, *The History of Tuscarawas County, Ohio, Containing A History of the County; Its Townships, Towns, Churches, Schools* (Chicago: Warner, Beers, 1884), 583, 895, lists Michael Uhrich as the founder of the city of Uhrichsville, Ohio. The town, which was originally called Waterford and was laid out by Michael Uhrich in 1833, was re-named six years later to Uhrichsville. EVD

5. According to Dennis Shuey, *History of the Shuey Family in America, From 1732 to 1876*, (Lancaster: Pub. for the members of the family, 1876), 164, Christian Shuey (*Christian Schuey*) was born in Germantown, Ohio, on September 22, 1822. He became a miller and a successful businessman in Germantown. EVD

6. The date of his arrival in Baltimore is documented by the following inscription, which was written into his diary by a fellow student on the day of his landing:

Contentment
        What children only desire from fate with fervor,
        What birth, grace, fortune bestows on us,
        What does not profit your wisdom,
        A heart, which owns you, learns easily to do without.
When reading these lines, remember, dear Köhne, your travel companion and friend
                                    Thomas Carstens, Ordinary Seaman

Written on September 15, 1824 in Chesapeake Bay on the ship Catharina from Bremen. HAR

7. Dianne Knipp, *Wapakoneta: Dianne Dodds Knipp with the Downtown Wapakoneta Partnership* (Charleston: Arcadia, 2010), provides more information about native Americans of this Shawnee village, city structures, industries, etc. of Wapakoneta, Ohio. Wapakoneta is known in history as the place where the Shawnee Indian Reserve was created after the *Treaty of Greenville*, which was signed August 3, 1795. The Shawnee Indians moved to Kansas in 1832 when they could no longer live with the immigrant European settlers. The first settlers to Wapakoneta were "German immigrants who purchased and cleared the land, established small businesses, and produced farm and industrial products, which were later distributed by rail throughout the country." 7. For more information about this resettlement and the history of the Shawnee, see Henry Harvey, *History of the Shawnee Indians, from the Year 1681 to 1854, Inclusive* (Cincinnati: Ephraim Morgan & Sons, 1855). Henry Harvey was a Quaker missionary. EVD

8. According to Patrick J. Jung, *The Black Hawk War of 1832* (Norman: University of Oklahoma Press, 2008), 3, about one thousand Indians with their Sauk chief, Black Hawk (1767-1838), protested the forced expulsion order by the federal government to leave western Illinois and relocate west of the Mississippi River in 1832. By the end of the short conflict, only half of the Indians remained alive. It was the last of the Indian wars in the *Old Northwest Territory*, north of the Ohio River. The short but violent conflict lasted from April to August 1832 between the United States and the Native Americans and the callous massacre "so affected neighbouring

Indian groups that by 1837 most had fled far west, leaving most of the Northwest Territory to white settlers." (*Britannica: Concise Encyclopedia*, 2006), 227. EVD

9. A Francis Arenz (*Franz Arenz*) is listed in the 1850 U.S. Census from Beardstown, Cass County, Illinois, as German native, born around 1800, with the profession of merchant. <https://familysearch.org/pal:/MM9.3.1/TH-267-12392-244768-46?cc=1401638&wc=MMY6-S8Y:1641528764>. William Henry Perrin, ed., *History of Cass County, Illinois* (Chicago: Baskin, 1882), 29-31, mentions that Francis Arenz was a business owner in Beardstown in 1834, although in 1833 there was not a single ad for a business in *The Beardstown Chronicle*, indicating that Francis Arenz was an early and successful settler. Francis Arenz, born in Blankenberg, Province of the Rhein, Prussia, on October 31, 1800, came to America in 1827 and stayed two years in Kentucky doing business as a merchant. When he arrived in 1829 in Galena, Illinois, he soon left for Beardstown where he saw the potential for a good future for himself and others. To attract more settlers, he began in 1834 *The Beardstown Chronicle and Illinois Bounty Advertiser* as the owner and editor. Besides starting the first newspaper, he also built the first schoolhouse with Thomas Beard in 1833, which also served as a church on Sundays. The *History of Cass County, Illinois* reports that Arenz provided supplies and arms for the army during the *Black Hawk War*, since Beardstown was a meeting place for the State troops. Francis Arenz also was instrumental in the construction of a canal from Beardstown to the Sangamon River. Francis Arenz was a leader and model citizen, but in 1835 he gave up being a merchant in Beardstown and lived on his farm, named *Recluze*, until 1839 (151). Arenz died on April 2, 1856, remembered as one of Beardstown's first settler (21). EVD.

10. Wright State University in Dayton, Ohio, has a collection, *Charles O. Wolpers Papers, 1817-1865* (Dayton: Wright State University Library Catalog, 1817). A guide to the collection, documenting Theodore Carl Otto Wolpers' (*Carl Otto Wolpers*) naturalization papers, residence documents, and business enterprises, can be accessed online <http://www.libraries.wright.edu/special/collection_guides/guide_files/ms126.pdf>. According to this document, Carl Otto Wolpers, born on January 15, 1790 in Maelstricht, Prussia, died in Germantown on December 21, 1868. He emigrated to the United States between 1810-1812. Frank Conover, ed., *Centennial Portrait* (1081), erroneously records the date of Charles O. Wolpers's birth as 1795. As soon as Wolpers arrived in Germantown, Ohio, he created a successful store in the vicinity of Gunckel's mill. Wolpers worked for many years in Bellefontaine, Ohio, which was then referred to as Bellville. Wolpers renamed Belville to Bellefontaine. Upon returning to Germantown, Wolpers "engaged in the drug business, and was also interested in distillery. He was a well-educated man, a classical and scientific scholar, and was a diligent student throughout his life." 1081. Conover continues to add that Wolpers manufactured in his chemistry laboratory "various articles for medical purposes." He had eight children with his wife Louisa Schwartz, whose father was born in Germany and was a Revolutionary soldier. EVD

11. Little is known about him. One can read the following in the *Deutsch-Amerikanische Geschichtsblätter*, ed. Julius Goebel, (1912), XII-XIII:298-299: "Dr. Ludwig Henrich, supposedly the son of the Grand Duchy of Saxony envoy to the Federal Assembly of 1819, had attained the Doctor of Philosophy degree from the University of Göttingen and was a lecturer in Leipzig. The beginning of the twenties ruling about *Demagogenriecherei* had driven him to

America in 1824. There is no information about his later life." (translation from German to English by EVD).

12. Ibid.,290: Eduard Schäffer, born in Frankfurt-on-the-Main, is closely connected to the German printing business in the United States. Eduard Schäffer arrived in Canton, Ohio, in 1821 with printing equipment and published the second German newspaper in Ohio, the *Westliche Beobachter und Stark und Wayne Counties Anzeiger*. He sold it in 1826 and moved to Germantown, Ohio, having heard about the intellectual German life there, and opened on September 4, 1826, a new German newspaper, the *National-Zeitung*. 301. Eduard Schäffer died from cholera in 1829. EVD

13. This is a quote from Friedrich Schiller, *Wallenstein*, Die Piccolomini, III, 4. EVD

14. According to H. A. Rattermann, *Abhandlunge, Vorträge und Reden: Bilder aus der Deutsch-Amerikanischen Geschichte* (Cincinnati: Selbstverlag des Verfassers, 1912), 226, Daniel Christian Lehmus was a former mathematician in Jena and Berlin, Germany, who came in 1826 to Germantown, Ohio, and was later working in Pennsylvania in the newspaper business. For additional extensive biographical information, see *Der Deutsche Pionier* (XI:348-350). The *Deutsch-Amerikanische Geschichtsblätter* (XII-XIII:291) add to Christian Lehmus' life that the professor of mathematics lost his teaching job in Jena, accused of *demagogische Umtriebe* (demagogic intrigues) and fled via Switzerland to America in order to escape persecution. Daniel Christian Lehmus also worked on translations of Franz Lieber's *Encylopaedia Americana* starting in 1830. He worked on the project for five years together with twelve other German translators. EVD

15. Mr. Köhne thinks he was the son of the Archduke Saxon Ambassador von Henrich, who in 1819, before the federal assembly, gave an explanation of the invalidity of the charges which were raised, in several documents, against the German universities, charging students and professors with demagogy. – One can find information about him in the book *Entlarvung der sogenannten demagogischen Umtriebe*, written by Rechtlieb Zeitgeist, Altenburg 1834, Vol. II, pp. 536-537. HAR

16. An uncle, Friedrich David Schäffer, D.D., had already settled in America in 1785 and was presently a preacher at *St. Michaels Kirche* in Philadelphia. HAR
According to Gustav Philipp Körner, *The German Element in the Ohio Valley: Ohio, Kentucky & Indiana; Translated and Edited by Don Heinrich Tolzmann* (Baltimore: Clearfield, 2011), Eduard Schäffer published between 1821 to 1826 the first German paper in Canton, Ohio, that was "not in the Pennsylvania German dialect." 60. The paper was called *Der Canton deutsche Beobachter*. EVD

17. Rector Lehmus was a priest in Adelshofen by Rothenburg, where he died in 1814. Information about him is contained in Jöcher's *Gelehrten Lexicon*, continued by Rothermund, volume V of the continuation. Appendix, p. CXXVII. HAR

18. For more information about Franz Lieber (1798-1872), see Don Heinrich Tolzmann, ed., *German-American Literature* (Metuchen: Scarecrow Press, 1977), 151-163. In his article on

Lieber, Thomas Kennedy points out that the first edition of the *Encyclopaedia Americana* was "Lieber's most ambitious enterprise" (153) and that Lieber wrote about twenty-three contributions for the *Encyclopaedia* (155). Franz Lieber worked with other scholars on the *Encyclopaedia* for about five years and although it oriented itself on the *Brockhaus Conversations-Lexikon*, Lieber rewrote articles so that they would specifically appeal to the American audience. (153). Kennedy also explains that the *Encyclopaedia* contains a large number of articles about German culture, philosophy, literature, art, theology, and science, which "was lacking in early English-language encyclopedias" (154). For more information about Franz Lieber's biography and his life's work, see *Der Deutsche Pionier* (1879, XI:3-11). EVD

19. Max Burgheim in *Cincinnati in Wort und Bild: Nach Authentischen Quellen Bearbeitet und Zusammengestellt* (Cincinnati: M. & R. Burgheim, 1888), 70, provides the reason for Christian Burkhalter's immigration to the United States in 1816, religious enthusiasm. Later Burkhalter joined the Shakers and helped establish the Shaker colony of Union Village in Warren County, Ohio, in 1820. According to Burgheim, Burkhalter returned to Cincinnati in 1837 and founded the *Westliche Merkur* (*Western Mercury*), a German Whig newspaper, which was changed in 1841 to *Der Deutsche im Westen* (*The German in the West*). EVD

20. According to Frank Conover, *Centennial Portrait* (141-142), Thomas Corwin (1794-1865), the twelfth governor of Ohio, was born in Bourbon county, Kentucky, on July 29, 1794. His father, Matthias Corwin, a judge, moved with his family four years later to Lebanon, Ohio, where young Thomas was educated in a small schoolhouse by Francis Dunlevy, the first schoolteacher in the Miami Valley. For more information about Francis Dunlevy (also *Dunlavy*), see Fred J. Milligan, *Ohio's Founding Fathers* (New York: Universe, 2003), 55-61. EVD

21. Conover, *Centennial Portrait*, states: about Thomas Corwin: "When he was seventeen years old he drove a wagon-load of provisions for the army to the headquarters of Gen. Harrison, and this event had a potential influence upon his subsequent career. In 1817, after having studied law one year, he was admitted to practice, and in March, 1818, was elected prosecuting attorney of his county." 141. The Corwin House in Lebanon, Ohio, has been on the National Register of Historic Homes since 1984. On 210 W. Main Street, in Lebanon, Ohio, is a historical marker in honor of Thomas Corwin. EVD

22. According to Max Burgheim, *Cincinnati in Wort und Bild: Nach Authentischen Quellen Bearbeitet und Zusammengestellt* (Cincinnati: Burgheim Pub. Co. 1891), 70, Albert (von) Stein (1785-1874), who came to Cincinnati in 1817, was one of the most influential engineers in the United States. Stein initiated and built the *Cincinnati Municipal Water Works*, the first in the country that was driven by pumps. The idea was to obtain clean drinking water and distribute the water throughout the city. Later Stein constructed many water pumps for other U.S. cities such as in Richmond, Lynchburg, Petersburg (Virginia), and New Orleans. Burgheim writes: "Ein deutscher Ingenieur hatte damit die erste künstliche Wasserleitung in Amerika, welche mittels Pumpwerken in Betrieb gesetzt wurde, geplant und erbaut." 388. For additional information about Albert Stein, see Ellen C. Merrill, *Germans of Louisiana; Foreword by Don Heinrich Tolzmann* (Gretna: Pelican Pub., 2005), 345. Gustav Philipp Körner in *The German Element in the Ohio Valley: Ohio, Kentucky & Indiana, Translated and Edited by Don Heinrich Tolzmann*, (Baltimore: Clearfield, 2011) adds that Albert von Stein also built water works for Nashville and Mobile. 4. EVD

23. Drury in *History of the City of Dayton* (1:886) states that Dr. Christian Espich, who came from New Philadelphia, Ohio, to Germantown in 1820, was the first physician in Germantown who permanently lived there as well. Beers, ed., *History of Montgomery County, Ohio* (III:50), adds that Dr. Espich had a partner, Dr. Brasacker, born in German, who practiced in Germantown, Ohio, from 1824 to 1827. Dr. Espich also printed with another German, George Walker, the statute laws of Ohio in the German language. The several volumes found few buyers and the business failed. According to Beers, however, this only attempt at book printing in Germantown, Ohio, failed. (48). Dr. Espich died on November 24, 1853. For more information about Montgomery County's pioneer physicians, see William Conklin, *Montgomery County Medical Society: Its Founders and Early Members* (Dayton: Montgomery County Medical Society, 1901). EVD

24. Rober Steele, *Early Dayton: With Important Facts and Incidents from the Founding of the City of Dayton, Ohio, to the Hundredth Anniversary, 1796-1896* (Dayton: W.J. Shuey, 1896), describes William Jennison (*Jenison*) as a naturalist, highly educated in Germany: "Mr. Jennison was an elegant and accomplished man, with the courtly manner of a gentleman of the old *régime*. He spoke English perfectly, which was probably due to the fact that his mother was an Englishwoman of rank, whom his father, Count Jennison, of Heidelberg, had married while minister of the Kingdom of Würtemberg to the Court of St. James." 168. EVD

25. Carl Becker reports in his book, *The Village: A History of Germantown, Ohio, 1804-1976* (Germantown: Germantown Historical Society, 1980), 12, that Dr. Wilhelm Frank, another German intellectual, who settled in Germantown around 1831, was a physician and botany professor from the University of Heidelberg. From Germantown, Dr. Frank organized expeditions around the Midwest for the purpose of gathering plants that he shipped to Heidelberg. According to Goebel, *Deutsch-Amerikanische Geschichtsblätter* (1912, XII:299), Dr. Wilhelm Frank, a former professor of botany at the University of Heidelberg, came with his pupil, Count Franz Jenison-Walworth to America in order to conduct botanical studies with him in Ohio. Dr. Frank went in 1839 to New Orleans as a voluntary physician to help patients during a yellow fever epidemic. Dr. Frank died the same year of yellow fever. Count Jenison later started a flower and fruit business in Dayton. EVD

26. An interesting and strange secret hovers over the birth of the count. HAR

27. Not to be confused with the theologian by the same name who published in 1837 in Heidelberg a religious polemic pamphlet: "Gutachten über den neuen Augsburger Katechismus." HAR

28. He was the former court physician of the Markgraf von Baden, in Rastatt (1796-83), then professor of physiology and medical policy in Göttingen (1784), clinical professor in Padua (1785), director of the general hospital in Vienna (1795), professor at the University of Wilna (1804), personal physician of the Emperor Alexander of Russia in St. Petersburg (1805) and finally again doctor and professor at the University of Vienna (1808), where he died in 1821. He is the author of numerous medical books, which all have an outstanding reputation. HAR
For additional information about Dr. Johann Peter Frank (1745-1821), father of Dr. Wilhelm Frank, see Victor Cornelius Medvei, *The History of Clinical Endocrinology: A Comprehensive*

Account of Endocrinology from Earliest Times to the Present Day (New York: Parthenon Pub. Group, 1993), 424. EVD

29. An older brother, Joseph Frank, also a highly respected physician, was professor of pathology in Wilna and is today the author of the *Grundriß der Pathologie nach den Gesetzen der Erregungstheorie* and several other books. HAR
The complete source of this book: Joseph Frank, *Grundriß der Pathologie nach den Gesetzen der Erregungstheorie, mit Erläuternden Zusätzen und Anmerkungen nach seinen Vorlesungen Bearbeitet* (Wien: Anton Doll, 1803). EVD

30. The exact information of this book is: W. Frank, *Deutschland in Amerika: Das Einzig Rechte Ziel Aller Deutschen Auswanderer* (Cassel: J. Luckhardt, 1839). EVD

31. According to Thomas W. Schmidlin, *Thunder in the Heartland: A Chronicle of Outstanding Weather Events in Ohio* (Kent: Kent State University Press, 1996), there was also a Lewis Groneweg, a meteorologist for the Smithsonian Institute in Germantown, who described the weather conditions to other German pioneers in the area with references they could understand and made sense to them. When referring to the cold temperatures from December to February of 1856 in Germantown, he did not just report that it was 8.7 degrees below normal, but that this was "nine degrees colder than the winter in Berlin, Prussia, and only five degrees warmer than the winter in Petersburg, capital of Russia." 84. However, the death certificate of this Groneweg from Germantown reveals that he was born on May 26. 1849 in Germany and died on January 5, 1931 in Oakwood, Ohio. "Ohio, Deaths, 1908-1953," index and images, FamilySearch (https://familysearch.org/pal:/MM9.3.1/TH-266-11772-16836-89?cc=1307272&wc=M9SV-PFC:n1287936619 : accessed 10 Jan 2014), 1931 > 03201-06200. EVD

32. George Hawes, *Ohio State Gazetteer and Business Directory for 1860-'61* (Indianapolis: G.W. Hawes, 1860), 126, shows a drugstore ad and lists L. Groneweg as the owner of a *Deutsche Apotheke* (German Pharmacy) in Cincinnati, Ohio. EVD

33. For an explanation about the *Free Soil Party*, see *Encyclopædia Britannica* (11th Edition, 1911), which describes it as a political party in the United States (1848-1854) that was against slavery in the new western territories and wrote their slogan on their banner: "'Free Soil, Free Speech, Free Labor and Free Man." The Free Soil Party was established in Columbus, Ohio, during the *Ohio Free Territory Convention* on July 21, 1848. EVD

34. According to Edgar, *Pioneer Life in Dayton and Vicinity* (154), Colonel John Johnston (1775-1861) was made Indian agent in Piqua, Ohio, in 1811. Hover, *Memoirs of the Miami Valley* (Chicago: Robert O. Law Co., 1919), I:340), reports that after Colonel John Johnston was in charge at Fort Wayne from 1800 to 1811. He became the Indian Agent at Fort Piqua from 1811-1833. It was his duty as Indian agent to keep a friendly relationship with the Indians. He accomplished this by treating them kindly, clothing and feeding them, and employing some Indian soldiers (525). According to Hover, Johnston's positive influence on the Indians, avoided massacres and contributed to the growth of the early Ohio settlement. Colonel Johnston, who was also a canal commissioner, worked tirelessly to expand the Miami canal construction further north: "as a citizen of Miami county he was very anxious to extend the benefits of the canal to his community." 505. EVD

35. *Ohio History: Ohio Historical Society* (Columbus: Fred Heer, 1905, XIV) refers to Caleb Atwater (1778-1867) as "Ohio's first historian," who wrote *A History of the State of Ohio* in 1838, was also a "minister, lawyer, educator, legislator, author and antiquarian." 247. He was born 1778 in North Adams, Massachusetts, and was related to the original pioneers of New Haven. He wanted to go west and came to Circleville, Ohio, in 1815. He practiced law there for six years, wrote articles for the Circleville newspaper and there was "no doubt that they had considerable influence in modeling the public opinion of the section." 250. Besides working for public growth, Caleb Atwater was also instrumental in education. He helped to give Circleville "its first school and their state its first system of education." 271. Atwater died on March 13, 1867, in Circleville, Ohio, and is remembered by a historical marker in Circleville. EVD

36. According to Hover, *Memoirs of the Miami Valley* (II:311-313), John McLean (March 11, 1785-April 4, 1861) was fourteen years old when he moved with his parents from Morris county, New Jersey, to Ohio. After working a few years on his parents' farm, he became an apprentice county clerk in Cincinnati, later a judge, then a House Representative, and finally U.S. Supreme Court judge. In Lebanon, Ohio, he also published a weekly newspaper, *The Western Star*, in 1807. According to Eliakim Littell, *Littell's Living Age* (Boston: Littell, Son, & Co., 1861), XIII:320, the Hon. Judge John McLean, one of the associate judges of the Supreme Court of the United States, was born in Morris County, New Jersey, in 1785. From there he moved to Virginia, Kentucky, before settling in Ridgeville, Warren County, Ohio, in 1797. Michael Les Benedict, ed., *The History of Ohio Law* (Athens: Ohio University Press, 2004), adds the detail that John McLean's father, a weaver from Ulster, was actually a squatter on the land in Warren County, Ohio, since John Cleave Symmes, the seller of the land, did not actually own the land (407-408). The editor also points out that John might have received a life lesson of what it means to be politically well-connected, "because Congress was persuaded by his father and the other 450 settlers in the county to sell them the land directly on very favorable terms." 408. John McLean received a good law education and even Arthur St. Clair, the future governor of the area, was his teacher and John C. Calhoun his friend. Among John McLean's many positions were "congressman during the War of 1812, federal lands commissioner, justice of the Ohio Supreme Court, candidate for U.S. Senator, postmaster general under three presidents, and most remarkably, an active candidate for president while serving on the U.S. Supreme Court." 408. McLean is also noteworthy for his strong beliefs in antislavery. Most Ohio settlers typically had such a view, but McLean "was intensely antislavery, for economic as much as moral reasons." 409. His views would be tested many times. McLean died in Cincinnati on April 4, 1861, and is buried in *Spring Grove Cemetery*, Cincinnati. For additional information, see Francis P. Weisenburger, *The Life of John McLean: A Politician on the United States Supreme Court* (Columbus: Ohio State University Press, 1939). For more information about the *Spring Grove Cemetery*, see Don Heinrich Tolzmann, ed., *Spring Grove and its Creator: H. A. Rattermann's Biography of Adolph Strauch* (Cincinnati: The Ohio Book Store, 1988). EVD

37. According to Hover, ed., *Memoirs of the Miami Valley* (II:627), Salmon Portland Chase (January 13, 1808 - May 7, 1873) was born in New Hampshire "of an American line of ancestry tracing back to the earliest days in our colonial history" and is well-known "in the history of the nation and in the annals of Cincinnati." His youth was difficult and he had to support his family by doing hard farm labor since his father, an owner of a tavern, died in 1817, leaving behind ten children. Salmon Chase was only nine years old. Despite hard farm labor, Chase received a good

education. He later became a politician, U.S. senator to Ohio, the 23rd governor of Ohio, and in 1864 he became Chief Justice of the United States Supreme Court. For more biographical information, see Frederick J. Blue, *Salmon P. Chase: A Life in Politics* (Kent: Kent State University Press, 1987). Blue mentions that the Chase family lived originally in England in the mid-seventeenth century and that the mother of Salmon P. Chase was a Scottish immigrant. (2). His mother was delighted when Salmon's uncle, an Episcopal priest and Bishop of Ohio, asked them to move to Ohio (3). Salmon P. Chase was also active in antislavery activities, the formation of the *Free Soil Party*, and the defense of escaped slaves. For more information about his involvement with the German-Americans specifically, see pp. 102-103 and pp. 109-110. There is also a *Salmon P. Chase College of Law* at the Northern Kentucky University in Highland Heights, KY, founded in 1893, and named in the honor of the U.S. Chief of Justice, Salmon P. Chase. His portrait is on the first one-dollar bill in the United States in 1862 when paper became the legal tender. His birthplace in New Hampshire was listed on the National Register of Historic Places in1975, and his grave can be visited at the Spring Grove Cemetery in Cincinnati, Ohio.
<http://en.wikipedia.org/wiki/Salmon_P._Chase_Birthplace>
<http://www.springgrove.org/salmon-chase.aspx> EVD

38. Liz Tilton, *Cincinnati's Historic Findlay Market* (Charleston: Arcadia Publishing, 2009) mentions that James Findlay (October 12, 1770 - December 28, 1835), an early pioneer and good citizen, came to Cincinnati from Pennsylvania in 1793 where he soon established a small shop close to the Ohio River, and later he "opened larger stores, served in the military, helped establish a public library in Cincinnati, became governor of Ohio and served in the U.S. Congress." 7. Fred Milligan, *Ohio's Founding Fathers* (New York: iUniverse, 2003), 118-120, states that James Findlay was born by Mercersburg, Franklin County, Pennsylvania on October 2, 1770 and had Scottish-Irish ancestry. After he arrived in Cincinnati in 1793 and opened a small shop, he bought real estate and laid out an area north of Cincinnati, called Northern Liberties. Milligan points to Findlay's entrepreneurial spirit when he lists his many businesses: "Findlay was a leading businessman of the town and engaged in a number of business ventures. He was associated with the organizations formed for civic betterment. He was a leader of the Presbyterian Church whose members included many of the town's leaders." 119. James Findlay was also "a director of the Cincinnati branch of the United States Bank." 120. Findlay was also active in the political life as justice of the peace and judge in Hamilton County in 1801, United States Marshall of the Territory in 1802, Mayor of Cincinnati from 1805-1806 and 1810-1811, a general in the War of 1812, and member of the Board of Trustees of Miami University. 119-120. Findlay died in Cincinnati, Ohio on December 28, 1835, and is buried with his wife, Jane Irwin Findlay, in the *Spring Grove Cemetery* in Cincinnati. In honor of James Findlay, a city was named after him and *Findlay Market* in Cincinnati was built on land donated by the estates of General James Findlay and his wife, Jane Irwin Findlay (1769-1851). For more information about the Findlay Market, which was opened in 1852, and is according to Tilton, "Ohio's oldest public market in continuous operation" (7), see Liz Tilton, *Cincinnati's Historic Findlay Market* (Charleston: Arcadia Publishing, 2009).
<http://www.springgrove.org/stats/3516.tif.pdf> EVD

39. Judge George Paull Torrence (1782-1855) was another prominent man of Cincinnati. For more information about the relationship between John Mclean and George P. Torrence, see Isaac

Cox "Selections from the Torrence Papers," in *Quarterly Publications of the Historical and Philosophical Society of Ohio* (Cincinnati: 1906-23, I-III). The *Torrence Papers* are a collection of letters belonging to Judge George P. Torrence that he wrote to many of his prominent friends. A letter between John McLean and George P. Torrence starts the collection. The letter is dated February 12, 1823. (1907, II:7). Gregory Parker Rogers, *Cincinnati's Hyde Park: A Queen City Gem* (Charleston: History Press, 2010) mentions that George Torrence (February 14, 1782 - August 27, 1855) served as a judge on the Hamilton County Court of Common Pleas for twenty-eight years and was honored by having a road named after him. He is buried in the *Spring Grove Cemetery* in Cincinnati, Ohio. <http://www.springgrove.org/stats/4650.tif.pdf>
Elisabeth Maxwell Paull, *Paul-Irwin: A Family Sketch* (n.p.: Privately Printed, 1915), daughter of Judge Torrence, writes that he was born on February 14, 1782 near Connellsville, Pennsylvania, studied law and arrived in Cincinnati in 1806 where he started to practice law until 1817. First he was elected in 1817 to the State senate, and in 1819 "he was elected presiding Judge of the Ninth Judicial District, and re-elected in 1826. His judicial career covered a period of twenty years." 160. EVD

40. According to the *History of Cincinnati and Hamilton County, Ohio: Their Past and Present, Including ... Biographies and Portraits of Pioneers and Representative Citizens, Etc.* (Cincinnati: S. B. Nelson and Co., 1894), 536 - 539, the Pendleton family is prominently linked to the history of Cincinnati and the country. It started with Henry Pendleton, a native of Norwich, England. His two sons, Nathaniel and Philip emigrated to America in 1674 and settled in Virginia. Many generations later, a Nathaniel Greene Pendleton (1793-1861) moved from "New York to Cincinnati, then but an inconsiderable village," where he began his law practice. 536. Pendleton was also a member of the Ohio State Senate in 1825, a U.S. Congressman in 1840, and a U.S. Army Officer in the War of 1812. Nathanial Greene Pendleton was born on August 25, 1793 in Savannah Chatham County, Georgia, and died in Cincinnati, Ohio, on June 15, 1861 where he is buried in the *Spring Grove Cemetery*. Pendleton is also a neighborhood in Cincinnati, Ohio. For additional information on Pendleton, see Andrew R. Dodge, *Biographical Directory of the United States Congress, 1774-2005: The Continental Congress, September 5, 1774, To October 21, 1788, and the Congress of the United States, From the First through the One Hundred Eighth Congresses, March 4, 1789, to January 3, 2005* (Washington: U.S. G.P.O.), 1719. <http://www.findagrave.com/cgi-bin/fg.cgi?page=gr&GRid=6921700>
<http://www.springgrove.org/stats/9634.tif.pdf> EVD

41. Nicholas Longworth (1783-1863) also belonged to Cincinnati's wealthy and influential families. Daniel Aaron, *Cincinnati, Queen City of the West, 1819-1838* (Columbus: Ohio State University Press, 1992), 63, points out that Nicholas Longworth, a Jersey native, was called the *Croesus of the West* when he came to Cincinnati to practice law, an occupation he abandoned to dedicate his time to real estate ventures. Aaron comments that the average German who came Cincinnati in the first wave, between 1830 and 1840, was not involved in the city life to a large extent: "But with the exception of a few literary figures, radical editors, and well-to-do businessmen, the average German in Cincinnati during the decade between 1830 and 1840 felt no great urge to participate in political and social affairs. Handicapped by language difficulties, these newcomers were apt to be docile." 167. To illustrate his point he provides the example of Nicholas Longworth who employed many Germans on his estate for very little money. Aaron has not much positive to say about Nicholas Longworth when it comes to his sponsoring of

young artists of Cincinnati as well: "Nicholas Longworth, the wealthiest man in Cincinnati and the most prominent *Maecceanas* in the West, had a peculiar facility for annoying mettlesome young artists." 255. Aaron continues with his opinion of Longworth by writing: "Nicholas Longworth, canny, realistic, and homely, could in no sense be called an aristocrat. In appearance he might have been a grubby and impecunious western lawyer instead of one of the richest men in the United States." 284. Thomas Pinney, *A History of Wine in America from the Beginnings to Prohibition* (Berkeley: University of California Press, 1989) adds one more dimension to the entrepreneur Nicholas Longworth, the leading American winemaker. According to Pinney, Longworth spent less time with his interest in horticulture while building his law practice when he came to from Newark, New Jersey, to Cincinnati in 1804. (157) He soon gave up being a lawyer because he made a fortune buying land, "property that he bought for a song became worth millions, and Longworth joined John Jacob Astor as one of the two largest taxpayers in the United States." 157. According to Pinney, Longworth gave up his law practice in 1828, picked up his interest in horticulture, specifically wine making, and started a vineyard in Delhi township with the assistance of a "German named Amen or Ammen." 157. Longworth aimed at a European-tasting wine and therefore also employed many "German immigrants flowing into the Cincinnati region and giving it that German flavor that it still retains." 159. Pinney points to two advantages of a collaboration with the Germans: "The Germans were in fact doubly necessary: they not only grew and made the wine, they drank it as well." 159. German immigrants liked his wine and they wanted an affordable table wine that reminded them of their homeland. Longworth's winemaking business in Cincinnati was successful and in 1859, the "peak year in the history of Cincinnati wine-growing," he and many of his German growers contributed to "putting Ohio at the head of the nation's wine production." 165. John Phin, *Open Air Grape Culture: A Practical Treatise on the Garden and Vineyard Culture of the Vine, and the Manufacture of Domestic Wine: Designed for the Use of Amateurs and Others in the Northern and Middle States: Profusely Illustrated with New Engravings from Carefully Executed Designs, Verified by Direct Practice* (New York: C.M. Saxton, Agricultural Book Publisher, 1862) calls Nicholas Longworth, the "father of American wine making." 251. Longworth died on February 10, 1863 and is interred in the *Spring Grove Cemetery*. Longworth's home is today the Taft Museum of Art in Cincinnati.
<http://www.springgrove.org/stats/11358.tif.pdf>
<http://tinyurl.com/kmagxy7> EVD

42. Rattermann cites a Heinrich Mundhenk as having founded Pyrmont, although three other sources list a Daniel Mundhenk. According to John Calvin Hover, ed., *Memoirs of the Miami Valley* (Chicago: Robert O. Law Company, 1919), 50, it was Daniel Mundhenk, Sr. (1777-1859), his father, who laid out the town of Pyrmont in Perry township in 1835 and not Henry Mundhenk as Rattermann states. A second source, Drury, *History of the City of Dayton and Montgomery County, Ohio* (1:909), also seems to indicate that Daniel Mundhenk established the city of Pyrmont in 1835. Conover, *Centennial Portrait and Biographical Record of the City of Dayton*, 1192, reports that Daniel G. Mundhenk, a German native from Pyrmont, Germany, arrived in Philadelphia in 1807, moved to Montgomery County, Ohio, in 1817 and laid out the town of Pyrmont on his estate, naming it after his hometown in Germany. Daniel Mundhenk died in Pyrmont, Perry township on March 1, 1859.
<http://tinyurl.com/pztw3je>
A Henry Mundhenk was born on April 17, 1816 and died on June 13, 1887 in Pyrmont, Ohio.

<http://www.findagrave.com/cgi-bin/fg.cgi?page=gr&GRid=27900096> EVD

43. Referring to the story of Henry Mundhenk and his wife, Rattermann points to Emil Klauprecht, *Deutsche Chronik in der Geschichte des Ohio-Thales, Und seiner Hauptstadt Cincinnati in's Besondere ... Zusammengestellt nach Authentischen Quellen von Emil Klauprecht* (Cincinnati: G. Hof & M. A. Jacobi, 1864), 162, who tells the story of Mrs. Klauprecht. She interrupted a festivity in honor of General Lafayette who toured the United States and stopped in Cincinnati, Ohio, just as he started his speech. Klauprecht comments that it was an inappropriate time that a German female vegetable farmer would run up the stage holding out her hand and saying: "Kennen Sie mich nicht mehr?" ("Don't you know me any more?"). That woman, Mrs. Mundhenk, reminded General Lafayette that she was the milkmaid who smuggled letters written by Mr. Bollmann to Lafayette while he was in prison in Ollmütz. The happy reunion with his former savior interrupted the celebration and Lafayette never completed his speech. Klauprecht identifies this woman as Mrs. Mundhenk, a farmer of the so-called hop garden who operated with her husband, Heinrich Mundhenk, a vegetable market in the early 1830's and who was well-known. EVD

44. Rattermann himself re-tells this anecdotal meeting of Mrs. Mundhenk and General Lafayette in *Der Deutsche Pionier: Erinnerungen aus dem Pionierleben* (Cincinnati, OH: Deutscher Pionier-Verein, 1876), VII:440. Rattermann again mentions Heinrich Mundhenk and his wife in *Der Deutsche Pionier*, VIII:125, while discussing Cincinnati's first gardener, the German Jonathan Stäbler. Rattermann then mentions two other skillful German gardeners, Jakob Kapp and Heinrich Mundhenk, and their idea to start a hop garden and thereby beginning a new era of agriculture, hop growing. Mrs. Mundhenk was praised as Lafayette's helper while he was in prison in the castle of Ollmütz. More detail is provided in a footnote about the prison situation of Lafayette and how Mrs. Mundhenk saved him from starvation. EVD

Sources

An extensive *Bibliography* was added to aid any historian in research or to indicate what was already written about the local history of Montgomery County, Ohio. A complete list of all books consulted is provided under the *Bibliography* heading, but the following titles were especially useful for my research.

Carl M. Becker, *The Village: A History of Germantown, Ohio, 1804-1976* (Germantown: Germantown Historical Society, 1980).

W.H. Beers & Co., *The History of Montgomery County*, Ohio (Chicago: W.H. Beers & Co., 1882).

Charlotte R. Conover, *Dayton, Ohio: An Intimate History* (New York: Lewis Historical Pub. Co., 1932).

_____, *The Story of Dayton* (Dayton: The Greater Dayton Association, 1917).

_____, *Some Dayton Saints and Prophets* (Dayton: United Brethren Publishing House, 1907).

Frank Conover, Frank, *Centennial Portrait and Biographical Record of the City Of Dayton and of Montgomery County, Ohio, Containing Biographical Sketches Of Prominent And Representative Citizens* (Logansport: A. W. Bowen, 1897).

John F. Edgar, *Pioneer Life in Dayton and Vicinity, 1796-1840* (Dayton: Shuey, 1896).
Albert B. Faust, *The German Element in the United States* (Boston: Houghton Mifflin, 1909).

L. H. Everts, *Combination Atlas Map of Montgomery County, Ohio: Compiled, Drawn and Published from Personal Examinations and Surveys* (Philadelphia: Hunter Press, 1875).

John C. Hover, ed., *Memoirs of the Miami Valley* (Chicago: Robert O. Law Company, 1919).

Henry Howe, *Historical Collections of Ohio* (Cincinnati: H. Howe, 1850).

Esther Light, *Miamisburg, Ohio, the Story of our Town: A Collection of Historical Essays from 1818 to 1993* (Miamisburg: Miamisburg Lions Club, 1993).

H. S. Reed, *Reed's Illustrated History of Montgomery County* (Dayton: H.S. Reed, 1880).
Clifford N. Smith, Early Nineteenth-Century German Settlers in Ohio (McNeal: Westland Publications, 1984.

Robert W. Steele, *Early Dayton: With Important Facts and Incidents from the Founding of the City of Dayton, Ohio, to the Hundredth Anniversary, 1796-1896* (Dayton: Shuey, 1896).

Additional sources were consulted:
Early Montgomery County, Ohio, Settlement History of the *Special Collections and Archives* at the Wright State University; the *German-Americana Collection Holdings* at the Blegen Library in Cincinnati; as well as archival holdings at Dayton History, Dayton Metro Library, Germantown Historical Society, Germantown Public Library and Miamisburg Historical Society.

Image Sources:
Most images are from the *Lutzenberger Image Collection*, the *Montgomery County Picture File Collection* or the *Portraits in Books Collection* of the Dayton Metro Library. The images were used with permission from the Dayton Metro Library, the owner of the digital collection.

Images and Text of Obituaries in Gedenkblätter (supplement of *Daytoner Volkszeitung*)
All images provided by Katharina Hargot, volunteer transcriptionist of the obituary entries of German settlers in the Gedenkblätter at the Dayton Metro Library. All image sources used with permission. *Die Daytoner Volkszeitung.* n.p.: Dayton, Ohio : Geo. Neder, 1866.

Image of Heinrich Böhm (Henry Boehm) used with permission from Rev. Helen Adams, Pastor of the Stehman Memorial UM Church Millersville, PA and Dolores Myers, executive director of the chapel society. The original painting is hanging in Boehm's United Methodist Church, Willow Street, PA.

Return from Indian Captivity
Cronau, Rudolf. *Drei Jahrhunderte Deutschen Lebens In Amerika : Eine Geschichte Der Deutschen In Den Vereinigten Staaten / Von Rudolf Cronau.* Berlin: D. Reimer (Ernst Vohsen), 1909. 167.

***Liberty Hall & Cincinnati Mercury* Newspaper clipping** (p. 14). Photocopy provided by the Public Library of Cincinnati and Hamilton County. Document in public domain.

Col. Robert Patterson's Signature
Signature of Col. Robert Patterson, 1813, Dayton, Ohio by Dayton Metro Library Local History, on Flickr (Dayton Metro Library, MS-015, Box 1, Folder 11)

Robert Patterson's Slave Case, 1805
Pasquinelli Rickey, Lisa. "Patterson's Slave Case, 1805." 17 February 2011. Online image. 27 June 2014. <http://www.flickr.com/photos/bellanox/5453594179/in/photostream/>

Handcuffs for African-Americans Brought by Col. Patterson from Kentucky, 1804
Conover, Charlotte Reeve. *Concerning The Forefathers; Being A Memoir, With Personal Narrative And Letters Of Two Pioneers Col. Robert Patterson And Col. John Johnston, The Paternal And Maternal Grandfathers Of John Henry Patterson Of Dayton, Ohio For Whose Children This Book Is Written By Charlotte Reeve Conover.* n.p.: [New York, The Winthrop press, 1902], 314.

Col. Robert Patterson Portrait
Conover, Charlotte Reeve. *Concerning The Forefathers.* n.p.: New York, The Winthrop Press, 1902, 349.

Alter Deutscher Orden der Harugari der Vereinigten Staaten Nordamerikas
Library of Congress; Date created: May 19, 1854; no known restrictions on publication.
<http://www.loc.gov/pictures/item/2004667960/>

Photo of Conrad Beissel's grave stone at the Ephrata Cloister (632 West Main Street, Ephrata, PA 17522), courtesy of Kerry Mohn, who describes the marker as a red sandstone slab.

Image of Chief Black Hawk or Sauk Chief Makataimeshekiakiah
McKenney, Thomas Loraine, and James Hall. *History Of The Indian Tribes Of North America.* Philadelphia, PA: J.T. Bowen, 1848-1850. Link to image: http://tinyurl.com/kemjp3b

Battle of Stillman's Run from an 1854 artist's rendering of that war. Created Dec. 31, 1853.
Link to image: http://tinyurl.com/6qc5cs

Hon. Thomas Corwin by J.A.J. Wilcox, Boston Engraving, published 1882. In public domain
Link to image: http://tinyurl.com/pk216dr

Thomas Corwin Estate from *Remarkable Ohio*. No copyright restrictions. Image used with permission from the *Ohio History Connection*. Link to image: http://www.remarkableohio.org/

Image of Cincinnati Water Works from the Collection of the *Public Library of Cincinnati & Hamilton County*. Used with permission.

Image of Johann Peter Frank (1774-1821) from a litography of a Johann Peter Frank by Adolph Friedrich Kunicke (Albertina, Vienna). Public domain image: http://tinyurl.com/npd4ytj

Image of the Cincinnati German Pioneer Society Composite Picture used with permission from the Campbell County Historical & Genealogical Society (CCH&GS). The original is the property and in the possession of The Campbell County, KY Historical & Genealogical Society, 8352 East Main St., Alexandria, KY 41006.

"Map of the States and Territories of the United States of America" by User:Golbez is licensed under CC BY 2.5. No changes were made to the map.
Link to image: http://tinyurl.com/lfukus2

All old images of Germantown, Ohio, courtesy of Gillian Izor, Assitant Director of the *Germantown Public Library*.

All photographs of Miamisburg, Ohio and Germantown, Ohio, taken by Nicole Mae Dona.
Used with her permission.

Bibliography

Aaron, Daniel. *Cincinnati, Queen City of the West, 1819-1838 / Daniel Aaron*. Columbus : Ohio State University Press, 1992.

Adam, Thomas. *Germany and the Americas [Electronic Resource] : Culture, Politics, and History*. Santa Barbara, Calif. : ABC-CLIO, 2005.

Adams, Willi Paul, La Vern J. Rippley, and Eberhard Reichmann. *The German-Americans : An Ethnic Experience / Willi Paul Adams ; Translated and Adapted by LaVern J. Rippley and Eberhard Reichmann*. Indianapolis : Max Kade German-American Center, Indiana University-Purdue University at Indianapolis, 1993; American ed, 1993.

American Catholic Historical Society,of Philadelphia. *Records of the American Catholic Historical Society of Philadelphia*. American Catholic Historical Society of Philadelphia, 1886.

Andrusko, Samuel M. *Der Deutsche Pionier: Membership Lists (1869-1887) of the Deutschen Pionier-Verein of Cincinnati and Branches in Dayton and Toledo (Ohio) and Covington and Newport (Kentucky) with Selected Additional Biographical Information from Obituaries and Biographhies [Sic] in the Deutschen Pionier / Abstracted, Translated, and Edited by Samuel M. Andrusko*. Washington, D.C. : S.M. Andrusko, 1989.

The Annual Cyclopedia of Insurance in the United States. H.R. Hayden, 1890.

Arndt, Karl John Richard, and May E. Olson. *The German Language Press of the Americas, 1732-1968: History and Bibliography by Karl J. R. Arndt and may E. Olson*. Pullach/München, Verlag Dokumentation, 1973.

---. *German-American Newspapers and Periodicals, 1732-1955; History and Bibliography, by Karl J.R. Arndt and may E. Olson*. Heidelberg, Quelle & Meyer, 1961.

Bach, Jeff. *Voices of the Turtledoves : The Sacred World of Ephrata / Jeff Bach*. University Park, Pa. : Pennsylvania State University Press ; Göttingen, Germany : Vandenhoeck & Ruprecht, 2003.

Bambakidis, Elli. *Montgomery County Horticultural Society : A Special Collection of Historical Materials at the Dayton & Montgomery County Public Library*. Dayton, Ohio : Dayton and Montgomery County Public Library], 1996.

Bateman, Newton, and Paul Selby. *Historical Encyclopedia of Illinois, Volume 2*. Chicago : Munsell, 1905; Cook County ed, 1975.

Becker, Carl M. *The Village, a History of Germantown, Ohio, 1804-1976 / Carl M. Becker*. Germantown, Ohio : Historical Society of Germantown : Distributed by Ohio University Press, 1981.

---. *The Village, a History of Germantown, Ohio, 1804-1976 / Carl M. Becker*. Germantown, Ohio : Germantown Historical Society, 1980.

Benedict, Michael Les, and John F. Winkler. *The History of Ohio Law*. Athens, Ohio : Ohio University Press, 2004.

Berger, Daniel. *History of the Church of the United Brethren in Christ. by Rev. D. Berger, D.D.* New York : Christian Literature Co., 1894.

Berry, Ellen T., and D. A. Berry. *Early Ohio Settlers : Purchasers of Land in Southwestern Ohio, 1800-1840 / Compiled by Ellen T. Berry & David A. Berry*. Baltimore : Genealogical Pub. Co., 1986.

Blair, Clifford George. *James Findlay, Politician*. 1941.

Blue, Frederick J. *Salmon P. Chase : A Life In Politics*. Kent, Ohio: Kent State University Press, 1987.

Boke, Liwwat, and Luke B. Knapke. *Liwwat Boke, 1807-1882, Pioneer : The Story of an Immigrant Pioneer Woman and Her Husband Who Settled in Western Ohio, as Told in Her Own Writings and Drawings / Compiled and Edited by Luke B. Knapke*. Minster, Ohio : Minster Historical Society, 1987.

Bowman, Carl Desportes. *Brethren Society: The Cultural Transformation of a "Peculiar People"*. Baltimore: Johns Hopkins Univ Pr, 1995.

Brancaforte, Charlotte Lang. *The German Forty-Eighters in the United States*. New York : P. Lang, 1989.

Buján, Carlos Pena. "Die Geschichte Der Deutschen in Amerika. Von 1680 Bis Zur Gegenwart. (German)." *Revista de Indias* 73.257 (2013): 274-7.

Burgheim, Max. *Cincinnati in Wort Und Bild : Nach Authentischen Quellen Bearbeitet Und Zusammengestellt / Von Max Burgheim ; Mit Zahlreichen Illustrationen*. Cincinnati, Ohio : Burgheim Pub. Co., 1891.

---. *Cincinnati in Wort Und Bild : Nach Authentischen Quellen Bearbeitet Und Zusammengestellt / Von Max Burgheim ; Mit Zahlreichen Illustrationen*. Cincinnati, Ohio : Burgheim Pub. Co., 1891.

---. *Cincinnati in Wort Und Bild [Microform] : Nach Authentischen Quellen Bearbeitet Und Zusammengestellt / Von Max Burgheim*. Cincinnati, Ohio : M. & R. Burgheim, 1888.

Centennial Anniversary of West Branch Monthly Meeting of Freinds, Established 1st Month, 7th, 1807. Held at West Milton, Ohio, 10th Month, 11th and 12th, 1907. n.p. 1907.

Church of the Brethren Eastern District,of Pennsylvania. *History of the Church of the Brethren of the Eastern District of Pennsylvania.* The New era printing company, 1915.

Cincinnati: A Guide to the Queen City and its Neighbors / Compiled by Workers of the Writers' Program of the Work Projects Administration in the State of Ohio. Cincinnati, Ohio : Wiesen-Hart Press, 1943.

Collins, Lewis. *Historical Sketches of Kentucky.* L. Collins; J. A. & U. P. James, 1850.

---. *Historical Sketches of Kentucky : Embracing its History, Antiquities, and Natural Curiosities, Geographical, Statistical, and Geological Descriptions with Anecdotes of Pioneer Life, and More than One Hundred Biographical Sketches of Distinguished Pioneers, Soldiers, Statesmen, Jurists, Lawyers, Divines,* Maysville, Ky. : L. Collins, 1848.

Conklin, William Judkins. *Montgomery County Medical Society: Its Founders and Early Members. by W.J. Conklin ...: Dayton, Ohio. in Commemoration of the Fifty-First Anniversary of the Montgomery County Medical Society.* Dayton, O.?] Printed by order of the Society, 1901.

Conover, Charlotte Reeve. *Concerning the Forefathers; being a Memoir, with Personal Narrative and Letters of Two Pioneers Col. Robert Patterson and Col. John Johnston, the Paternal and Maternal Grandfathers of John Henry Patterson of Dayton, Ohio for Whose Children this Book is Written by Charlotte Reeve Conover.* New York, The Winthrop press, 1902.

---. *Dayton, Ohio: An Intimate History.* New York : Lewis Historical Pub. Co., 1932.

---. *Some Dayton Saints and Prophets.* Dayton, Ohio, United Brethren Pub. House, 1907.

Conover, Frank. *Centennial Portrait and Biographical Record of the City of Dayton and of Montgomery County, Ohio, Containing Biographical Sketches of Prominent and Representative Citizens, Together with the Biographies and Portraits of the Presidents of the United States and Biographies of the Governors of Ohio.* Logansport, Ind.] A. W. Bowen, 1897.

Crawford, Martin, and William Howard Russell. "William Howard Russell's Civil War: Private Diary And Letters, 1861-1862." (n.d.): *Biography Reference Bank (H.W. Wilson).*

Crew, Harvey W. *History of Dayton, Ohio : With Portraits and Biographical Sketches of some of its Pioneer and Prominent Citizens.* Dayton, Ohio : United Brethren Pub. House, 1889.

Croll, P. C., Henry Addison Schuler, and Howard Wiegner Kriebel. *The Pennsylvania-German: a Popular Magazine of Biography, History, Genealogy, Folklore, Literature*, Lebanon, Pa., P.C. Croll; 1900-11, 1900.

Cronau, Rudolf. *Drei Jahrhunderte Deutschen Lebens in Amerika : Ruhmesblätter Der Deutschen in Den Vereinigten Staaten / Von Rudolf Cronau*. Berlin : D. Reimer (Ernst Vohsen), 1924; 2., neu bearbeitete Aufl, 1924.

Curwen, Maskell E. *A Sketch of the History of the City of Dayton, by Maskell E. Curwen*. Dayton, J. Odell, jr., 1850.

Dalton, Curt. *The Breweries of Dayton : An Illustrated History*. Dayton, OH : C. Dalton, 1995.

---. *Dayton / Curt Dalton*. Charleston, SC : Arcadia, 2006.

Daly, Walter J. "The Black Cholera Comes to the Central Valley of America in the 19th Century - 1832, 1849, and Later." *Transactions of the American Clinical and Climatological Association* 119 (2008): 143-52.

Darbee, Jeffrey T., Nancy A. Recchie, and Judith B. Williams. *German Village Guidelines : Preserving Historic Architecture / the German Village Commission ... [Et Al.] ; [Text and Text Photographs by Jeffrey T. Darbee, Nancy A. Recchie, and Judith B. Williams of Benjamin D. Rickey & Co.*, Columbus, Ohio : German Village Society, 1989.

Dayton Liederkranz-Turner Collection, 1880-2007. n.p.: n.d. Wright State University Library Catalog.

Dayton Liederkranz-Turner Verein 110Th Anniversary Concert And Celebration Of 10Th Anniversary Of German Unification October 28, 2000. n.p.: Dayton, Ohio : The Verein, 2000.

Deutsch-Amerikanische Geschichtsblätter. / Deutsch-Amerikanische Historische Gesellschaft Von Illinois. Chicago : Die Gesellschaft, 1901.

Der Deutsche Pionier : Erinnerungen Aus Dem Pionierleben Der Deutschen in Amerika. Cincinnati, Ohio : Deutschen Pionier-Verein, 1869-1887, 1869.

Di Grazia, Donna Marie. *Nineteenth-Century Choral Music*. New York ; London : Routledge, 2013.

Dictionary of American Naval Fighting Ships [Electronic Resource]. Washington, D.C. : Dept. of the Navy, Naval Historical Center, 2004.

Dodge, Andrew R., and Betty K. Koed. *Biographical Directory of the United States Congress, 1774-2005 : The Continental Congress, September 5, 1774, to October 21, 1788, and the Congress of the United States, from the First through the One Hundred Eighth Congresses,*

March 4, 1789, to January 3, 2005, Inclusive. Washington, D.C. : U.S. G.P.O. : May be purchased from the Supt. of Docs., U.S. G.P.O., 2005.

Drury, A. W. *History of the City of Dayton and Montgomery County, Ohio, by A.W. Drury*. Chicago, S.J. Clarke Pub. Co., 1909.

---. *The Life of Rev. Philip William Otterbein, Founder of the Church of the United Brethren in Christ*. Whitefish, Mont. : Kessinger Pub., 2008.

---. *The Life of Rev. Philip William Otterbein, Founder of the Church of the United Brethren in Christ*. Dayton, Ohio : United Brethren Pub. House, 1890, 1884, 1890.

Durnbaugh, Donald F. "The German Journalist and the Dunker Love-Feast." *Pennsylvania Folklife* 18.2 (1968): 40-8.

Edgar, John F., and Patricia Ann Schlipf. *Pioneer Life in Dayton and Vicinity, 1796-1840*. Columbus, Ohio : Genealogy Services, State Library of Ohio, 2000.

Everts, L. H. *Combination Atlas Map of Montgomery County, Ohio / Compiled, Drawn and Published from Personal Examinations and Surveys by L.H. Everts*. Philadelphia : L.H. Everts, 1875.

---. *Combination Atlas Map of Montgomery County, Ohio / Compiled, Drawn and Published from Personal Examinations and Surveys by L.H. Everts*. Philadelphia : Hunter Press, 1875 ; Evansville, IN : Unigraphic, Inc., 1972.

Faust, Albert Bernhardt. *The German Element in the United States*. Boston and New York, Houghton Mifflin company, 1909.

---. *The German Element in the United States : With Special Reference to its Political, Moral, Social, and Educational Influence*. Baltimore, MD : Clearfield Company, 1995.

Fetters, Paul R. *Trials and Triumphs : A History of the Church of the United Brethren in Christ*. Huntington, Ind. : Church of the United Brethren in Christ, Dept. of Church Services, 1984.

Ford, Henry A., and Kate B. Ford. *History of Cincinnati, Ohio : With Illustrations and Biographical Sketches / Compiled by Henry A. Ford and Kate B. Ford*. Cincinnati, Ohio (726 Main St., Cincinnati 45202) : Ohio Book Store, 1987.

Ford, Henry A. *Every Name Index, History of Cincinnati, Ohio : With Illustrations and Biographical Sketches, Compiled by Henry A. Ford, A.M., and Mrs. Kate B. Ford, Published by L.A. Williams & Co., Publishers, 1881*. Cincinnati, OH : Hamilton County Genealogical Society, 2005.

Fortin, Roger A. *Faith and Action : A History of the Catholic Archdiocese of Cincinnati, 1821-1996 / Roger Fortin*. Columbus : Ohio State University Press, 2002.

Frank, W. *Deutschland In Amerika, Das Einzig Rechte Ziel Aller Deutschen Auswanderer. Von W. Frank. Cassel, Ger., J. Luckhardt, 1839.* n.p.: San Francisco, R & E Research Associates, 1970.

German American, Historical Society, et al. *German American Annals.* German American Historical Society, 1903.

Germanistic Society, of America, and von Illinois Deutsche-Amerikanische Historische Gesellschaft. *Deutsch-Amerikanische Geschichtsblätter.* Die Gesellschaft, 1901.

Germantown Notes of Marcella Henry Miller. Germantown, Ohio : n.d.

Girardey, G. *Höchst Nützliches Handbuch Über Kochkunst, Fabrication Der Liqueren, Weine, Cider, Essig, etc. : Oder, Allgemeine Magasine Über Landwirthschaft Und Andere Verschidenen Beschäftigungen, Nebst Eine Vollständige Darstellung Alles Zu Fabriciren was Dem Land-, Geschäft- Oder Hausman Nothwendig Ist, Und Mit Beysatz Einer Menge Selbstgeprüfte Mittel Über Verschiedene Kränkliche Umständen, Und Physische Auslegung was Dem Menschen Als Lebensgenuss Am Besten Dienet / Verfasst Und Herausgegeben Von G. Girardey.* Cincinnati, O., 1842.

Girardey, George. *Manual of Domestic Economy, Or, House-Keeper's Guide : Comprising a very Large Collection of Original Receipts, Derived from the Practical Experience of the Author.* Dayton, O. : John Wilson, Printer, 1841.

Greve, Charles Theodore. *Centennial History of Cincinnati and Representative Citizens, by Charles Theodore Greve.* Chicago : Biographical Pub. Co., 1904.

Hanna, Charles A. *Historical Collections of Harrison County, in the State of Ohio, with Lists of the First Land-Owners, Early Marriages (to 1841), Will Records (to 1861), Burial Records of the Early Settlements, and Numerous Genealogies.* New York : Privately printed, 1900.

Hargis, Wm Michael. *Covington's Sisters of Notre Dame / Wm. Michael Hargis.* Charleston, S.C. : Arcadia Pub., 2011.

Harvey, Henry,missionary to the Shawnee Indians. *History of the Shawnee Indians.* E. Morgan & sons, 1855.

Hawes, George W. *Geo. W. Hawes' Ohio State Gazetteer and Business Directory for 1860-'61.* Indianapolis, G.W. Hawes, 1860; 2d ed, 1860.

Heinsius, Wilhelm, et al. *Allgemeines Bücher-Lexikon, Oder Vollständiges Alphabetisches Verzeichnis Der Von 1700 Bis Zu Ende ... [1892] Erschienen Bücher, Welche in Deutschland Und in Den Durch Sprache Und Literatur Damit Verwandten Ländern Gedruckt Worden Sind. Nebst Angabe Der Druckorte, Der Verleger Und Der Preise. Von Wilhelm Heinsius.* Leipzig, 1812-94, 1812.

Henkel, Paul, Frederick E. Cooper, and Clement L. Martzolff. *Rev. Paul Henkel's Journal. His Missionary Journey to the State of Ohio in 1806. Tr. from the German by Rev. F.E. Cooper ... and Ed. by Clement L. Martzolff,* 1914.

Hentz, J. P. *History of the Evangelical Lutheran Congregation in Germantown, Ohio, and Biographies of its Pastors and Founders, by J. P. Hentz.* Dayton : Christian Pub. House, 1882.

Hentz, John P. *Twin Valley : Its Settlement and Subsequent History, 1798-1882 / by J.P. Hentz.* Dayton, O. : Christian publishing house, 1883, 2001.

High Street United Brethren Church (Ohio) Ladies',Aid Society. *Good Things to Eat.* The Otterbein Press, 1915.

Hildreth, Samuel P., and Ephraim Cutler. *Biographical and Historical Memoirs of the Early Pioneer Settlers of Ohio : With Narratives of Incidents and Occurrences in 1775.* Cincinnati : H.W. Derby, 1852.

History of Cincinnati and Hamilton County, Ohio; their Past and Present, Including ... Biographies and Portraits of Pioneers and Representative Citizens, Cincinnati, S. B. Nelson, 1894.

The History of Montgomery County, Ohio : Containing a History of the County; its Townships, Cities, Towns, Schools, Churches, Chicago, W.H. Beers & Co., 1882. Evansville, IN : Unigraphic, Inc., 1973.

The History of Montgomery County, Ohio, Containing a History of the County; its Townships, Cities, Towns ... etc.; General and Local Statistics; Portraits of Early Settlers and Prominent Men; History of the Northwest Territory; History of Ohio; Map of Montgomery County, Chicago, W. H. Beers, 1882.

History of the Church of the Brethren of the Eastern District of Pennsylvania, by the Committee Appointed by District Conference. Lancaster, Pa., The New era printing company, 1915.

History of the Police Department of Dayton, Ohio : From Earliest Times to October First 1907, Roster of the Officers and Members of the Present Force, a Souvenir. Dayton, Ohio : John C. Whitaker, 1907.

Holian, Timothy J. *Over the Barrel : The Brewing History and Beer Culture of Cincinnati / Timothy J. Holian.* St. Joseph, MO 64506 (610 Tanglewood Drive) : Sudhaus Press, 2000.

Houser, Howard R. *From Blacksmith to General : General Edmund Munger and the War of 1812 in Ohio.* Centerville, Ohio : Centerville Historical Society, 1985.

---. *The Royal Rebels : The Sunderlands in America.* Centerville, Ohio : Centerville Historical Society, 1992.

---. *A Sense of Place in Centerville and Washington Township the Centerville Historical Society; [Howard R. Houser, Editor]*. Centerville, Ohio : The Society, 1977.

Hover, John C. *Memoirs of the Miami Valley / Ed. by John C. Hover ... [Et Al.]*. Chicago : Robert O. Law company, 1919; Butler County ed., 1919.

Howe, Henry. *Historical Collections of Ohio: An Encyclopedia of the State: History both General and Local, Geography with Descriptions of its Counties, Cities, and Villages, its Agricultural, Manufacturing, Mining and Business Development, Sketches of Eminent and Interesting Characters, etc., with Notes of a Tour Over it in 1886. Illustrated by about 700 Engravings. Contrasting the Ohio of 1846 with 1886-90. from Drawings by the Author in 1846 and Photographs Taken Solely for it in 1886, 1887, 1888, 1889 and 1890*. Cincinnati, O., Pub. by the state of Ohio, 1904; The Ohio centennial ed. By Henry Howe, 1904.

Index to the "Journal of German-American Studies" and the "Yearbook of German-American Studies," 1969-92 Edited by Don Heinrich Tolzmann, J. Anthony Burzle, Helmut E. Huelsbergen and William D. Keel : Reprinted from the "Journal of German-American Studies" and the "Yearbook of German-American Studies," 1980-92. Cincinnati : University of Cincinnati Libraries, 1994.

Ingersoll, Robert Green. *The Works of Robert G. Ingersoll*. New York, The Dresden pub. co., C. P. Farrell, Dresden edition, 1903.

Jahresbericht Des Vorstandes Des Deutschen Pionier-Vereins Von Cincinnati, Ohio Für Das Verwaltungsjahr. Cincinnati, O. : S. Rosenthal, 1887-1889, 1887.

Johnson, Peter Leo. *Crosier on the Frontier; a Life of John Martin Henni, Archbishop of Milwaukee*. Madison, State Historical Society of Wisconsin, 1959.

---. *Stuffed Saddlebags; the Life of Martin Kundig, Priest, 1805-1879*. Milwaukee : The Bruce Publishing Company, 1942.

Jung, Patrick J. *The Black Hawk War of 1832 / Patrick J. Jung*. Norman : University of Oklahoma Press, 2008; First paperback edition, 2008.

Karstaedt, Karl, and Don Heinrich Tolzmann. *Dayton's German Heritage : Karl Karstaedt's Golden Jubilee History of the German Pioneer Society of Dayton, Ohio*. Bowie, Md. : Heritage Books, Inc., 2001.

Klauprecht, Emil, Steven W. Rowan, and Don Heinrich Tolzmann. *Cincinnati, Or, the Mysteries of the West : Emil Klauprecht's German-American Novel / Translated by Steven Rowan ; Edited by Don Heinrich Tolzmann*. New York : Peter Lang, 1996.

Klauprecht, Emil, and Don Heinrich Tolzmann. *German Chronicle in the History of the Ohio Valley and its Capital City Cincinnati in Particular*. Bowie, Md. : Heritage Books, 1992.

Klauprecht, Emil. *Deutsche Chronik in Der Geschichte Des Ohio-Thales : Und Seiner Hauptstadt Cincinnati in's Besondere : Umfassend Eine Ausführliche Darstellung Der Abentheuer, Ansiedlungen Und Des Allgemeinen Wirkens Der Deutschen Im Flussgebiete Von Der Entdeckung Des Mississippi-Thales an Bis Auf Unsere Tage / Zusammengestellt Nach Authentischen Quellen Von Emil Klauprecht*. Cincinnati, Ohio : G. Hof & M.A. Jacobi, 1864. Knepper, George W. *The Official Ohio Lands Book / Written by George W. Knepper ; Cover Art by Annette Salrin*. Columbus, Ohio : Auditor of State, 2002; 1st paperback ed, 2002.

Knipp, Dianne Dodds. *Wapakoneta / Dianne Dodds Knipp with the Downtown Wapakoneta Partnership*. Charleston, SC : Arcadia Pub., 2010.

Körner, Gustav Philipp, and Don Heinrich Tolzmann. *The German Element in the Ohio Valley : Ohio, Kentucky & Indiana*. Baltimore, Md. : Clearfield, 2011.

Lamech, Brother, Johann Peter Miller, and J. M. Hark. *Chronicon Ephratense : A History of Seventh Day Baptists / Brother Lamech*. Bedford, Mass. : Applewood Books, 2009.

Lamott, John H. *History of the Archdiocese of Cincinnati, 1821-1921*. New York : F. Pustet Co., 1921.

Light, Esther, and Mady Ransdell. *Miamisburg, Ohio, the Story of our Town : A Collection of Historical Essays from 1818 to 1993*. Miamisburg, Ohio : Miamisburg Lions Club, 1993.

Littell, Robert S., and Eliakim Littell. *Littell's Living Age*. Boston, T. H. Carter & Co., 1844.

Löher, Franz von. *Geschichte Und Zustände Der Deutschen in Amerika*. Cincinnati, Eggers und Wulkop, 1847.

Lowry, R. E. *History of Preble County, Ohio: Her People, Industries and Institutions by R.E. Lowry. with Biographical Sketches of Representative Citizens and Genealogical Records of Old Families*. Indianapolis, B.F. Bowen, 1915.

Mansfield, John Brandt. *The History of Tuscarawas County, Ohio, Containing a History of the County; its Townships, Towns, Churches, Schools, etc; General and Local Statistics; Military Record; Portraits of Early Settlers and Prominent Men; History of the Northwest Territory; History of Ohio; Miscellaneous Matters*, Chicago, Warner, Beers, 1884.

Martzolff, Clement Luther. *Caleb Atwater. By Clement L. Martzolff*. n.p.: 1905.

McBride, James. *Pioneer Biography : Sketches of the Lives of some of the Early Settlers of Butler County, Ohio*. Cincinnati : R. Clark, 1869-71, 1973.

Medvei, Victor Cornelius, and Victor Cornelius Medvei. *The History of Clinical Endocrinology : A Comprehensive Account of Endocrinology from Earliest Times to the Present Day / Victor*

Cornelius Medvei. Carnforth, Lancs., UK ; Pearl River, N.Y., USA : Parthenon Pub. Group, 1993.

Menzel, Gottfried. *Die Vereinigten Staaten Von Nordamerika, Mit Besonderer Rucksicht Auf Deutsche Auswanderung Dahin Nach Eigener Anschauung Beschrieben Von Gottfried Menzel*. Berlin, G. Reimer, 1853.

Merrill, Ellen C. *Germans of Louisiana*. Gretna : Pelican Pub., 2005.

Miami Township / 175th Anniversary Committee. Charleston, SC : Arcadia Pub., 2004.

Mikesell, Shirley Keller. *Early Settlers of Montgomery County, Ohio / Compiled and Edited by Shirley Keller Mikesell*. Bowie, MD : Heritage Books, 1991-1993.

---. *Early Settlers of Montgomery County, Ohio : Genealogical Abstracts from Common Pleas Court Records, Civil and Probate / Compiled and Edited by Shirley Keller Mikesell*. Bowie, MD : Heritage Books, 1992.

---. *Early Settlers of Montgomery County, Ohio, Volume III : Genealogical Abstracts from Marriage and Divorce Records 1803-1827, Early Deeds Recorded Late, Election Abstracts, Obituary of an Early Settler / Compiled and Edited by Shirley Keller Mikesell*. Bowie, Md. : Heritage Books, Inc., 1993.

Miller, Daniel, and Don Heinrich Tolzmann. *Early German-American Newspapers / Daniel Miller's History ; Edited by Don Heinrich Tolzmann*. Bowie, Md. : Heritage Books, 2001.

Miller, Marcella Henry. *Facts About Germantown from 1798-1950*. Germantown, Ohio : Historical Society of Germantown, n.d.

---. A History of Germantown, Ohio, and Biographical Sketches. Germantown, Ohio : n.p., 1962.

Milligan, Fred J. *Ohio's Founding Fathers / Fred J. Milligan*. New York : IUniverse, 2003.

Mitter, Sonja. *German-American Organizational Culture in Present-Day Madison*, 1991.

Montgomery County Ohio 1990 : A History Written by the People of Montgomery County, Ohio ... / Compiled and Published by the Montgomery History Planning Committee. Dallas, Tex. : Taylor Pub. Co., 1990.

Newcom Tavern. Dayton, Ohio : Carillon Park, 1965.

Newcom Tavern at Carillon Historical Park. Dayton, Ohio : Carillon Historical Park, 1996.

Nunley, Debbie, and Karen Jane Elliott. *A Taste of Ohio History : A Guide to Historic Eateries and their Recipes*. Winston-Salem, N.C. : John F. Blair, 2007.

Ogle, Maureen. *Ambitious Brew : The Story of American Beer / Maureen Ogle*. Orlando : Harcourt, 2006.

Ohio Auditor, of State, and Joseph W. Tannehill. *Ohio Interrogation Points*. The F. J. Heer printing co, 1917.

Ohio Historic Places Dictionary. Hamburg, MI : State History Publications, 2008.

Ohio History. Kent, Ohio : Kent State University Press, 2007.

Ohio Source Records from the Ohio Genealogical Quarterly. Baltimore, Md. : Reprinted for Clearfield by Genealogical Pub. Co., 2007.

Ohio Valley History : The Journal of the Cincinnati Historical Society. Cincinnati, Ohio : Cincinnati Museum Center, 2001.

Onuf, Peter S. *Statehood and Union : A History of the Northwest Ordinance / Peter S. Onuf*. Bloomington : Indiana University Press, 1987.

Our Landmarks. n.p.: Germantown, Ohio : Historical Society of Germantown, 1978.

Overman, William D. *Ohio Place Names : The Origin of the Names of Over 500 Ohio Cities, Towns, and Villages*. Akron, Ohio : s.n., 1951 (Ann Arbor, Mich. : Edwards Bros.), 1951.

Owen, Lorrie K. *Dictionary of Ohio Historic Places / [Lorrie K. Owen, Editor]*. St. Clair Shores, MI : Somerset Publishers, Inc., 1999.

Patterson, family. *Patterson Family Papers, 1785-1960*. n.p.: 1785. Wright State University Library Catalog.

Paull, Elisabeth Maxwell. *Paull-Irwin*. T. R. Marvin & son, printers. Priv. print, 1915.

Pearce, John Ed, and Richard Nugent. *The Ohio River / John Ed Pearce ; Photographs by Richard Nugent*. Lexington, Ky. : University Press of Kentucky, 1989.

Pennsylvania-German Society. *Proceedings and Addresses*. Pennsylvania-German Society, 1891.

Perkins, James H., John Mason Peck, and James R. Albach. *Annals of the West*. W.S. Haven, book and job printer, 1837.

Perrin, William Henry. *History of Cass County, Illinois*. Chicago : O. L. Baskin, 1882, 1975.

Petticrew, Gary L. "St. John's Evangelical Lutheran Church, Miamisburg, Montgomery County, Ohio: 195 Years." 2011. <http://tinyurl.com/p6eqcqt>

Phin, John. "Open Air Grape Culture : A Practical Treatise on the Garden and Vineyard Culture of the Vine, and the Manufacture of Domestic Wine : Designed for the use of Amateurs and Others in the Northern and Middle States : Profusely Illustrated with New Engravings from Carefully Executed Designs, Verified by Direct Practice." New York : : C.M. Saxton, Agricultural Book Publisher, 1862.

Pinney, Thomas. *A History of Wine in America from the Beginnings to Prohibition / Thomas Pinney.* Berkeley : University of California Press, 1989.

Pocock, Emil. "Slavery and Freedom in the Early Republic: Robert Patterson's Slaves in Kentucky and Ohio, 1804-1819." *Ohio Valley History* 6.1 (2006): 3-26.

Pohlmann, Marcus D., and Linda Vallar Whisenhunt. *Student's Guide to Landmark Congressional Laws on Civil Rights / Marcus D. Pohlmann and Linda Vallar Whisenhunt.* Westport, Conn. : Greenwood Press, 2002.

Portrait and Biographical Album of Fulton County. Fulton County Historical and Genealogical Society, 1979.

Quarterly Publications of the Historical and Philosophical Society of Ohio, 1906-1923, v. 1-18. Cincinnati, Ohio 1906-23, 1906.

Randall, E. O., and William Henry Venable. *Ohio Centennial Anniversary Celebration at Chillicothe, may 20-21, 1903 : Under the Auspices of the Ohio State Archæological and Historical Society : Complete Proceedings.* Columbus, : Ohio State Archaeological and Historical Society, 1903 (F.J. Heer), 1903.

Rattermann, H. A., and Mary Edmund Spanheimer. *The Letters of Heinrich Armin Rattermann to the German-American Poet-Priest, John E. Rothensteiner; Edited with Notes and Introduction by Sister Mary Edmund Spanheimer, with a Foreword by Albert B. Faust.* Joliet, Ill., College of St. Francis, 1938.

Rattermann, H. A., and Don Heinrich Tolzmann. *Spring Grove and its Creator : H. A. Rattermann's Biography of Adolph Strauch.* Cincinnati, OH : The Ohio Book Store, 1988.

Rattermann, H. A. *Abhandlungen.* Selbstverlag des Verfassers, 1912.

---. *Gesammelte Ausgewählte Werke / Von H. A. Rattermann.* Cincinnati, O. : H. A. Rattermann, 1906-1912, 1906.

Records of the American Catholic Historical Society of Philadelphia. Philadelphia : American Catholic Historical Society of Philadelphia, 1887-2000, 1886.

Reed's Illustrated History of Montgomery County : From its Earliest Recollections to the Present Time : Complete Compilation of the Present most Important Business Interests, with Faithful Illustrations. Dayton, Ohio : H. S. Reed, 1995.

Ritter, Frédéric Louis. *Music in America*. New York : Johnson Reprint Corp., 1970.

Rogers, Gregory Parker. *Cincinnati's Hyde Park : A Queen City Gem / Gregory Parker Rogers*. Charleston, SC : History Press, 2010.

Rupp, I. D. *A Collection of Upwards of Thirty Thousand Names of German, Swiss, Dutch, French, and Other Immigrants in Pennsylvania from 1727-1776, with a Statement of the Names of Ships, Whence they Sailed, and the Date of their Arrival at Philadelphia, Chronologically Arranged Together with the Necessary Historical and Other Notes, by Prof. I. Daniel Rupp*. Philadelphia, I. Kohler, 1876; 2d. rev. and enl. ed. With German translation, 1965.

Salisbury,Pa.New Jerusalem Union Church of Western Salisbury., and John Baer Stoudt. *History of Jerusalem Lutheran and Reformed Church of Western Salisbury*. H.R. Haas, 1911.

Salzbacher, Joseph. *Meine Reise Nach Nord-Amerika Im Jahr 1842*. In commission bei Wimmer, Schmidt & Leo, 1845.

Schlipf, Patricia Ann, and John F. Edgar. *Complete Name Index to John F. Edgar's 1896 Pioneer Life in Dayton and Vicinity / Compiled by Patricia A. Schlipf*. Dayton, OH : Montgomery County Chapter, Ohio Genealogical Society, 1994.

Schmidlin, Thomas W., and Jeanne Appelhans Schmidlin. *Thunder in the Heartland : A Chronicle of Outstanding Weather Events in Ohio / Thomas W. Schmidlin and Jeanne Appelhans Schmidlin*. Kent, Ohio : Kent State University Press, 1996.

Schonberg, Marcia. *Ohio History / Marcia Schonberg*. Chicago, Ill. : Heinemann, 2010.

Sell, Donna-Christine, and Dennis F. Walle. *Guide to the Heinrich A. Rattermann Collection of German-American Manuscripts*. Urbana : University of Illinois Library, 1979.

A Sense of Community : In Celebration of the Bicentennial of Centerville/Washington Township, 1796-1996 / the Centerville Historical Society. New York : American Heritage Custom Publishing, 1996.

Sharts, Joseph W. *Biography of Dayton*. Dayton, O., Miami Valley Socialist, 1922.

Shea, John Dawson Gilmary. *The Hierarchy of the Catholic Church in the United States Embracing Sketches of all the Archbishops and Bishops...also, an Account of the Plenary Councils of Baltimore and a Brief History of the Church in the United States*. New York : Office of Catholic Publications, 1886.

Shea, John Gilmary. *History of the Catholic Church in the United States*. New York : J. G. Shea, 1890-1892, 1890.

Shuey, Dennis Boeshore. *History of the Shuey Family in America, from 1732 to 1876, by D.B. Shuey, A.M.* Lancaster, Pa., Pub. for members of the family, by the author, 1876.

Skocpol, Theda, and Morris P. Fiorina. *Civic Engagement in American Democracy / Theda Skocpol, Morris P. Fiorina, Editors.* Washington, D.C. : Brookings Institution Press ; New York : Russell Sage Foundation, 1999.

Smith, Clifford Neal. *Early Nineteenth-Century German Settlers in Ohio (mainly Cincinnati and Environs), Kentucky, and Other States / Clifford Neal Smith.* Baltimore, MD. : Clearfield, 2004.

Smith, William Henry. *The First Fugitive Slave Case of Record in Ohio.* Washington, D.C. : American Historical Association, 1950.

Sobel, Robert. *Biographical Directory of the United States Executive Branch, 1774-1989 / Robert Sobel, Editor-in-Chief.* New York : Greenwood Press, 1990.

Spanheimer, Mary Edmund, and Don Heinrich Tolzmann. *The German Pioneer Legacy : The Life and Work of Heinrich A. Rattermann.* Oxford ; New York : P. Lang, 2004.

Spanheimer, Mary Edmund. *Heinrich Armin Rattermann, German-American Author, Poet, and Historian, 1832-1923, by Sister Mary Edmund Spanheimer.* Washington, D.C., The Catholic University of America, 1937.

St. Joseph's Orphan Society / Children's Treatment Center Records, 1849-2004. n.p.: n.d.

Steele, Robert Wilbur, and Mary Davies Steele. *Early Dayton; with Important Facts and Incidents from the Founding of the City of Dayton, Ohio, to the Hundredth Anniversary, 1796-1896.* Dayton, O., W.J. Shuey, 1896.

Strassburger, Ralph Beaver, and William John Hinke. *Pennsylvania German Pioneers : A Publication of the Original Lists of Arrivals in the Port of Philadelphia from 1727 to 1808.* Camden, Mo. : Picton Press, 1992.

Surminski, Marc. *Heinrich Armin Rattermann Und "Der Deutsche Pionier".* n.p.: 1988.

Taylor, Charles Lewis. "Early Presbyterians in Montgomery County." *Smithfield Review* 14 (2010): 5-21.

Thornton, Richard H. *An American Glossary; being an Attempt to Illustrate Certain Americanisms upon Historical Principles. with an Introd. by Margaret M. Bryant.* New York, F. Ungar Pub. Co., 1962.

Tilton, Liz. *Cincinnati's Historic Findlay Market / Liz Tilton.* Charleston, SC : Arcadia Pub., 2009.

Tolzmann, Don Heinrich, H. A. Rattermann, and Gustav Philipp Körner. *Kentucky's German Pioneers : H.A. Rattermann's History / Translated and Edited by Don Heinrich Tolzmann.* Bowie, Md. : Heritage Books, 2001.

---. *Cincinnati's German Heritage.* Bowie, MD : Heritage Books, 1994.

---. *Festschrift for the German-American Tricentennial Jubilee, Cincinnati, 1983.* Cincinnati : Cincinnati Historical Society, 1982.

---. *German Cincinnati / Don Heinrich Tolzmann.* Charleston, SC : Arcadia, 2005.

---. *The German-American Experience / Don Heinrich Tolzmann.* Amherst, NY : Humanity Books, 2000.

---. *The German-American Forty-Eighters, 1848-1998 / Don Heinrich Tolzmann, Editor.* Indianapolis : Max Kade German-American Center, Indiana University-Purdue University at Indianapolis : Indiana German Heritage Society, 1998.

---. *German-American Literature / Edited by Don Heinrich Tolzmann.* Metuchen, N.J. : Scarecrow Press, 1977.

Troup, Erin. *Obituary Translations For Gedenk-Blaetter : Sonntagsblatt Zur Volkszeitung : A Selection Of Obituaries From The Sunday Supplement To The Daytoner Volks-Zeitung / Translated By Erin Troup.* n.p.: Dayton, Ohio, 2005.

Vaughn, Stephen L. *Encyclopedia of American Journalism / Stephen L. Vaughn, Editor.* New York : Routledge, 2008.

Willen, Henry. *Henry Armin Rattermann's Life and Poetical Work, by Henry Willen.* Philadelphia, 1939.

Wittke, Carl Frederick, *The History of the State of Ohio, Edited by Carl Wittke. Published Under the Auspices of the Ohio State Archaeological and Historical Society. Publication Committee: H. Lindley, Chairman, Carl Wittke, William Utter.* Columbus, O., 1941-1944.

Wolpers, Charles O. *Charles O. Wolpers Papers, 1817-1865,* 1817.

Yoder, Don. *Pennsylvania German Church Records of Births, Baptisms, Marriages, Burials, etc. : From the Pennsylvania German Society Proceedings and Addresses / with an Introduction by Don Yoder.* Baltimore : Genealogical Pub. Co., 1983.

Index

Names of individuals, important events, recurring themes, cities, counties, townships, and buildings mentioned in the main text are indexed. Counties and Townships are indexed under their name and not under the state they belong to. German words appear in italics. If the text describes a "first" event, this is marked in the index for ease of use. Names and references in the *Notes* and *Bibliography* sections are not indexed.

A
Accola, O.J. 40
Adam, Edmund 16
Adams 6
Adler, J. 33
African descent 16
Agniel 45
Ahrens 46
Aigenbrecht, Friedrich 16
Albrecht, C. 22
Allen County 5
Ambos, Mrs. 50
America 51, 52
Americans 53
Anglicized 10
Anglo-Americans 6, 9, 10, 17, 18, 25, 42
Appomatox Channel 50
Archbishop of Cincinnati 25,
Archbishop of Milwaukee 24
Archer, Benjamin 5
Arenz, Franz 45
Arnetz, Thomas 3
artist family 27
attorney 3,
Atwater, Caleb 52
Auglaize County 5
Austria 38

B
Bachmann 10
Badin, Stephan Theodor 24
baker 31, 41

Banest, Hans 16
Bansell, Hans 6
Bär, Heinrich 43
Bartels, G. 22
Battle of Stillman's Run 45
Bauer, C.R. 37
Baumann (Bowman)
  Bernard 6
  David 23
  C.L. 37
  Christian 8
  Christina 17
Baumheckel, Franz 37
Bauzer (Bowser, Bouzer), Daniel 17
Beck 7
  Philipp 33
  Samuel 16
Beckel's Hall 33
Beissel, Conrad 44
Beisselites 43
Belgian 24
Bene Jeschurun Temple 40
Benz, Hans 9
Berk
  F.W. 33
  Friedrich Wilhelm 31
Bert, F.W. 30
Best, H. 30
Bettelon, Johann 34, 35, 36
Biechler 44
Bierfritz 26
Big Bear Creek 11
bilingual 2
Bishop of Alton, Illinois 24, 25

Bittmann, Johann 36
Black Betty 13
Black Hawk
  chief 45
  War 45
block houses 2, 3, 4
Block, Isaac 33
Blücher. Prince 49
Bohlender, Johann 30, 37
Böhm
  Heinrich 2
  Martin 23
Bonebraker (Beinbrecher), Georg 23
book printer 21, 47
Boonbrick (Beinbrecht) 9
Born, F. Reverend 40
botany 50, 51
Bourne, Wm. 27, 28
Boyer, Jacob 27, 28
brandy distillery 25, 41
Braun, Jacob 16
Braunschweiger, Jacob 33
Breidenbach, D.G. 37
brewer(s) 38, 44
brewery 25, 26, 41
  business 41
  first 25
  Germantown 25
bricklayer 20, 35
Bromwell & Kielmeier Manufacturing C. 42
Brunner, Louis A. 20
Bummelreisen eines Lunch-Reporters 37
Bummerschein, Wilhelm 43
Burkhalter, Christian 49
business 21, 25, 36, 37, 41, 42, 47
Butler
  County 3, 22, 42
  Township 7, 19
Buttler, Paul D. 18
Butz, Lorenz, Jr. 37

C

cabin 8, 17, 20,
canal 21, 30,
Canary, Carl W. 37

Captain A. Kothe tavern 11, 29
Carillon Historical Park 3
carpenter, first 3, 9
Catholic
  clergymen 24
  priest, first 24
Catholic(s) 24, 38, 39, 40, 41
Catrow
  Michael 43
  Zebulon 43
Centre Street, Germantown 25
ceremony 12, 33
Chase, Salmon P. 52
Chenoweth, Wm. 11
Chevalier, Anton 6
child, white, first 9
choir 11, 28, 29, 45
cholera 21
church
  first 9
  music 27
  services 7, 24
cigar factory 41
Cincinnati Water Works 50
Cincinnatier Volksblatt 36
Cincinnatier Volksfreund 37
cistern-prison 16
citizens 3, 4, 42, 43, 52
Claussen, Peter 16
Clay Township 9, 19
Clegg 27
  brothers 29
  John 28
  Josias 28
  Samuel 28
Clemer 9
clergymen 19, 24, 40
clerk 5, 33, 37
Cohn, M. 33,
Columbus-Haus 41
Columbus Männerchor 31
Congregation of the House of Jacob 40
Congress 2, 3, 15
constitution 16, 33
contract 1, 2
Cooper 4

138

Daniel C. 1, 17
Corwin, Thomas 49, 52
county poor house 40
court
   documents 13, 18
   files 3
   of law 3
   prosecutor 5, 13
   session, first 5
Cromwell 18
Curtner, Christ 13
custom 42, 43, 52, 53

D

Darke County 5, 36
Darst
   Abraham 17
   Johannes 23
daughters 17
Davis
   John 1
   Thomas 1
Dayton Anzeiger 37
Dayton Grocers' Baking Company 6
Dayton Harmonie 33
Dayton, Jonathan 23
Dayton Township 8
Dayton Turner Society 34
Daytoner Harmonie 33
Daytoner Turnverein 34
Daytoner Volkszeitung 37
death, first 7
Dechant
   Christoph 20
   Friedrich 44
   Rev. 20, 21, 25
Decheron 8, 21, 22
Defiance County 5
Dein, Philipp 35
Deis, Georg 37
Delacourt 37
Delaware 1, 2
Democratic Party 49
Denis, J.R. 20
Der Deutsch-Amerikaner 21

Der Hochwächter 21
Der Protestant 21
Deschler, Joseph 31, 33
Deutsche Sängerbund von Nord Amerika 31
Deutsche Evangelische Gemeinschaftskirche 40
Deutsche Journal 36
Deutsche National Garde Bande 28, 29
Deutsche Nationalgarde 28
Deutsche Pionier-Verein 41, 42
Deutsche Republikaner 36
Deutschland in Amerika 52
Die Volksbühne 21
Diehl, Wilhelm 16
Dietz
   Johann 30
   Johann Peter 36, 37
Dill, Johann C. 22
Dilley 7
Dilts, Franz 13
Discher, Katharina 41
doctor 7, 29, 45, 47, 50, 51
doctorate degree of Medicine 51
Dodds 6
Döpker, G. 22
Dorough, John 1
Dötschmen 42
Dreher 10, 11
Dreifaltigkeits-Schule 38
Dunlap, John 1
Dunlavy, Francis 5
Dutch 24
Dutchman 5

E

Eagle Creek 45
East Third Street, Dayton 36
Ebel, August 33
education 22, 33, 37, 50, 53
Egry, Captain Dr. 29
Elizabeth Hospital 38
Emanuel Church, Dayton 24
Emerich
   Christopher 11

Wilhelm 8
Emmanuel Catholic Church 38
Emmerich
  Christoph 44
  brothers 45
Encyclopaedia Americana 47
Engel (Eagle, Engle), Fabian 16
Englert, G. 33
English 7, 8, 9, 18, 19, 22, 24, 25, 40, 42, 43
entertainment 19, 27, 28, 29
epidemic 27, 51
Ephrata Cloister 44
Episcopal Church 18, 23
Erhardt, Martin 13
Espich, Christian Dr. 21, 50
Etter, Michael 23
Euchenhöfer, Friedrich 41
Euchenhofer, Mr. 29
Eversole, Josias 27, 28, 29
Ewing, John 5

F

farmer 9, 12, 17, 20, 29
Father of Forensic Science 51
Feigst, Johann 37
Felix, Peter 3, 16,
Ferneding
  Heinrich 41,
  Henry Brewery 41
Ferrell, Daniel 1
festivals 11, 29, 35
Fifth Street, Dayton 4, 32
Findlay, James General 43, 53
Fink 52
Finkeln 52,
First German Baptist Church 40
First Reformed Church 19
Fischer
  Adam 14
  Daniel H. 8, 16
  E. 40
  Mrs. 13
Flickersdorf, Joseph 7
Flock, Johannes 16

Flory, Emanuel 9
flourmill(s) 9, 38, 41
first 7
Flotow, Friedrich von 34
Folkerth (Volkert?)
  Johannes 13, 16
  Justice of Peace 28
Forty-Eighters 30, 37
founder(s) 1, 8, 13, 14, 34, 35, 41, 50
frame house, first 9
Frank
  Johann Peter 50, 51
  Wilhelm Dr. 50, 51, 52
Franklin Hain No. 2 35
Franklin House 29
Franz, Heinrich 29
freedom 14, 15
Freemason 45
Frey, Heinrich Joseph 23
Freyberger 10
Fritsch, Franz 33
Fritz Loge of the Druids 35
Fritz, Christian 16
Fröhliche Botschafter 37
Front Street, Dayton 3
Frybarger 10
Fulcus 8
Fulton County 5

G

Gahagan, Wm. 1
Gaisser, Jacob 33
Gans, Dr. 28
Gärtner (Cartner)
  Christopher 17
  Johann 13
Gebhard 13
Gebhardt, Emanuel 21
Gebhart
  Daniel 6
  Philipp 6
Gedenkblätter 31, 38
Geisbauer, Karl 26
Gemünn, Wilhelm 28, 29
Gerhard, Johann 13

German
  amateur theatre, first 33
  barn, German-style, first 7
  Catholic Orphan Society 41
  Catholic Parish, first 24
  congregation 19, 24
  doctors 29
  engineer 50
  language, 2, 9, 20
  national character 11
  origin 21
  press 36
  school 9
  settlement 6
  taverns 18
  teacher 29
  theatre 34
  writers 21
German Methodist Preacher 2
German National Guard 28, 29
German newspaper, first 21, 36, 37, 47
German Pioneer Society of Dayton 36, 42
German Protestant 23, 40
German Protestant-Lutheran 21
German publication house 25
German Reformed Church 19, 28, 30
German Reformed Preacher, first 19
German Riflemen Company 29
German Sisters of Notre Dame 38
German St. Johannes Church 40
German Township 20, 43
German Whigs 28
German-American 10, 21
German-Lutheran 8, 9, 21, 22, 40
Germann, Friedrich 26
Germany 10, 11, 20, 22, 37, 43, 45, 47, 50
  Achem by Rehstatt, Baden 30
  Alsace-Lorraine 25, 37, 41
  Bavaria 20, 36, 46, 50
  Bielefeld 52
  Braunschweig 27, 46
  Bremen 44
  Cuxhaven at the Weser 22
  Diepholz by Hannover 44
  Dinklage, Oldenburg 41
  Düsseldorf 50
  Elsass 16
  Fort Ollmütz 53
  Frankfurt am Main 36, 47
  Glan-Münchweiler 31
  Göttingen 47
  Hannover 22, 27, 29, 44
  Heidelberg 51
  Hesse-Darmstadt 37
  Hessian Oldendorf 30
  Jena 47
  Kingdom of Würtemberg 21, 41
  Kurpfalz 50
  Müsbach 42
  Neu-Wied 49
  Oldenburg 41
  Rastatt 50, 51
  Remscheid, Duchy of Berg 45
  Rhenisch-Bavaria 31
  Rhineland Palatinate 28, 29, 36
  Rothenburg ob der Tauber 46, 47
  Sigmaringen 37
  St. Johann by Saarbrücken 25, 26
  Steinweiler Rhineland Palatinate 29, 36
  Urach near Reutlingen 21
  Walddeck 34
  Westphalia 7
  Wilna 51
  Wolfenbüttel 46
  Würtemberg 21, 41
  Würzburg 44
  Zweibrücken 1
Getter, Johann G. 40
Gewert, Johannes 3
Geyer (Guier)
Girardey 42
Glaßmeier, Abraham 1, 2
Goß, Salomon 1, 2
Götz, F.J. 40
Grand Jury 16, 17
Great Miami River 2, 6,
Greter, Fritz 33
Gripe
  Jakob 8
  Reinhart 9
grist mill, first 8
grocery store, first 9, 29, 45

Groneweg 52
Großkurdt, August 22
Gruber 25
   Jacob 22
Gunkel (Gunckel), Phillip 8, 13, 21
Gutheil, Karl 33

H

Haberstich
   Philipp 33
   Wilhelm 30, 31
Hahne, Johann F. 24, 40
Hähnle, Johann 8
Haick, Hanns 16
Hamer 2
Hamilton County 2, 3, 5, 14
Hammer
   Salomon 1
   Thomas 1
   Wilhelm 2, 17
Harbor of Baltimore 22
Hardorf, Andreas 22
Hardorff, Andreas 22
Harmonie Dayton 33, 34
Harries 7
Harrison Township 7, 8, 19
Harrison, General 52
Harter, Jacob 16
Harugari Lodge 35
Hauser 9
Heck, Jacob 13
Hehr, Johann 29
Heidrich, Elisabeth 9
Heinke, Christoph Heinrich Daniel 22, 25
Henkel, Andreas 20, 21
Henni, Johann Martin 24, 25
Henrich, Ludwig Dr. 46, 47
Henry County 5
Herchelrode, Christian 42
Hergenröther, Wilhelm 33
Herrentisch 43, 46, 49
Hermann, Heinrich 30
Herrmann & Herchelrode Manufacturing Co. 42
Hessian soldiers 43

Hildebrand, Abraham 16
historian 25, 52
Höfer, J. Ch. 33
Hoffmann, Georg 33
Hole
   Isaias 7
   J. Dr. 7
   Jakob 6
Hole's Creek 11
Hole's Station 7, 11, 16
Holland, Johann 8
Holt, Hieronymous 16
Holy Trinity Church 38, 39, 40
homestead 20
Hormel, Louis 28
hospital 29, 38
house 2, 3, 4, 8, 9, 11, 12, 14, 17, 25, 29, 30, 33, 37, 40, 41, 43
   first 4
Huber (Hoover), Daniel 7
Huesmann, Ludwig 30, 31,33, 34
Huet, Heinrich 6
Huey, Norbert 13
Huston Hall 34
Hutfeld 7
hymns, German 27

I

identity 25, 27, 53
Illinois
   Alton 24, 25
   Beards Ferry 45
   Beardstown 45
   Chicago 33, 38
immigrant(s) 17, 50, 52
Indian(s) 1, 4, 7, 9, 11, 12, 45, 52
   captivity 7
Indiana
   Indianapolis 33
   Fort Wayne 45
   Madison 25
   Vincennes 15
Infirmary, Dayton 38
instrumental music 27
instruments 27, 28, 29, 34

insurance 25, 42
intellectuals 52
Irish 2
ironworks 42
itinerant preacher 22

J

Jacob, Richard 28
Jackson Township 9, 19
Jahrling, Peter 33
Jaunt
  Georg 6
  Heinrich 7
Jefferson Township 8, 11, 19
Jefferson, President 9
Jenison-Walworth, Franz 50
Jenison, Count 50, 51
Jenner, A.E. 37
Jersey man 2
Jewish Temple of Jeshurun 39
Johantgen, P. 37
Johnson 37
Johnston, John 52
Jones, Abijah 7
Jordan, Friedrich 16
Jugend-Pilger 37
jungle 17, 45
Junker
  Father 24
  Heinrich Damian 24, 25
justice 5, 14, 28, 46
Justice of the Peace 13, 15, 17, 28, 46

K

Kaste, Conrad 16
Kaufmann, Johann 40
Keck
  Jacob 9
  Michael 9
Keiser, Bernard 16
Kelse 7
Kentucky
  Blue Licks 7
  Convington 26
  Hinkston Creek 49
  Lexington 8, 16
  Louisville 21, 26, 27, 31
  Scott County 45
Keßling, Johannes 23
Kielmeier, C.H. 42
Kienzle, Jacob, Sr. 9
Kimmel 10
Kindelbier 11
Kinzer, Heinrich 13
Kirchner, Jacob 6, 11, 21
Kirchner's Tavern 12
Kistner 35
Klein
  Adam 28, 29
  Johann 28
Kleine Schulgrammatik 47
Kleine, J.P. 40
Knaub, Wilhelm 37
Knecht, Christ 28, 30,
Kneisly, Dr. 27, 28,
Köhne, Jakob 43, 44, 45, 46, 47, 49, 51, 52
König, Joseph (King) 9
Kothe, Captain 11, 29
Krehe, Johannes 31
Kreher, H. 33
Kreib, Daniel 17
Kreutzer, Conradin 32
Kronemann, Wilhelm 35
Küfer, Joseph 7
Kugler, Adam 16
Kuhlmann, Louis Captain 31, 34
Kumler, Henry Jr. 23
Kümmel 10
Kummler 43
  Heinrich, Jr. 23
Kundig, Martin 24, 25
Kuns 10
Kuntz 10
  Elias 20
  Georg 6
  Jacob 8, 43
Kunz
  Georg 16
  Jacob 9

L

Lack, Andreas 16
Lafayette, General 53
Lagerbier 25
Lake Superior 51
Lamarche 36
Lamb 6
Lambertine 10
Lammers, David 17
landowner, first 3, 8, 9
Langstedt, Dr. 34
Laubach, H.H. 37, 40
Lauer, J. 33
Ledermann
   Heinrich 16
   Johannes 9
legal matter 2
Lehmann, Benjamin 16
Lehmus
   Christian Balthasar 47
   Daniel Christian 46, 47, 49
Lenz, Peter 37
Leonhard
   C.P. 28
   Daniel 30, 31
   Wilhelm 33
Leonhardt
   Daniel 33, 34
   P. 33
Liberty Hall 13, 14, 50
Liberty Hall and Cincinnati Mercury 13
Library of Congress 15
Lieber, Franz 47
Lily Water 38
Link, Adam S. 22
Linxweiler, Jacob 30, 31, 33, 42
Little Miami River 1
Little Sisters 38
Löb
   Jacob 33
   Philipp 33
log cabin 3, 4, 17, 20
   first 3, 8
Löhninger, Friedrich 38
Longworths 53
Lorenz, Eduard 40
low-fermentation beer 25
Löwenstein, Gottfried 40
Ludlow, Israel 1
Lumpp, August 33
Lutheran Church 18, 20

M

Mad River 1, 7, 29,
Mad River Township 7
Madison Township 7
Malby 7
Manger 7
Marian School 38
Marien Institut 38
Markart, Louis 22
Markgraf, Ludwig 34, 35
Marquard, Heinrich 16
Marschall, Theodor 43
Maryland
   Fredericksburg 2
mathematician 47, 49
Mayer 10
   Anna 17
   Daniel 17
   Elisabeth 17
   Heinrich 8, 17
   Jacob 17
   Johannes 17
   Jonas 17
   Michael 17
   Peter 17
Mayflower 18
mayor 37, 46
McCarthy, Margaret 2
McClure
   James 1
   John 2
McLean
   John 52
   Judge 53
medical forensic science, founder 50
medicine 38, 51
Mentges, J.D. 40
Mercer County 5
Methodist 2, 18, 21, 23, 40

Episcopal Church 23
Mettauer, Franz 41
Metz, Nikolaus 37
Mexican War 28, 29
Meyer
  Anna 11
  Johann 23, 37
  Martin 8
Miami countries 1, 3
Miami County 5, 6, 20
Miami Rivers 1, 2
Miami Township 6, 11
Mickesell
  Johann 17
  Joseph 9
mill, first 7, 8, 9, 25
Miller, Daniel 7
Missouri
  St. Louis 27, 38, 45
Montgomery County 10, 11, 13, 14, 15, 18, 19, 20, 21, 22, 24, 25, 27, 29, 36, 37, 40, 41, 43, 47, 50, 53
Morris, James 1
Mosbrugger 37
Moses 16
  Peter 33, 34
Moß, H.W. 33
Moyer 10
Müller 9
  Daniel 23
  David 16
  Heinrich 35
  Jacob 5, 17
  Joseph 33
  Stephan 9
  Xaver 33
Mundhenk
  Heinrich 53
  Margaretha 53
Mungen, Edmund 17
Muselmann, Peter
music 19, 27, 28, 29, 33, 45
  choir 28, 29, 45
  directors 34
  lessons 27
  organization 28
  school 28
  teacher 27, 34
musician(s) 11, 27, 28, 30, 34, 45

N

Nägeli, Captain 45
namesake of Dayton 1
national character 11
National Zeitung der Deutschen 36, 47
Nauerth
  Johann Valentin 29
  Wilhelm 38
Neder, Georg 37
negroes 14, 15, 16
Neukomm
  (Newcom) 1, 4, 10
  Colonel 16
  Christian 1, 2
  Georg 1, 2, 3, 5
  Georg, Tavern
  Sheriff 14
  Wilhelm 1, 2
Neukomm's Tavern 11
Neumann, Thomas 7
New Orleans 27, 38, 51
Newcom 1, 2
Newcomer 2
newspaper 13, 21, 35, 36, 37, 47, 49
Nickers, Elias 20
Niehaus 35
Nippen, Michael 37
Nold, Val. 33
Northwest 7, 14, 18, 36
  Ordinance 15
  Territory 1, 3
Null, Christian 16
Nutz (Nut)
  Franz 7
  Friedrich 7

O

Oblinger 43
Oehlinger 8

Ohio
  Canton 24, 36, 47
  Centreville 5
  Cheviot 27
  Chillicothe 24
  Cincinnati 1, 2, 3, 4, 7, 8, 11, 13, 14, 15,
    21, 24, 25, 27, 28, 29, 30, 33, 34, 36,
    37, 41, 42, 43, 45, 50, 52, 53
  Columbus 24, 31, 32, 33, 41, 50
  Dayton 1, 2, 3, 4, 5, 6, 7, 8, 10, 11, 13, 14,
    16, 17, 19, 21, 22, 24, 25, 27, 28, 29,
    30, 32, 33, 34, 35, 36, 37, 38, 39, 40,
    41, 42, 43, 49, 50, 51
  Deercreek 29
  Finchtown 10
  Eaton 45
  Ford Washington 1
  Germantown 8, 10, 11, 13, 19, 21, 22, 25,
    26, 27, 36, 43, 44, 45, 46, 47, 49, 50,
    51, 52, 53
  Göttersburg 8, 10, 11
  Greenville 1, 47
  Hamilton, town 27, 29, 37, 42
  Harschmannville 10
  Honey-Creek 2
  Jimtown 10
  Lebanon 49
  Lewisburg 43
  Liberty 11
  Little York 7
  Miami City 8
  Miamisburg 6, 7, 8, 11, 21, 22, 27, 29,
    40, 41, 50, 51
  Middletown 19
  Philippsburg 10
  Piqua 52
  Portsmouth 24
  Pyrmont 10, 34, 53
  Salem, city 9
  Salem Springs 9
  Schneidersburg (Taylors Borough) 10
  Springboro 38
  Springfield 2, 27, 28, 50
  Stillwater 7
  Troy 29
  Union Village 49
  Wapaghkonetta 45
  Washington 16
  Westwood 27
  Wolf Creek 7, 8
  Xenia 27, 32
  Yellow Springs 27, 33
Ohio River 14, 36, 45
Ohmer
  Franz 42
  Nikolaus 42
Ordinance of 1787 14, 15
organ, first 27
organist 29, 34

P
Page
  Eduard 16
  Lucy 16
Pansing, Friedrich 40
pastor(s) 9, 12, 20, 21, 22, 23, 24, 29, 40
patent 2, 9
Patterson Farm 15
Patterson, Robert, Colonel 8, 14, 16
Paulding County 5
Paully, Johannes 17
Peck 37
Peine 25
  Johannes 20
Pendletons 53
Pennsylvania
  Altoona 38
  Berks County 6, 7, 20
  Elizabethtown 30
  Ephrata 43, 44
  Lancaster County 9, 30
  Philadelphia 1, 7, 9, 25, 28, 36, 41
  Pittsburgh 41
  Reading 36
  York 7
Pennsylvanian-German 43
Perry Township 9
person, first, died 7
petition 10
Pfautz, Michael 8
Philippsohn, Jacob 16

physician 38, 51
Pilcher, Heinrich Ernst 23
pioneer 3, 7, 12, 29, 30, 36, 37, 41, 42, 43
   ladies 11
   woman 17, 18
pioneers 2, 7, 11, 12, 13, 17, 25, 27, 30, 36, 40, 41, 43, 53
   first 2
pirogue 4
political
   life 37
   newspaper 36
Post, Michael 7
postmaster 46
Pottawatamies 45
preacher(s) 2, 7, 8, 9, 12, 18, 19, 20, 21, 22, 23, 43
   first 7
Preble County 5, 43, 45
Presbyterian 18, 23, 34
preservation 25, 27, 33
Pressel, Daniel 8, 16
prisoner(s) 14
Pritz, W.H. 37
property 9, 14, 16, 17, 54
Protestant-Lutheran Synod of Ohio 22
Puffenberger, Louis 43
Purcell
   Bishop 24
   J.B. 25
purchase 2, 9, 10, 11, 28, 29
Puritan
   customs 52
   hypocrites 19
   ideas 18
Putnam County 5
Pythias Ritter 35

Q
Quaker 7
quarrel 9, 11, 13, 14
Quillian, Johannes 7

R
rabbi 17, 33, 40
Rack, Lorenz 33
railroad(s) 32
Randolph Township 7, 9
Raßmussen, N. 33
Rauh
   Hermann 37
   Leopold 37
Reformatory School 38
Reformed
   Church 7, 19, 28, 30, 40
   minister, first 21
   preachers 19
Rehbaum, Joseph 17
Reiß (Reuß), Friedrich 22
Religion
   Brothers of Nazareth 38
   Duncards 18
   Dunkards 7, 9, 23, 43
   German Baptist 40
   German *Beisselites* 43
   German Dunkards 7, 9
   German Lutheran(s) 8, 9, 21, 22
   German Lutheran preacher, first 21
   German Lutheran St. Johannes Church 40
   German Lutheran St. Paulus Church 4
   German Methodism 2
   German Methodist Church 40
   German Methodist(s) 2, 23
   Methodist(s) 2, 18, 21, 23
   Presbyterian 18, 23, 34
   United Brethren 18, 21, 23, 25, 37, 40
religious life 18
Renz, Alexandrine 41
Reuß 28
   Friedrich (Reiß oder Reuß) 22
Rex
   Carl 34
   Uncle 34
Ringel, Mathias 8, 16
Ritter, Johann 33
Rodefer 27
   John 28

Rohrer 44
   Christian 25. 28
   Christian Jr.
   Karl J. 25
   Samuel C. 25
Rosenmüller, Peter 22
Roser, Heinrich 33
Rübsamen, Heinrich 23
Rüfele, Georg 18
Rüffle, David 13
Rundstock, Jacob 33
Rush, Dr. 7
Ruß, Rupert 33
Rutz 30

S

saloon 9, 35
Sander, Wilhelm 33
Sau-Kuntz 43
Sauerbrei (Sourbray), Georg 16
Sauter, Heinrich 30
savages 9
saw mill, first 8, 9
Schäffer, Eduard 36, 46, 47
Schantz, Adam 37, 38
Schaub, Georg 16
Scheibenzuber
   Anton, Dr. 37
   Dagobert Anton, Dr. 38
Scheick
   Louis 25, 26
   Philipp 25, 26
Scheidacker (Scheidecker), Johannes 13
Scheidler 10,
Scheidler's tavern 11
Schellenberger, David 23
Schellhammer 30
Schenk 37
Scheu, Jacob 28, 29
Schewe, Martin 8, 13
Schiebele, Franz 35
Schiffermann 30
Schiller Loge 35
Schlei (Sly), Jacob 16

Schmidt
   Balthasar 8
   Conrad 29, 30
Schold, Lazarus 33
Schön, Johann 37
Schönberg
   Jacob 33
   S. 33
Schönfeld
   Emilie 40
   Johann Dr. 40
Schönle, Hermann 20
school
   hours 3
   teacher, first 9
   tuition 3
   private 3
schoolmaster, first 3, 8, 9
schoolteacher 7
Schorndorf 41
Schreiber, Daniel 44
Schröer 10
Schuey, Michael 44
Schulz Brewery 25
Schwab, Jacob 33
Schwartzel
   Mathias 8
   Philipp 8
Schweger 35
Schweinfurth, Johann 40
Schweinhirt, Adam 9
Schweizer, Georg 33
Schwind, Cölestin 35
Scott County, Illinois 45
Scott, Benjamin 5
Second United Brethren Church 40
Seebohm, Louis 3
Seibert, Albert F. 40
sermon 9, 21, 43
   first 2
servitude 15, 16
settlement(s) 1, 6, 7, 8, 9, 10, 20
settler(s) 1, 3, 4, 6, 7, 8, 9, 11, 15, 16, 18, 45
   first 4, 7, 9, 10, 16, 45
seventh range
Shaker community 49

Shank 10
Sharp, David M. 16, 17
Shelby County 5
sheriff 5, 13, 14
Shideler 10
shoemaker 30
    first 3
Shuey, W.J. 37
Sidicker (Scheidacker, Scheidecker) 13
singing festival(s) 31, 32, 33, 34
Singing Society 30, 31, 33
slave(s) 14, 15, 16
    case 15
slavery 14, 15, 16
Smith, Amor 27, 28
Snyder 37
social life 30
Social Singing Society 31, 33
Sociale Sängerbund 31, 33
Söhner,
    Captain 29
    Ferdinand 29
    H. 37
Sonntagmorgen 37
Sortmann, J. 37
Spanish 49
Speck
    Bernhard 14
    Elisabeth 14
Spinning, Isaac 5
Spittler, Jacob 13
Spitzbuben Marsch 52
Spring Valley Street 11
Springfield Turnpike 2
St. Clair, Arthur, General 1
St. John's Reformed Church of Germantown 19
St. Mary's Catholic Church 40
Stammel, Maria 7
Steele 27, 44
Stein, Albert 50
Steiner, Joseph 20
Stephan, Jacob 37, 38
Stiehl (Steele), Jacob 44
Stillwater River 7
Stiver (Stöver), Pastor 9

store, first 7
Straub, Joseph 33
Stroup (Straub) 10
Stuckenberg, H. Father 40
Stumpe, Leonhard 8
Stutzmann 52
    Wilhelm 44
Sultz 7
Sunday worship 18
Sunderland 5, 6, 11, 12
    ranch 13
    Peter 5, 6, 7, 9. 11
Supreme Court of Illinois 15
surgeon 38
surveyor 1, 3, 8
Swiss 44, 45
Switzerland
    Geneva 51
Symmes
    Daniel 5
    John, Cleves 1, 2,
Symmes' Purchase 3, 9, 10

T

tannery 32, 43
tavern(s) 3, 11, 12, 18, 19, 29, 30, 41, 43, 52
tavern, first 3
teacher(s) 7, 9, 28, 29, 34, 38, 45
Teltow
    Edwin 27
    Emiline 27
    Herman 27
    Mrs. 27
    Otto 27
    Wilhelm 27
temperance
    laws 19
    movement 33
Tennery, George F. 3
territories 15
Teutonia Loge 35
Teutonia Versicherungs-Gesellschaft 42
Theobald, Peter 33
theologian 21, 22

theology 21, 22, 47
Thienpont, Emanuel Father 24, 25
Thomson, Samuel 1
Tisch
   Karl Th. 33
   Wilhelm 31
Tobe 9
Toby's Church 9
Tom's Run 9, 11
Torrences 53
trade 3, 22, 25, 29, 30, 35, 36, 41, 45
trademark 38
tradition(s) 11, 12, 43
Treaty of Greeneville 1
Trebein, Wilhelm 30
Treon
   Peter, Dr. 21
   Thomas Dr. 21
Tschudi, Jakob 44
Tull, Karl 16
Tunkers 23
Turner(s) 10, 34, 35
Tuscarawas County 21

U

Unabhängige Orden der Rothmänner 35
Unger, F. 37
United Brethren Church 9, 21, 23, 37, 40
United Western Indian Tribes 1
University of Heidelberg 51
University of Tübingen 21

V

Van Buren 46
Van Buren Township 9
Van Cleve
   Benjamin 1, 5
   Wm. 1
Van Horne, David 19
Van Wert County 5
Vernosdell 6
Viot, J.E. 37

W

Wach, Wilhelm 16
Wagener 7, 43, 49, 52
   Johann 43
Wagener's tavern 43
Wagon-Boy 49
Waldruhe Park 38
Walker
   Georg 22
   Hans Georg 21
Walnut Street, Germantown 25
Walz, Philipp 29, 34, 35
War of Independence 7
Warren County 3, 16, 22
Washington County, Pennsylvania, 2
Washington Township 5, 7
Water Street, Dayton 3
Water Works 50
Wayne Township 9
Wayne, Anthony 1
weaver 2
Weber
   Johannes 16
   Peter 8
   Philipp 30
   Uncle Abe 11
wedding(s) 11, 12, 13
   first 9
Wegemann, Catharina 30
Wehmeier, Andreas 7, 10
Wehner, Julius 37
Weil, H.F. 37
Weiß, Israel S. 20
Welsh, John 4
Werner, Johann 30, 31
West Virginia 28
   Wheeling 45
Westermann, Wilhelm 28, 29
Westfahl 4
   Andreas 3
   Cornelius 3
   Georg 3
   Jobst 3
Westliche Beobachter 36
Westphal
   Jobst 17

Mr. 7
Whig Party of Ohio 49
Wilhelm, Balthasar 16
Wilkinson Street 3
Wilkinson, Jakob, General 1
Williams County 5
Williams
  Balzel 16
  Stephan 7
Wilmington, Delaware 1
Winter
  David 19, 20
  Ludwig 13
  (Winters) Reverend 19
  Thomas 19, 20
Winters, David 19
Wirz, Mathias 25
Wodemann, Johann 16
Wolf
  Jacob 23
  Karl 33
  Leonard 17
Wollenhaupt, H. 33
Wolpers
  Carl Otto 45, 46, 47
woman 2, 9, 17, 18, 53
women 11, 12, 13, 17, 18, 30
Wrampler, Philipp 23
Wyandots 45

Y
Yankee(s) 5, 43
Yecki, Jacob 16
yellow fever 27, 51

Z
Zehring, Peter 10, 43
Ziegler
  Major 7
  Friedrich 33
Zimmer, Leo 29
Zink, Georg 7
Zwisler, Joseph 41

About the Author

Dr. Elfe Vallaster Dona is an Associate Professor of German at Wright State University, Ohio, who has taught German language, literature, culture, and business courses at three Ohio universities for the last 20 years. She holds an M.A. in Germanic Studies from the Ohio State University and a Ph.D. in Germanic Studies and Literature from the University of Cincinnati, Ohio. Her special interests besides German-American cultural studies include language pedagogy, exile studies, international business, and the integration of instructional technology in education. She is also the author of *Hilde Domin: Ein Zimmer in der Luft* (1994) and co-author of *Deutsch Immer Besser* (1996).

Dr. Elfe Vallaster Dona has been involved for numerous years with the *Society for German-American Studies* where she also served as editor. Her interest in local history and German-American contributions to the United States resulted in multiple articles, presentations and college course creations around that topic. Experience and training in the field of German-American studies include active memberships in four genealogical societies, dedicated participation in the oldest German-American club in Dayton, Ohio, the *Dayton Liederkranz-Turner Society*, intellectual discourse with several German-American researchers, archival work in public libraries and at the Universities of Cincinnati and Wright State University. Wright State University granted her a one-year leave of absence to complete this book project successfully.

She was born and raised in Austria and is herself a first-generation immigrant to the United States living in Ohio with her husband and two daughters, Nicole and Krista.